Chicken Soup for the Soul.

Attitude of Gratitude

Chicken Soup for the Soul: Attitude of Gratitude
101 Stories About Counting Your Blessings & The Power of Thankfulness
Amy Newmark

Published by Chicken Soup for the Soul, LLC www.chickensoup.com
Copyright ©2022 by Chicken Soup for the Soul, LLC. All Rights Reserved.

The publisher gratefully acknowledges the many publishers and individuals who granted Chicken Soup for the Soul permission to reprint the cited material.

Front cover photo of open door courtesy of iStockphoto.com/Ralwel (©Ralwel), photo of landscape courtesy of iStockphoto.com/Nomadsoul1 (©Nomadsoul1)
Back cover and interior photo of woman courtesy of iStockphoto.com/kieferpix (©kieferpix)
Photo of Amy Newmark courtesy of Susan Morrow at SwickPix

Cover and Interior by Daniel Zaccari

Publisher's Cataloging-In-Publication Data
(Prepared by The Donohue Group, Inc.)

Names: Newmark, Amy, compiler.
Title: Chicken soup for the soul : attitude of gratitude : 101 stories about counting your blessings & the power of thankfulness / [compiled by] Amy Newmark.
Other Titles: Attitude of gratitude : 101 stories about counting your blessings & the power of thankfulness
Description: [Cos Cob, Connecticut] : Chicken Soup for the Soul, LLC, [2022]
Identifiers: ISBN 9781611590937 (print) | ISBN 9781611593310 (ebook)
Subjects: LCSH: Gratitude--Literary collections. | Gratitude--Anecdotes. | Attitude (Psychology)--Literary collections. | Attitude (Psychology)--Anecdotes. | Conduct of life--Literary collections. | Conduct of life--Anecdotes. | LCGFT: Anecdotes.
Classification: LCC BF575.G68 C45 2022 (print) | LCC BF575.G68 (ebook) | DDC 179.9--dc23

Library of Congress Control Number: 2022937119

PRINTED IN THE UNITED STATES OF AMERICA
on acid∞free paper

27 26 25 24 23 22   01 02 03 04 05 06 07 08 09 10 11

Chicken Soup for the Soul

Attitude of Gratitude

101 Stories About Counting Your Blessings & The Power of Thankfulness

Amy Newmark

Chicken Soup for the Soul, LLC
Cos Cob, CT

Changing lives one story at a time ®
www.chickensoup.com

Table of Contents

3

~Everyday Miracles~

4

~Live in the Moment~

5

~The Right Words~

❻

~Simple Pleasures~

❼

~Eye-Openers~

8

~Saying Thanks~

9

~The Joy of Giving~

10

~A Change in Perspective~

Introduction

Why are we presenting you with this new collection of stories focused on gratitude? It's because in our twenty-nine-year history of publishing personal, revealing stories we've come to understand that gratitude is essential to happiness and wellbeing.

As Marcus Tullius Cicero said, "Gratitude is not only the greatest of virtues, but the parent of all others." I don't think you can be truly happy if you're not grateful, if you're not counting your blessings on a regular basis. And you may have trouble cultivating other desirable attributes, such as forgiveness and a sense of humor, if you're not feeling thankful.

According to a web posting by Harvard Health Publishing, "In positive psychology research, gratitude is strongly and consistently associated with greater happiness. Gratitude helps people feel more positive emotions, relish good experiences, improve their health, deal with adversity, and build strong relationships."

Gratitude helps people focus on what they have instead of what they feel is missing from their lives. The journalist Germany Kent said, "It's a funny thing about life, once you begin to take note of the things you are grateful for, you begin to lose sight of the things that you lack."

With an attitude of gratitude, every day comes bearing gifts. And, although it may feel a bit forced at first, your attitude of gratitude will grow stronger with use.

The wonderful thing about counting your blessings and practicing gratitude is that you don't have to be *born* with that tendency; you can *learn* how to be a thankful person and enjoy all the emotional benefits of gratitude. It only takes a little practice to make it a regular part of your outlook — a daily habit.

Here are some ways you can cultivate your own attitude of gratitude:

- Keep a gratitude journal.
- Make a list each day of three good things that happened.
- Write thank-you notes. Or verbally explain to people why you are thanking them.
- Expect and actively look for the silver linings even when things aren't going your way.
- If you're religious, pray and thank God for the big, and small, good things in your life.
- Review all the things you're thankful for, including health, family, friends, employment, financial security, and whatever else you have. Don't forget to feel grateful for indoor plumbing, food on your table, your car... these are things that are not guaranteed to everyone.
- Fill your life with grateful, positive people who will help you be the same.
- Let yourself be delighted by the sun warming your body, by birdsong, by budding flowers. These everyday pleasures are free and are always there for you to enjoy.

In this book, you'll meet people who have learned to focus on thankfulness and found deeper joy and happiness as a result. They used various methods. Sarah Budka Ammerman, for example, wrote down the good things that happened to her throughout the year and threw the slips of paper in a Mason jar. Each New Year's Day she sits down and reads all the notes she wrote during the previous year. Dana Drosdick started a gratitude practice after her grandmother died by writing down ten things that had given her joy each day. And Jane McBride realized that instead of praying to God every day and *asking* for things, she should instead *thank* God for the good things already in her life. She discovered that she became a much happier person as a result.

The English writer and philosopher G.K. Chesterton said, "I would maintain that thanks are the highest form of thought; and that gratitude is happiness doubled by wonder." We hope you will find your own "happiness doubled by wonder" as you exercise your gratitude muscles. These 101 stories are a great way to get started.

— Amy Newmark —
May 1, 2022

Chapter
1

Count Your Blessings

The Rolls

*The life that counts blessings discovers
its yielding more than it seems.*
~Ann Voskamp, One Thousand Gifts Devotional

The horn on my mother's car tooted from the driveway, but I didn't move. I was propped up in bed, my splinted legs set atop pillows while I browsed the Internet from my laptop. It was my only means of escape from the hours I spent sulking.

Day after day, for three years, I holed up in a 10x12-foot bedroom in my mother's house. I had undergone seven unsuccessful surgeries and a slew of complications to combat degenerating bones and soft-tissue ruptures in my feet and ankles. The prospect of getting back on my own two feet was dimming.

I felt lost. Broken. My days of playing tennis and taking bicycle rides and long walks on the beach seemed like a lifetime ago.

I mourned for the old me whom I feared was dead and might never be resurrected.

"Kath, you're missing a beautiful day outside." My mother's cheery, enthusiastic footsteps charged up the stairs to my dimly lit bedroom. "Let's take a spin in The Rolls."

"In the *what*?" I swept my gaze away from the computer and into the hall. I was waiting for my mother's body to catch up with her voice, much the way the sound of thunder chases a burst of lightning.

"The Rolls-Royce. She's a beauty," Mom said. "I picked her out myself." She burst through my bedroom door, beaming. She clapped her hands together like two cymbals. "C'mon, up and at 'em."

I watched as she dug into my dresser drawers. She yanked out a clean pair of sweatpants and a T-shirt and threw them my way. They landed, draping like curtains over the laptop monitor.

"Let's go!" she said.

I didn't move.

Mom reached for my crutches. They loomed a good four inches over the wisps of her poufy, blond hair.

"C'mon, you're being sprung from your cell."

"I happen to like my cell."

"Well, don't worry. It'll still be here when we get back." My mother propped the crutches against the bed. Then she leaned over and pulled the pillows from beneath my splinted legs.

"Mother, please," I fought. "Maybe later, okay?"

"But The Rolls is top-of-the-line. Light as a feather — even you can lift her. She's got high-tech lumbar support and these padded, long-leg extensions. C'mon, we'll take her for a spin at the park. Let's get some fresh air."

I suddenly connected the dots to all this mysterious Rolls talk. It was a wheelchair, the very thing I had been resisting.

"You heard what that doctor said. It's bad enough about your feet, but it's even worse with the tendonitis in your hands and arms from always using those crutches." She closed the lid on my laptop. "You can't just give up like this."

I flailed my arms, shouting, "Leave me alone!"

My words fired, curt and fierce. As my gaze bored through her, I spied a sense of my own defeat and disappointment etched on her face.

Neither my mother nor I said another word about The Rolls for weeks afterward. We didn't have to. My mother's positioning of The Rolls in the garage — beneath my cobweb-covered bicycle and tennis racket on the wall — spoke volumes.

Every time I piled into her car so she could drive me to the doctor, physical therapy or the pool, I'd gaze at The Rolls through the windshield. It was cloaked in a white bedsheet, shrouding it as if it were a ghost or some sort of sacred statue awaiting its official unveiling.

My mother knew me well enough to know that the sight of The Rolls would eventually wear me down. Yet, I remained resistant to the whole idea and what it represented for my life. If I started to rely on a wheelchair, I feared it might mean that my disability had won. But every time I spied The Rolls, I knew I'd have to find some way to let go of my pride in order to transcend my physical limitations. I'd have to start accepting help — from a wheelchair or other people — if I wanted to live again.

After dinner one night a few weeks later, my mother asked what I wanted for my twenty-seventh birthday. I swallowed hard when I told her that I'd like to go to The Metropolitan Museum of Art in nearby New York City to see an exhibit and then maybe go out to lunch at an over-priced Manhattan restaurant. All of this would be her treat, of course.

With my pronouncement, my mother dropped our dirty dinner plates into the kitchen sink. They landed with a clatter.

"Oh? And just how do you propose to accomplish such a feat? Pun intended." She grinned as an aside. "I mean, the Met's enormous, with lots of long corridors. How do you intend to do all that walking and standing?"

She turned to face me, crossed her arms, and leaned against the kitchen counter, as if bracing herself for battle.

"The Rolls," I said, eyeing her squarely. "You win, Mother."

"No, Kath. Don't you get it? It's you who wins."

It wasn't until my mother pushed me, seated in The Rolls, upon the smooth, marble floors set below the high-vaulted ceilings of The Metropolitan Museum of Art that I realized how much I'd missed a sense of motion and speed those three years — the ability to get somewhere quickly without having to hobble, step by painful step, on crutches. The dreariness of all the time I'd spent confined to that 10x12-foot room in my mother's house dissolved amid the sprawling, ornate stateliness and beauty that surrounded me at the Met that day. That moment held as much excitement for me as riding a roller coaster where I thrust up my arms into a V shape of victory.

— Kathleen Gerard —

The Gratitude Jar

Simple blessings are all around us. Once we receive
them with thanksgiving and appreciation,
we experience true joy.
~Krystal Kuehn, Giving Thanks

I started the jar the winter after I was told my cancer was in remission. I thought it might be a good way to stay upbeat while I recovered from cancer and navigated my divorce. I used a medium-sized Mason jar and filled it periodically with notes listing the things for which I was grateful.

Years later, the jar has become an important part of my routine. Every year on New Year's Day, I start with an empty jar and scribble notes on scraps of paper detailing the things I'm grateful for or moments that brought me joy. I empty it the following New Year's. It's the perfect way to cultivate gratitude and keep myself focused on positivity.

Some weeks, I don't add any notes. Other times, I'm tearing paper and adding note after note. Every January when I open the jar it's like re-reading my diary. Some years, by the time I open the jar my circumstances have drastically changed. I might have written about a nice phone call with a family member, only to have lost them by the time the jar is opened. Those are the notes I keep tucked away in a drawer.

I remember writing a note of gratitude that my friend Alli was able to conceive her son after chemotherapy. A few years later, I attended her funeral, watching her young son place a single pink rose on her casket.

The jars aren't just filled with happiness and joy. The jars are life: the good and the bad. They remind me of the things I have, as well as the things I've lost. They remind me to hold on with both hands to the memories of the people and places I love. They remind me that, even during the darkest winter, there will still be moments worth writing down.

Every January, when I open the jar and smile, I realize that I have forgotten many of the moments that inspired me to add a note months earlier. For a fleeting moment, I get to relive each blip on the radar. The time someone sent me a card unexpectedly; the time I ate at a new restaurant, and it was simply fantastic; the time a friend came to visit me on a sunny day. The jar hasn't just helped me to cultivate a sense of gratitude. The jar has helped me to notice the seemingly insignificant moments. Through the jar, I am transported to the time when I petted a friend's new dog or found an empty playground with my daughter.

Honestly, I never really cared much for New Year's Eve. But now I look forward to it every year. It isn't just the start of a new calendar year and all that comes with it. It is the chance to reflect on and enjoy all the moments that filled the past twelve months. And every year, when I add that first note, always on New Year's Day, I realize that one of the things I am most thankful for in my life is an inexpensive Mason jar.

— Sarah Budka Ammerman —

Standing Room Only

Always count the blessings in your life.
Never take them for granted.
~Buffy Andrews, A Grandmother's Legacy

I t had been a long day in the most magical place on Earth, filled with shopping and walking and eating and standing and — most of all — waiting. Waiting in line to purchase tickets to enter the park. Waiting in line to get a picture with Pooh (during which my friend Marni asked me, "You do realize this is just a man in a costume, right?"). Waiting in line to ride Space Mountain, and then waiting in another one to choose the souvenir photo of the three of us screaming while careening down a hill.

There was waiting in line to get a table for dinner at the Rainforest Cafe, waiting in line to buy an ice-cream pop shaped like Mickey's ears, and waiting in line to pay for three bags of souvenirs, which I then had to lug through the park and hold as I waited in yet another line for the bus that would take me back to the Polynesian Village.

After a ten-hour day filled with walking and standing and stepping and dashing, my legs were on fire. All I wanted was a seat before I had to yet again wend my weary bones through the mock Polynesian village to my hotel room.

But the bus was packed. Not only were there no seats left, but all the passengers were crammed tightly together, pressed up against each other, some hands overlapping as we jockeyed for pole space. I looked at Marni and Lisa, my fellow Disney World vacationers, and let out a pathetic whine. I may have even stomped my feet.

"Seriously?" I huffed, as the handle on one of my shopping bags tore, sending half the contents onto the floor. There was a caramel-colored, sticky substance in the grooves of the rubber runner, and I prayed it wouldn't stick to my Ranger Pooh stuffed animal's synthetic fur.

Suddenly, there was some shuffling and re-positioning as the bus driver asked us to make room for one more passenger.

"Is he kidding?" I complained.

Lisa scoffed, "Exactly where would he like us to go?"

Just then, I caught sight of the person we were making room for: an eight-year-old girl in a wheelchair wearing a Disney princess dress and clutching a stuffed Minnie Mouse. Her smile was luminous, contagious, and I found myself smiling back at her through my shame.

If I had asked her why she was smiling, I'm sure her answers would have been limitless. If, at that moment, someone had asked the same of me, only one answer shouted loudly through my brain: I am smiling because I have working legs.

Every day, I wake up with legs that move me out of bed and to the bathroom and all over my house. They moved me all through Disney World, and they held me the whole bus ride back to my hotel. They were aching and stiff, but they did whatever I asked of them. I was even grateful for the charley horse that woke me out of a deep sleep that night and had me stomping all over the room at 3:00 in the morning.

When I walk, run, skip, shuffle or limp, I am reminded that movement is a blessing, and I won't ever take it for granted again. Pain, fatigue, muscle cramps — any messages my legs want to send me, I now receive them gratefully.

— Rachel Remick —

Chemo Mondays

*Better to lose count while naming your blessings than
to lose your blessings to counting your troubles.*
~Maltbie D. Babcock

My friend's cancer is back. Stage 4. He has a three-day treatment every other week. He gets the chemo on Monday, wears a pump and tubes on Tuesday, and gets it all taken out on Wednesday.

For the most part, I know the routine, but sometimes I forget and need to ask if it is a chemo week or an off week.

My friend, Wes, is remarkable. He doesn't refer to his chemo schedule that way. He calls his chemo weeks "good weeks" and his off weeks "great weeks." Until recently, those labels irritated me. Every time he referred to his routine that way, I would fuss. "You don't have to be strong all the time. It's okay to be angry."

I gave that man lots of sermons.

I thought he was trying too hard to be positive. I thought he was being false or putting on a brave but fake face. Every time I called him out, he would say he really didn't care what I thought. He was sticking to his description: The chemo weeks were good, and non-treatment weeks were great.

Everything changed for me last week. I gained clarity. Wes was coming over to help me with some projects on a Sunday afternoon, the day before his chemo Monday. Even in the middle of cancer treatment, he was thinking of others. That's the kind of man he is.

On that particular Sunday it was cold but the sun was shining. I was in my kitchen cooking and listening to Pandora, watching the birds at the feeder outside my kitchen window. I was basically enjoying life when it hit me: Wes wasn't trying to be falsely positive. He considers his chemo weeks good weeks because those treatments keep him alive. Wes is thankful to be here on Earth. It's just that simple.

Maybe cancer does that to you. A stage-4 diagnosis certainly gets your attention. The second time around hits harder than the first.

I think Wes has made his peace with cancer. Every two weeks, my sweet friend can sit in a chair for six hours while chemicals pour into his beautiful body. He can nap and sip on ginger ale when he gets home. He can deal with a fanny pack on his waist and a port under his skin because those things keep him alive. Those three days every two weeks are the price he must pay.

What I considered the "awful chemo days" are necessary days. Because of those three days every two weeks, he will live to see his two grandchildren grow. He will coach and watch football and walk his dog. He will listen to good music, play the piano and sing with his church group. He will attend his men's group on Tuesday mornings, and he will be in church every Sunday. He will flirt with the ladies, and the ladies will flirt back. He will take the boat on the water, and he'll find a quiet cove and pause long enough to say, "Thank you, Lord, for giving me this day."

Nobody wants cancer. But if we let it, maybe cancer can have one redeeming quality: Maybe the threat of death will snap us into living. Maybe cancer will get our attention and serve as a wake-up call. Maybe cancer will help us see that there are no bad days — as long as we are living, breathing and loving.

Good days and great days. Wes Dorton might be onto something. Maybe there are only two types of days — good ones and great ones. Even days filled with chemicals and tubes are days to be cherished.

On that project-filled Sunday afternoon, I apologized to my friend. I should not have accused him of being fake, and I promised not to do it again.

Because of his tremendous faith, I'm trying to banish the term "bad day" from my vocabulary. No more bad days for me. I might have a day full of headache and aggravation. I might have a day filled with problems that need a solution, but even those days are good days. I'm having a day. God has given me a day. I will rejoice and be glad in it.

—Tammy Davis—

When One Door Closes, Another Opens

To have faith is to trust yourself to the water.
When you swim you don't grab hold of the water,
because if you do you will sink and drown.
Instead you relax, and float.
~Alan Watts

There was a time in my life when I lost everything. And I don't mean that in an exaggerated, dramatic way. I mean, I lost *everything*.

My physical health was the first thing to go. I had always had a history of underlying autoimmune conditions, but it was now exacerbated by a rare bacterial infection that wreaked havoc on my body. I lost the ability to walk and ended up in a wheelchair. I lost the ability to brush my hair and eat certain foods. For a year of my life, I was bedbound. I lost my ability to drive a vehicle or have that freedom of the open road before me.

After that, I lost everything else.

I lost friends who lost patience with me, who grew tired and weary of waiting for a recovery that might never come. I lost friends who got tired of me canceling plans. I couldn't go places and do the things we used to do.

I lost my career, which I had worked for decades to build — my source of independent income. There went my sense of purpose, too.

I lost my marriage. Sometimes, when people take their wedding vows, they don't actually pay attention to the fine print about "in sickness and in health." So, when your health leaves, they leave, too.

I lost my house after the divorce. I had nowhere to live and had to move back in with my parents.

With no job, health, friends, romantic partner, or house to come home to, most people would fall into a deep pit of despair. And I did experience depression. But, most of all, I experienced hope. Relief that my life could start over, completely new, from the ground up. Hope that I could heal not only physically but in all ways.

I think it was my ability to keep this faith that allowed that faith to be rewarded in the end.

My health returned slowly but surely. I deliberately made my health a top priority. I no longer neglected myself or put my body last. I ate healthier foods, exercised more regularly, and constantly integrated new ways to reduce stress like meditation and yoga. I was so grateful for the opportunity to heal that I researched natural medicine and became devoted to helping others heal, too. I was grateful that I could now see how important my health was, and that it was okay to prioritize myself over a paycheck.

New friends entered my life — people with authentic hearts and kind understanding. People who had experienced similar suffering in life, so we were able to connect at deeper levels. People who didn't leave when things got tough, but instead toughed it out with me. People who accepted me as I was and didn't expect me to be anything different to make them more comfortable. I was grateful that I lost people along the way to make room for the people who were supposed to be there all along.

A new job presented itself as well — one where I wasn't working seven days a week. I could pace myself and allow my creativity to unfold. Life was too short to spend the majority of it working a job that drained me. I was so grateful that I lost my old job so that one better suited to my hobbies could unfold before my eyes.

A new romantic partnership presented itself — one that was way more genuine and longer lasting than the one I was in during my disintegrating marriage. I was grateful that God revealed people's true colors and true integrity, and He led me to calmer waters.

New ways of thinking became my reality. When bad things happen, it doesn't mean that better things aren't down the line. We just need the strength to hold on to hope.

Yes, there was a time in my life when I lost everything — everything except my faith. But the new perspective that I gained was more important than anything that I lost.

— Kate Hodnett —

Twice Loved

We are born of love; Love is our mother.
~Rumi

In the upstairs bedroom of the olive-green house
surrounded by trees, cornfields and a small pond,
he wakes with a start, tosses off his weighted dinosaur blanket,
lunges from his twin bed over the carpeted floor full of Legos,
and plops on his big brother's bunk.

Small brown hands shake the sleeping boy.
Straddling the covered bundle, he bounces up and down.
"Wake up! It's my birthday! It's my birthday! Wake up!"

Scampering down the steps, running through the house,
he is in awe of the Baby Yoda birthday paper chains
Daddy hung from the ceiling and across the French doors
as Teddy the cat looks in from the cold,
observing the little Filipino's joy
with the delightful décor.

The morning sun's rays hit the beautifully boxed
birthday donuts on the kitchen counter
beside the spicy noodles and fried rice
Momma will fix as his favorite dinner
when everyone returns home from a hectic day.

The dinosaur sketch lying on the counter
proclaims his sister's devotion
and hope of forever happiness.

Across the deep waters
on a little island in the Pacific,
a young woman places her small brown hands
on her abdomen and caresses the extra skin
that once covered her little boy.
And she prays that he is loved
as she loved him.

— Donna Arthur Downs —

Sgt. Navarro

*A hero is someone who has given his or her life
to something bigger than oneself.*
~Joseph Campbell

"Can some of you take a little time to write to him? He is having such a rough time." Bella's words immediately touched my heart. She was writing about her nephew, Sgt. José Navarro, a young man who had been wounded in Afghanistan and was now at Walter Reed beginning what would be years of surgery and therapy.

I became acquainted with Bella through an online religion & spirituality forum and its companion social-media site. I had been taking part in the forum for a few years and had formed a number of friendships. The spiritual dimension of the forum appealed to me, finding as I did that people seemed to have a need to express the good in themselves. Given such a forum, people seemed to open up without hesitation, to lean on each other.

And now Bella was asking some of us, a few people whom she trusted, to write to her nephew. José had been in an ambush while out on patrol with his troop and had suffered extensive injuries. This young man now faced an even greater battle than he had in Afghanistan. With the contact information provided by his aunt, I wrote him, all the while wondering what I could possibly say or do to help.

My background did include experience with individuals facing challenges in their lives. I had previously worked for a decade with patients dealing with Alzheimer's disease and had spent more time than that with people fighting HIV, but this was something new. I decided to write José as I would write anyone. I wasn't exactly a shy person and was never at a loss for words. I would let José decide how much he wanted to share, and I would let him set the pace.

José was immediately open about all that he had gone through and continued to go through. His wounds were horrific. At one point, he posted pictures on the forum that showed extensive damage to his legs, and I was heartbroken to think of this young man caught up in the carnage of war, his life now shattered. One of the most difficult things that he shared with me was his mourning over the fact that he could never father children. "My privates got pretty messed up" was his simple summary of a lost future.

Inevitably, a lot of our correspondence pondered a reason for everything he had gone through and was going through. I knew that I couldn't give him an answer to this question, but I tried to help him see that he would find his own answer.

"Joe, I'm not sure I would say that you were singled out, that somehow God marked you to have this happen. I do think that you can use all of this to make a reason for your future; you can be in control of how these experiences help you to reach out to others. You are still a soldier, Joe. Your brothers need you, and that will never change. You will be able to help so many of them because you have been there. I don't know how it will all happen, but I can guarantee that you will be right there beside them — in combat on a new battlefield, one that is every bit as important as any overseas. Joe, I know that it is hard to see right now, but your soldiers need you more than ever. Don't give up; hang in there because they won't make it without you."

I tried anything I could think of to cheer up José, and a lot of the time we just talked about inconsequential things, silly things. I never wanted him to feel as though I wrote him out of pity. In truth, I enjoyed writing him because he was an intelligent, warm individual. He was funny. He still had plans for the future. He was so much more than a casualty of war, and I didn't want him to think that he had been written off one hot day in the mountains outside of Kabul. He deserved more than to be defined by one terrible moment in his life.

He took part in the forum with some hesitation, and I tried to get others to make him a part of it all. Ultimately, though, too many of the others on there let it get in the way — they saw him only as someone who had been injured. As he put it, "...It stinks that people can't forget about my injuries. I'm sure as hell trying my best to forget about it all." I remembered to let him set the pace and share what he felt comfortable with; I didn't talk about his experiences unless he did.

He opened up about little things, such as his love for birds. He hoped to one day open an aviary and breed birds. I sent him one of my drawings: a parrot made just for him. He also jumped right in when the forum got in the spirit for Halloween. I Photoshopped the profile pictures of those taking part into appropriately ghoulish characters. I wasn't sure if he wanted to participate, but he was enthusiastic, so I made his picture into the zombie soldier he requested. "Man, I love it!" he wrote to me. "That's me, undead — you can't kill off Sgt. Navarro!"

I count that as one of the happiest moments of my life.

Over time, as José's therapy progressed and he wasn't confined to bed as much, he didn't answer back as often. I knew that his life was moving on, and I accepted that this was as it should be. His brothers and sisters in the service needed him. And the day that I read about him taking part in a new military exercise, "Operation Proper Exit," I knew that he had found his reason for the future. In Operation Proper Exit, José returned to Afghanistan and reunited with the soldiers on the battlefield. He, along with other returning wounded men and women, took his proper place among his comrades.

I saw pictures of José standing proud in his uniform, striding from his helicopter and shouldering his weapon. There was José, smiling as he posed with the others, and there was José, with his arm around a soldier in a field hospital. José had been there before, and now he was back to help another young man who also found himself with an uncertain future. They needed him, and he was still a soldier, still there doing his duty, still on the battlefield.

I cannot express deeply enough the privilege that I feel I have been blessed with in being allowed to share part of Joe's life. Sgt. Navarro has an armful of medals testifying to his valor and commitment, but none of them do justice to his warrior heart. He continues to fight, a comrade-in-arms, always at the ready—a soldier you can depend upon to be there. José was right—you can't kill off Sgt. Navarro.

—Jack Byron—

Someone Else's Fairy Tale

*Beginning today, make it a habit to count
your blessings every day.*
~Shadonna Richards, R.N., A Gift of Hope

A s Wale Ayeni once said, "Be thankful for what you have. Your life, no matter how bad you think it is, is someone else's fairy tale."

Often, I find myself wishing I was living other people's lives. Scrolling through Instagram stories and seeing influencers travel to exotic places like Bora Bora or flying on their private planes. I sit there and say to myself, "Why can't I do that? That's not fair."

I'm sure many of us wish that we could step into a luxurious private plane and fly to a private island. However, I'm also sure that many of us wish to have a bigger house, or wish to be able to work fewer hours, or maybe even wish to eat three meals a day.

When many of us picture New York City, we think, *It's unsafe. There are lots of homeless people everywhere.* I've lived in the city for almost ten years, and I can't say that I haven't thought about it that way. I've seen numerous homeless people on the street and in the subways. When I was younger, I never understood the reality of their lives. I was just scared of them and walked on the opposite side of the street. As I've grown older, I've come to ponder how difficult and painful their lives must be and how much they struggle.

I take the subway home every day after school, and when I get off, I take the same route to walk home. A few days ago, I noticed a young man on the side of the road holding a sign asking for money. I had seen him a couple of times in that spot, and now I saw the sadness in his face. He looked distraught. I immediately looked in my wallet to see if I had cash to give him, but I didn't.

I finally realized that this guy's wants are things that come to me so easily every day. He probably never gets to eat three meals in a day. He doesn't have a home to live in. He doesn't have a family to spend time with.

I went home and continued to think about that look on his face and knew that I had to bring cash with me the next day to give to him. Hopefully, it would make his day and buy him a meal. For him, it might be the best meal ever, even though it would be just a normal, everyday meal for me.

The next afternoon, when I got off the subway to walk home, I hoped he would still be there, and he was. He was standing in the same spot with that same look on his face. I took the money out of my backpack and waited until he came back from begging people in cars to give him money. I was a little scared to walk over to him at first, but I knew I needed to or I'd later regret not doing it.

I walked over and handed him a five-dollar bill, and his face lit up. He thanked me four times. I was so happy knowing that I had made his day just a little bit better. I had done a good deed and helped someone who was in despair.

After that day, I began to reflect on the things I'm grateful for. I became more aware of the fact that nothing in life should be taken for granted. So many people don't get to live the life I get to live as a sixteen-year-old, and I often forget that. There are children who are sick and must spend their lives in hospital beds. There are families living in poverty who must spend their nights in shelters.

I get to go on nice vacations once in a while. I get to live in a nice apartment in New York City with my family. Yes, I share a room with my brother. Yes, maybe I wish I had more space, but I still have what others dream of. These are the things that some people will never get to experience.

The next time you complain about something small or become

upset because you saw a famous person flying on their private plane to the island you've always wanted to visit, take a minute and appreciate the circumstances you're currently in. Live in the moment. Be thankful that you have a roof over your head. Be thankful for your own life, which many people, including the homeless man I walk by every afternoon, would view as their fairy tale.

— Alexis Farber —

9

The Gratitude List

I am happy because I'm grateful. I choose to be grateful.
That gratitude allows me to be happy.
~Will Arnett

I nearly dropped the phone. Instead of listening to my daily litany of grief and upset, my friend had suggested I try practicing more gratitude. Hadn't she heard what I'd said?

Her next few words literally changed my life.

"You already know all that is going wrong in your family life right now," she said. "I promise you there is still beauty around you that you never notice. Doing a nightly gratitude list will help you find that beauty again."

She told me to get a small notebook, the kind used for writing grocery lists or daily tasks. Number each page from 1–10, she said, and write down ten things you are grateful for. She also warned me that I might have difficulty finding ten in a single day at first. Just keep at it, she said.

I trusted my friend enough to know she spoke from compassion and love. The family I had married into had been rocked by the recent death of my husband's older sister. Rather than bringing the extended family together, her death just drove them further apart. Many nights, my phone rang more than once, with different family members offering different versions of their latest upset. Each nightly call seemed angrier than the last, and many demanded I provide a solution.

Each morning, I called my friend, telling her the latest bad news.

And she'd always listened patiently—until this particular morning when she gave me her gratitude advice.

I had exactly the sort of notebook she described, so that evening, right before bed, I sat in the bathroom, numbered the first page, and tried to recall ten things I could honestly be thankful for. She was right. It *was* hard at first. I was ashamed to run out of blessings halfway through.

The next night, I had to start over and list ten more. My first notebook has more gaps between dates than it does daily entries. My friend's counsel to focus on each day's lived experience gave me a framework to use. Rather than list by rote "big-ticket" items like a roof over my head or my husband's love, I began to search for small, specific pleasures I had scarcely noticed. Early lists included such blessings as the taste of cranberry juice, a bird feather found, a grandson's hug, my husband's early morning smile, and a cool breeze on a hot August day.

I recalled that my mother would mark special days every year on her kitchen calendar—the first daffodil, the first robin. Robins are year-round birds here, but the spring's first ladybug made a later list, as did the annual emergence of sea oats on the coastal dunes where I live. Looking for gratitude-list items became a quest that took me through the hours of each day as I wondered, *What will I find to give thanks for tonight?*

More than seventeen years have passed since my first gratitude list. I still sit quietly for a few minutes in the bathroom right before bed and write out my daily blessings in a little notebook. Living through the COVID-19 pandemic, I've had plenty to worry about—my health, and the health of my family, business, and community. Every time I felt overwhelmed by all I had no control over, my gratitude list grounded me. It readied me for sleep and the next day's challenges by shifting my focus again to nature's beauty and bounty. I date each entry and start my list with these simple words, "Tonight, I am grateful…"

Gratitude brings me both joy and hope. Sometimes, my lists chronicle what I have received from others or from nature. I have learned to say "thank you" in the moment, which helps me remember the experiences and encounters that make up my later lists. I re-experience these joys every night when I pause to write down my thanks. On other days, my lists outline what I have been blessed to share with others. Just this week, my list included safe travels for a dear friend, a beach walk at first light, a serendipitous heart shape in the curl of a breaking wave, and a young deer with extremely large ears and eyes peering at me through grasses on the dunes. Many nights, as I am writing out my thanks, I can sense God saying, "You're welcome, and wait until you see what's in store tomorrow!"

Tonight, my list will include the chance to share this reflection for possible publication, knowing that someone who reads it may be inspired to start gratitude lists of their own.

—Eve Turek—

10

Prayers of Thanksgiving

Everything we do should be a result of our gratitude
for what God has done for us.
~Lauryn Hill

"Father in Heaven, please bless my children. Please bless my friends who are struggling. Please do this and do that ..." And so my prayers went. They were less about thanksgiving than they were a list of things for the Lord to do.

Who was I to give the Lord instructions?

A moment of reflection following one of my typical prayers brought me up short. Shamed, I realized that my prayers acknowledged little gratitude and praise to the Father at all.

What could I do to change that?

I challenged myself for a week to give prayers that were 100 percent ones of gratitude. Could I do that? Could I suppress my natural tendency to ask for things?

I was determined to find out.

I started small. I thanked the Lord for a sunny day and the flowers outside my window. I thanked Him for the change of seasons. I thanked Him for the gift of prayer itself.

Something happened along the way. Gratitude, it turns out, is contagious. As I became more aware of His hand in my life, I also became more cognizant of the blessings that others brought into my life as well.

A bouquet of flowers from a friend for no occasion.

An unexpected phone call from a distant relative.

A note from a grandchild saying that he loved me.

Another unexpected consequence resulted along the way. The more grateful I became to the Father for His many blessings, the happier I grew.

—Jane McBride—

I've Got What I Need

11

Who Do You Think You Are?

Gratitude turns what we have into enough, and more.
It turns denial into acceptance, chaos into order,
confusion into clarity...
~Melody Beattie

The 23andMe DNA test that my ex-husband had gifted me for my sixtieth birthday sat on my desk for several weeks before I finally opened it. I spit the required saliva into the tube, registered online, and sent off the sample. Over the next few weeks, I got periodic e-mail updates on the progress of my specimen, and I was invited to participate in some surveys, which I would sometimes do when I had some free time.

When I opened the online results I found nothing that startling. I was shown to have 44% French and German and 37% British and Irish ancestry, with a bit of Scandinavian, Spanish, Portuguese, and Eastern European thrown in. There was an option to create an account and connect with possible relatives in their database, but I decided to put that off for a while.

Then, late one night, I went for it. I created the account and clicked the "DNA Relatives" button. When the list of names popped up, I stared at it, confused. All of my four siblings are sisters, but the first name on the list was a name I didn't recognize. It was labeled "half brother." The second unidentifiable name was labeled "aunt."

I struggled to make sense of what I was seeing for several minutes before I clicked on my half-brother's name to see his profile. It said he was born two years before me, was from a town very close to where I was born, and was adopted. He had found his mother's name, which he shared, but his father's name was left blank on his birth certificate, which had just become available to him a few years earlier.

So, the logical conclusion, once I was able to form one, was that my father had had a dalliance before I was born, which resulted in the birth of this child who was given up for adoption. It was a startling revelation, but not really all that surprising since my parents divorced when I was fifteen because my dad had found someone else. I sent a brief note to this newly found brother and thought how strange it would be to tell him about his father and our family.

The next day, I received an excited message back from my brother, and we exchanged e-mail addresses to continue the conversation. He let me know that he had learned his birth father's name not that long ago, so I sent him a brief outline of my family, thinking it would fill in some of the blanks for him. After a few exchanges, he said, "It is apparent that your birth father is [name] as he is my birth father." The name that filled in that blank was not my father's name but the name of a close family friend who was my godfather.

This second shock derailed me. I spent the rest of the day swimming through a vast sea of emotions. I reached out to some friends who helped to hold my head above water as I floundered around with the enormity of this new truth. I talked to my sisters (whom I now know are half-sisters), and we sorted through what this all meant.

By the end of the day, I was calmer but still reeling. Thoughts filled my head. How does this affect my identity, my sense of self, the very foundation of my life? How could my mother withhold this from me her whole life? We were very close, and I thought we shared everything. Did the birth father know? Did they make a pact to keep it a secret forever? Or did she really believe that her husband was my father? I don't look that much different from my siblings, which I'm sure was a relief to her. But she must have suspected, perhaps until the day she died at age eighty in 1997.

In fact, they're all dead now (except for that second name on the list, my birth father's elderly sister whom I don't intend to contact).

My father died in 1990, and my birth father died in 2016. This means that the story behind my birth will remain a mystery, and there's no one left to blame — which is truly a blessing in many ways.

In fact, when I woke up the next morning, I decided to see the whole thing as a blessing.

One of the most profound things I've learned in my sixty years is that everything that shows up in our life's path offers a gift, an opportunity, or a blessing. Usually, though, these events appear as challenges, sometimes even tragedies and shocks. And there is no way to understand them as anything other than immense challenges when we are immersed in the necessary emotions surrounding them. The grief, sadness, anger, disappointment and other powerful reactions must be fully realized and expressed for as long as it takes to wade through them. Eventually, we will find that we're able to make decisions again about how to proceed, what to do with what has shown up, and how to start to move toward a better place.

The next day, I still felt the swirl of conflicting emotions, but I realized that I was still *me*, that the father who raised me was still my father, and that whatever happened sixty years ago and led to my arrival here on this Earth was truly a blessing, no matter how it happened or what was kept hidden. I decided that my life was still my life, and that this truth has always been. It's just that now I know it, and I also know that shining light on a truth can offer tremendous healing and growth. I realized that I had found this new brother, who amazingly shares many similar views on life and spirituality, and that if he has come into my life at this particular time, there must be something for us to experience together as brother and sister.

I still periodically find myself in that swirling vortex of emotions, but those moments are becoming less frequent as I choose to focus on the opportunities that I know will continue to emerge from this situation. My newly found brother and I communicate via e-mail regularly. Although we live far apart, I know we'll arrange to meet in person soon. He is getting to know my children as their uncle, and we continue to be amazed at the similarities we are discovering in each other. And, just recently, I had a dream that my father (the one who raised me) communicated to me that he's still my father, that he loves me and that all is well. And I truly believe they were the words of his spirit.

Here, in this experience, is the true opportunity to consider who I really am. I can truly live my life in a state of gratitude and peace.

— Tracy Farquhar —

12

Some Don't

The moments of each day, are a special gift to us. And
should never be wasted, we should feel very blessed.
~Julie Hebert, Living in the Moment

I wake up with a roof over my head.

Some don't.

I have my husband — a good and decent man — by my side.

I have an indoor bathroom with running water for my shower. I have hot coffee with milk and toast. I have electricity and air-conditioning. I have a refrigerator, and I cook on a stove. My pantry is overflowing. I have way more than I need.

Some don't.

I have kids who need me. They may disobey me and argue with me, but I know they love me still.

Some don't.

I have two arms and two legs. I can embrace, and I can walk.

I have walking shoes and dancing shoes and fancy-shmantzy, high-heeled shoes (that I do not need).

I have lacy lingerie, designer jeans, party dresses and coats to keep me warm.

There were times when my closet only held hand-me-downs. I never noticed it. Even then, I felt blessed.

Sometimes, I'm almost overwhelmed for having so much. So, I donate to friends, charities, neighbors, animal shelters and other countries. Giving makes me happy. But it's not enough. It's never enough.

I have a job. I don't have a fortune, but I share what I have. I should share even more.

Some don't.

I walk in the park with my dog. I see beauty in nature, taste the snowflakes on my lips, and smell the fresh air. I feel the gentle breeze in my hair, and I hear the cheerful chirping of the birds. I appreciate the simple things.

Some don't.

I have friends, relatives and strangers who greet me in the street. I hug a senior, kiss a baby, and cuddle a pet.

I breathe, I smile, I cry for others, and I cry for me.

Some don't.

I've lost loved ones, including my beloved parents whom I took for granted, and treasured soul mates I never thought I'd lose. Yet they remain in my heart. I have memories.

Some don't.

I laugh and cry. I love, forget and forgive — and then I try harder. I hurt, I feel, but I choose to smile.

I feel compassion for those who suffer. I find joy in helping others. I pray for myself and others. I give thanks.

Some don't.

I go to sleep with a full stomach.

I don't have a million dollars, but what I have is worth so much more. I have a family, friendship and health. I have those who love me.

Some don't.

I believe in a greater power.

With the grace of God, I'll wake up tomorrow with my good and decent husband still by my side.

Some won't.

My cup runneth over.

—Eva Carter—

13

More Yesterdays than Tomorrows

Memory is the diary we all carry with us.
~Oscar Wilde

My husband and I recently sold our house in an effort to downsize. Although it was a difficult decision, we agreed the time had come to make the change. The continual upkeep both inside and out was wearing us down.

As we packed, we sorted through our belongings, determined to whittle down the number of possessions to those most needed and important. We sold furniture, donated household items, and gave family members items they wanted. We were amazed at how much we had accumulated, and we reminisced about some of our purchases.

The weeding-out process prompted us to share memories of our years together. We recalled family vacations when we bought mementos and questioned why we felt this particular item was important. Did I really need an overpriced Christmas ornament of a skating mouse to remind me that we visited a theme park?

We sorted through more photos and memorabilia, grabbing one another's arms and laughing at the silliness of some of the pictures. Had I really thought that hairstyle was flattering? Did he really wear that shirt?

One photo in particular caused us to pause. It was a picture of our six-year-old son and his best friend climbing into a Honda Civic we had owned. We recalled a mishap involving the car and the two boys. Long ago, while driving to town one day, we had hit a deer, totaling our car. When my husband lamented that he had just had the transmission fixed on the vehicle, our son's friend stated, "I wouldn't have done that if I was going to go out and hit a deer." We saw no humor in the comment at the time, but now we laughed hysterically at his innocent remark.

Other photos brought deeper emotions. Our eyes brimmed with pride as we looked at pictures of our sons and their milestones. Graduations, promotions, marriage, grandchildren. So many incredible memories.

After a while, my husband stood up, deciding to tackle another project. Before he left the room, he turned to me. He was silent for a moment, and then he squeezed my shoulder and kissed the top of my head. "Looking through all this cements the fact that we are moving on to another chapter in our lives. We have more yesterdays than tomorrows." There was no sadness in his voice, no regrets. He simply stated a realization.

I mulled over his words and continued to sort through photo albums, news clippings, and random pictures. He was right. We had been blessed with our yesterdays. They included laughter, celebrations, and excitement. Birthdays, graduations, accomplishments, family vacations, anniversaries, and so much more. Moments of sadness are sprinkled throughout. Overall, though, our memories bring smiles to our faces and contentment to our hearts.

As I consider our tomorrows, I recognize the insignificance of mementos purchased in years past. I'm determined that our tomorrows will focus on creating memories and feelings that last a lifetime for us and for others. Laughter, cheers, celebrations, and lots of hugs.

My husband and I have been blessed with many yesterdays, and we hope to make the most of however many tomorrows we are allowed.

— K.M. Waldvogel —

14

This Card Has Been Declined

Count your blessings. Once you realize how valuable
you are… you will finally be able to move forward
the life that God intended for you...
~Og Mandino

"I'm sorry, miss, but this card has been declined," the cashier said sympathetically but firmly as she handed back my card. My confusion turned to fear after I dug my "Emergencies Only" credit card out of my wallet, only to have it declined, too. The shoppers behind me in line cleared their throats and sighed. The message was loud and clear: Either pay for your stuff—or get out of line.

The cashier suggested I call the customer-service number on each card, and she volunteered to push my cart aside until I could figure out what was going on.

Fear and panic are never welcome emotions when they barrel into our lives and upend everything—particularly when you are a young, scared twenty-something, fresh out of military training, and a thousand miles from home, trying to figure out why you can't buy groceries and a few essentials.

With my proverbial tail between my legs, I found a deserted corner of the store next to the gardening section and called customer service.

Neither credit card had an outrageous limit. One was $1500, while the emergencies-only card had a limit of $3,000.

I have moved across country, I whispered to myself. *That must be it.*

They must think the cards were stolen and have been declined. After all, I was in California, and the cards had been registered in Texas.

"Customer service," a very chipper voice sang as she came on the line.

I explained that my cards had been declined — and that I had moved due to military training. To my knowledge, there would have been a few hundred bucks on the card for some military gear I'd had to purchase until the Air Force reimbursed me, but there shouldn't be any other charges.

"Well, let's take a quick look," she said. I waited and listened to the sound of fingertips hammering away at a keyboard.

I had just graduated college after putting myself through school on cobbled-together scholarships, hardship grants, and student loans. Being poor didn't mentally bother me. Instead, it was a powerful motivator. If my life was to change, it would be up to me to get it done. Finishing college and earning an officer's commission in the Air Force seemed like good starts.

But not to my husband.

Just before graduation, my college boyfriend had proposed marriage. I'd accepted, mainly because I believed it was expected and the next thing to do in life. Go to school. Graduate. Get married.

We'd had problems immediately over the arguably next-expected step: children. I wanted a career; he and his family wanted children.

He was dead set against me competing for an officer's commission — partly because he had just tried to compete for one himself and had been denied. He didn't get into any programs. To say he was livid that I, first, wanted to apply and, second, had been accepted with flying colors was an understatement, to say the least. He was so angry that he'd refused to even hug me goodbye at the airport.

"Ah, here we go," the agent chirped, drawing my thoughts back to the present. "Yep, this card has been maxed to the gills — that part is accurate."

Suddenly, a horrible, knowing realization settled on my shoulders. "Can you read the charges to me?" I asked, voice shaking.

"Sure! Let's see, we've got several charges for a Lone Star Liquors.

There's a handful here for some nightclubs, tattoos, and video-game stores. Does that sound accurate?"

I dissolved into tears as I sank down against bags of potting soil. My backside would be filthy, but I couldn't care less. Between sobs, the agent pieced together the timeline for the charges. Every single one was made during my three-month period of military training. While I'd been locked down 24/7 on an Air Force training campus, my good-for-nothing, jealous husband had treated himself to quite a little escapade and used my credit cards to foot the bill.

And, idiot that I was, I had added him as an authorized user on my accounts just before I left in case he needed to pay any bills for me while I was in training.

I explained the horrible mess to the agent, absolutely dejected that my "for better or worse" partner had done this to me.

"Well, I can't help you with disputing any of these charges, but I think I can help you with your next decision," she said. "The charges get worse."

I nearly fell off my mound of potting soil. "Worse?" I blubbered. "How could they possibly be any worse?" I swiped at my eyes again, feeling grit against my face from a leaking bag of dirt.

"The most recent charge is a recurring one, and that's what maxed out your card. It's a monthly subscription to a dating website."

Any lingering feelings of pity for myself evaporated into pure rage. This idiot had not only maxed out my card, but he'd used my own money to start cheating! He'd signed up for the website less than two weeks after I'd started military training and had been using it the entire time.

"Honey, just be glad you found out when you did," the agent offered as she suspended the account and removed my soon-to-be-ex-husband as an authorized user. She issued a forbearance on the account due to military hardship and wished me luck.

I stood and straightened myself up, dusting the potting soil from my clothes the best I could. My next stop was going to be a rent-to-own furniture store next door to get a bed, as my unaccompanied officers' quarters were unfurnished. The ability to purchase furniture was definitely out, verified by the meager cash I had in my wallet. It was a little under a hundred bucks.

"Okay, think. Bed and a little food for under a hundred. I can do this," I said to myself.

And just then, in a dusty corner of the garden section, I spotted a lawn hammock with a telltale bright orange sticker tacked to the box. My brain locked onto it immediately. Clearance inventory. It was fifteen dollars and came with its own frame. I snatched that dusty, little box off the shelf and held it to my chest like a gold medal.

A fleece blanket and pillow set, a twenty-four pack of off-brand canned ravioli, and a set of plastic picnicware completed my shopping spree.

Later that evening, in my lonely quarters, I ate cold ravioli straight from the can with a plastic fork. My dinner "centerpiece" was my now maxed-out credit card, and I gazed at it with a newfound appreciation.

Against the hurt, against the betrayal, I smiled. The universe had "declined" my plan in order to give me a better one. And as I stretched out on the little garden hammock that would be my bed for the foreseeable future, I smiled in the darkness.

"Declined," I whispered to the silent, barren room. Declined, declined, declined.

— Kristi Adams —

15

Chicken Soup for the Soul

Attitude Adjustment with a Single Snap

Count your blessings — not your troubles.
~Hendrik de Vries

According to one theory, if our prehistoric ancestors weren't apprehensive while conducting their daily routines, if they weren't worried while foraging for food, if they weren't fearful as darkness approached, their gene pool might have ended millions of years ago. However, fast-forward to the second millennium, and those traits no longer served the person I wanted to be.

Nevertheless, no matter how much I longed to be a carefree, lighthearted, happy-go-lucky individual, I knew deep down that altering that fight-or-flight response would be no easy task. I gave a lot of thought to how to change this behavior. Knowing how deeply ingrained my thought process was wired, I knew the task would be monumental. Hence, I started big by using a simple but effective tool: a humble rubber band.

One day, I slipped a rubber band around my left wrist. Every time I caught myself thinking of a dire outcome or scenario, I snapped the rubber band, causing a mild discomfort. This simple exercise served three purposes: It immediately disrupted my doomsday thought process; it taught me to associate such thinking with discomfort; and it helped me track the frequency of this destructive behavior. Later that day, I started to think of myself as one of Pavlov's dogs in reverse. Those canines heard the bell and then reacted; I reacted and then felt the snap. But, after a few weeks, I did notice something else: I seemed to be snapping the band less.

That looked like progress to me, so I continued to the next step. As long as I was interrupting my negative thoughts, why not replace them with something else? Something light, bright, and optimistic? And a quick glance out the nearest window held the answer. Springtime was in full bloom. Trees were just beginning to blossom, birds were building nests, and the sky was a cerulean blue. Yes, nature, which is known to abhor a vacuum, filled my immediate thoughts with beauty.

Once I began to notice the power of such positive thoughts, it was easy to expand my horizons. I started to take note of new, brightly painted signs and homes. I took notice of people taking time out of their daily routines to smile, assist others, or give a neighborly wave. Finally, I even appreciated the traffic patterns of our main street — the ebb and flow of cars, buses, and emergency vehicles during rush hours, off-hours, and weekends. There was a comforting rhythm to the world outside when I was able to take the time to notice it. It did not have to be perceived as chaotic, menacing, or fearful.

Finally, as my thoughts shifted, I started to journal. I went slowly at first, jotting down a few phrases at a time right before I drifted off to sleep. I made note of the positive things that I had noticed that day, such as the colorful goldfinch in the birdfeeder, the new coffee shop that opened downtown, and the toasted, sesame bagel I had for lunch.

As my list grew, I decided to expand my thinking once again. In addition to reflecting upon the positive parts of the day, I wanted to project what good things might be in store for tomorrow. What did I want tomorrow to look like? What could I do to make my typical day in the office a better one? Bring in an extra coffee for the receptionist? Leave the house a few minutes early and take the scenic route to work? Take a walk at lunchtime and enjoy the beautiful day? Send a complimentary e-mail to a colleague for a job well done?

Once I started to journal, I realized that the possibilities were endless. More importantly, they were within my control. Though I would not consider myself a religious person, I remember reading a quote that is a cornerstone to those who practice Buddhism. That saying, attributed to the Buddha, is: "The mind is everything. What you think, you become." I have found there is truth in that statement. By working to control what occupied my mind, I truly changed. What was incredulous to me was the power of little things — a steaming cup of coffee, a bouquet of yellow daffodils, the scent of a vanilla candle — to influence the course of my day in the most positive way.

It's been several years since I launched this self-improvement project. Looking back, I'm proud to report that I have come a long way. That's not to say that there are not days when I feel as if the sky is ready to fall, but I seem to be able to recover quickly. Yes, I continue to wear that simple elastic band on my left wrist. And when such thoughts threaten, I quickly snap that band, adjust my thinking, and get back on track, counting my blessings.

— Barbara Davey —

16

What Goes Around Comes Around

Develop an attitude of gratitude. Say thank you to
everyone you meet for everything they do for you.
~Brian Tracy

With a grunt, I turned off my handheld reader. I had just finished reading a story called "What Goes Around Comes Around," which made me both sad and frustrated. The story had been about a man who stopped to help a stranded but obviously wealthy woman sitting in a Mercedes on a deserted back road. Her car had a flat tire, and she was at an age when changing it was impossible for her, even if she had known how. Although frightened, she had no other choice but to accept his offer of help.

As he changed her tire, she noticed that his clothing was tattered and worn from wear, not fashion, and his hands were bare in the winter cold. When he finished, despite her insistence, he refused to accept any tip or payment, telling her simply to "help someone else, and when you do, think of me." She thanked him and then drove away.

After reaching the main road, she saw a diner in the distance and pulled in. The young waitress, very pregnant, kindly gave her a towel to dry off after she was soaked by the rain. Inspired by the young man's words, the older woman slipped four one-hundred-dollar bills under her plate and paid for her meal with another hundred, leaving before the waitress could return with her change. Unknown to the wealthy woman, the pregnant waitress turned out to be the wife of the good Samaritan who had helped the older woman earlier.

"What goes around comes around."

"Yeah, right!" That was my assessment. How many times had I done the right thing and never been rewarded? Mom had raised me to always do the right thing, even if no one was watching. In that spirit, I had grown up trying to help where I could.

I had once literally given the coat off my back to a homeless woman who had been given the bum's rush when she had taken refuge in a local business, seeking only to warm up during a bitterly cold day. I had assisted the elderly, not for pay but because I knew that they couldn't afford to hire anyone to do much-needed chores around their homes.

During a time in my life when I could have desperately used it, I had found nearly a thousand dollars in cash on the sidewalk in a wet, trampled envelope. I called the police, who contacted the man who had lost it. He arrived at the office where I worked within minutes, flushed and agitated. He didn't even thank me, which was surprising. But I was really taken aback when he simply seized the money, counted it and then, to my horror, asked me where the rest was. I found out later that the poor guy had dropped close to three thousand dollars in cash on the way to his bank.

Although he didn't thank me that afternoon, my day still turned out better than his. I still had a job. After dropping the deposit, I doubt that he did.

The day I read that story I was depressed. The past six months had been a real trial. Everything seemed to be spiraling out of control with non-stop emotional and financial losses. My mom, who suffered from dementia, died unexpectedly. Shortly before her death, my dog and my mom's beloved cat had died as well, along with all my chickens after a predator got into the henhouse.

My heating system had ruptured, pouring rusty water onto my carpet, which ruined it and caused my vinyl flooring to lift and swell. My carpet and flooring would have to be replaced as well as the entire heating system. I had also been stuck in a wheelchair for six months. It was just one horrible thing after another.

Bitterly, I thought, *Where's my what-goes-around-comes-around moment, God? I have served You and tried to live right, but where's my reward? Where's my compensation? Where is my acknowledgment that You know I did a good thing?*

Burying my face in my hands, with my heart burdened and heavy, I felt like crying, but it was too cold in my house. My tears would probably freeze. I felt completely hopeless and helpless as I sat there, too overwhelmed to even pray.

It wasn't a tangible voice, but I heard it nonetheless. "Look around you."

Lifting my head, I saw a gleaming new faucet. My brother had replaced it when it couldn't be repaired, refusing reimbursement. I saw a cabinet beside the stove, crafted by another brother. The walls of my home had been cleaned and painted by my family when I had purchased this house, my first home.

The house had been a foreclosure — beyond filthy and desperately in need of repairs. So, my family had dug in to help repair, clean and make it livable. I had purchased the house for half its value in a rural paradise where I would never have been able to afford a home. Everything had just fallen into place for its purchase. Upon reflection, I realized that things in my life had seemingly just "fallen into place" too many times to be a coincidence.

For a believer, there are no coincidences. My life has His handiwork written all over it. So often, things fall into place, achieving almost impossible results.

There were little things and big things, but they all proved to me that I was blessed. Last spring, my mower threw a belt, and I was unable to mow. My neighbor rolled up on his mower, cut my grass, and refused any pay. He then repaired my mower.

When I had surgery and was stuck in a wheelchair, my cousin and aunt drove to my home nightly for months, tending to my hens and ducks. They also refused compensation. These are just a few examples that I have indeed received favor.

So, that morning it was brought to my bone-headed attention just how blessed I truly am. I have appealed to God in my needs and completely missed His obvious response so many times. I'm surrounded by daily blessings!

Every month, I'm able to buy groceries, pay my utility bills, and purchase gas for my car. They're not dramatic, but they are blessings, nonetheless. Imagine what would happen if I couldn't?

If we look around, the everyday blessings are there.

Did I mention that the COVID stimulus check will cover my insurance deductible so I can repair my heating system and flooring? What goes around does come around.

— Laurel L. Shannon —

17

Rooted in Gratitude

Using your fire to ignite someone else's,
will not dim your light... It will illuminate
the room and you will shine, together.
~B.K. Sweeting

When the anniversary of our grandson's death was approaching, I decided to return to my local grief group. I felt the need to talk about my sadness again and get some support from others who share similar feelings.

It had been a while since I had attended. The format was familiar, but the faces were new to me. It didn't take long for the common bond of grief to draw us together, though.

After the large group met and the speaker had finished, we broke into small groups. The leader of our group began by asking that we each "check in" by sharing the sadness that brought us to the group and relate how we were doing.

When the turn came for the large, teddy-bear-like man sitting next to me, he cited his sorrow over recently losing his only remaining family member. Then he looked up over his large, horned-rimmed glasses and said with gentle sincerity, "I'm thankful to be here. I'm thankful for each of you. I'm thankful I have shelter and food. Happy Thanksgiving."

Instantly, warm tears came from a deep, holy place in my heart and ran down my cheeks. I had an urge to reach out and hug this tender-hearted man.

Someone in the group responded by asking, "Do you have somewhere to go for Thanksgiving?"

"Yes, I will find a meal at one of the churches," he answered with confidence. No one spoke, and the turn passed to me.

I wiped my tears, controlled my urge to hug, and felt my sorrow settle.

Soon, the meeting was over, and I made my way to my car.

While walking, I felt the bright autumn sun on my face, looked up to see the clear blue sky, and realized I felt so different from the way I had felt when I arrived.

My mind was calm, and my heart was still. I felt close to my grandson and grateful for the joy he had brought to me and the love we had shared. In fact, I felt grateful for everything: the cool, crisp weather, the trees, the people at the meeting, my neighborhood, my car, my life in general!

Teddy-Bear Man's heart was filled with sadness and ached with missing his loved one, yet he seemed to know there was more to his story. He was thankful. His words of gratitude were a saving moment for me. His gratitude opened my heart.

Gratitude is powerful.

I'm not talking about the denial of reality. Sadness is real. Anger, depression, annoyance, and discouragement are all real.

Leaning into our feelings, whatever they are, nourishes our humanity. But gratitude is the bedrock for these feelings, as well as for our experiences. It keeps us grounded.

Gratitude roots us in hope, and hope is what keeps us living.

I want to be more like Teddy-Bear Man. I want to be so rooted in gratitude that even when I'm experiencing the hardest parts of life, gratitude will be my "check in."

"Gratitude turns what we have into enough," someone said wisely, no matter what we have lost or don't have.

— Norma Bourland —

18

Dinner with My Dad

Confidence is half the victory.
~Yiddish Proverb

My late father was a complex man who died more than two decades ago. In many ways, I'm still trying to get to know him; the true bonding moments we shared were few and far between. One conversation will always stand out in my mind, as it not only represents who he truly was but who I am to this day.

The third of four siblings raised by hard-working Russian immigrants, Dad grew up in the Bronx during the Depression. As an adult, he survived Japanese air raids on the 58th United States Naval Construction Battalion (Seabees) in the South Pacific during World War II; the tragic capsizing of party fishing boat, *Pelican*, which killed dozens of men, women, and children just off Long Island's Montauk Point on Labor Day of 1951; as well as the numerous challenges of building and sustaining a successful New York City-based fur-manufacturing business that served loyal customers for more than forty years.

Worldly and well-read, his self-acquired knowledge made him very opinionated and, on occasion, a bit of a bully. But Dad easily held his own in discussions on almost any subject despite never having attended college. He lived with an assortment of personal demons — some quite obvious and others, for the most part, left unspoken — but I admired his strength, courage, and ability to press on even through the most difficult circumstances.

Happy to share his positive life outlook with anyone he encountered, my father was always able to cheer me on to complete any task or overcome any obstacle. I was his firstborn, and he expected a lot from me.

Whether I was learning to ride a bike, baking his favorite cookies, or completing a tough homework assignment, I tried to make him proud. No matter what I confronted, "Tomorrow will be a better day" were the words he repeated to me hundreds if not thousands of times.

In my mid-twenties, living in Manhattan and still trying to figure out what I wanted to do with my life, I found myself between jobs due to a difficult economic downturn. Even though I lived in a modest apartment on the Upper West Side, money was tight.

When my father called one morning to invite me out for dinner, I almost declined. But I will always be grateful that I pulled myself together and joined him that evening.

It wasn't the restaurant's great Szechuan menu and bustling ambience. It wasn't the hundred-dollar bill that Dad always managed to slip into my pocket "just to help out" every time he saw me. What changed my life and entire perspective were the words he said to me as we sat in his huge Buick outside my building when he finally drove me home.

"What's really got you down, honey?" he asked.

I looked at him with tears in my eyes and said, "I feel so poor."

Hugging me to his side, he lifted my chin with one finger and told me, "You aren't poor at all. You may be broke, but you aren't poor. Broke means you don't have any money, but poor means you don't have any hope."

I still get choked up every time I share those wise words with others.

There have been more hard times and plenty of other hurdles in my life since that cold winter night, but I've never forgotten the lesson my father taught me. Hope has kept me going through thick, thin, and even thinner. Thanks to that dinner with my dad, I know it always will.

— Jane R. Snyder —

19

In Search of New Friends

God doesn't move in your life when you struggle;
He moves when you pray.
~Author Unknown

Our family shed a lot of tears in 2020. Tears when our home-school co-op was canceled. Tears when the soccer season was canceled. Tears when birthday plans changed. Tears when grandparents couldn't visit. But mostly tears when our best friends moved. Best friends, plural — two families with whom we had shared our lives for the past several years.

We spent most of our time together in a church small group, with the adults talking and studying the Bible while the kids played. We shared our Thanksgiving dinners and hid Easter eggs in each other's yards. We knew we could call on them when we needed help. We prayed together, played at the park together, and laughed together. We cried together when we lost loved ones. And our kids were best friends.

Then, one of the families moved 2,000 miles away. The second family announced that they were moving, too, 1,700 miles away.

Our kids mourned through the summer as they anticipated the departure of their remaining friend. They declared they would never make a friend again — partly to avoid the heartache and partly because they genuinely believed it was impossible. After all, 2020 was not an easy year for social gatherings and spontaneous friendships.

Nevertheless, as we counted down each day to our friends' move, we prayed that God would send us new friends. We went swimming with our friends, and we prayed God would send new friends. We hiked with our friends, and we prayed God would send new friends. We rode bikes at the park with our friends, and we prayed God would send new friends.

We continued to meet as a church small group, and our kids dreaded the day when there would be no other kids left to play with. We prayed harder. At our last small-group meeting, the adults took turns telling each other what we appreciated about our friendship. The kids exchanged homemade gifts. We unveiled a bag of surprises for our friends' drive across the country. We still had a few days of special outings planned, so our family left for an outdoor worship service on the church lawn.

We sang and prayed and listened to the pastor. At the end of the service, I turned around to pick up my camp chair. Behind me and to the right sat a family I had never seen. Three kids. My own three had already spotted them and hurried to introduce themselves. Within minutes, they were running around the lawn, playing games, and laughing.

Our new friends joined our small group the following week. They were new to the area, and their kids were very close to our own kids' ages. They were also a homeschool family, and the kids quickly discovered that they all enjoyed riding scooters, climbing trees, and reading many of the same books. We all love the new friends who came into our lives at the exact right time.

We still miss our old friends, but now we have more friends. More joy. More laughs. And fewer tears.

— Melissa Cutrera —

Three Minutes

Anything is possible when you have
the right people there to support you.
~Misty Copeland

Each morning, I hear my phone ring around 8:00 A.M. Instead of answering it, I let it go to voicemail. Anyone who is not familiar with this practice will think I am avoiding the caller and usually say, "Aren't you going to answer that?"

I listen to the message when I have time to relax and be alone. It is a call from my friend Tina. After listening to her talk, I call her cell and leave a similar message.

This practice started ten years ago when I came to a crossroads in my life. I had been sober for twenty years, but the AA meetings that I attended didn't satisfy me anymore. I had helped other suffering alcoholics as the program taught me, but I felt empty. I enjoyed being around nature more than sitting in a church basement. At the meetings, I sounded like a broken record, saying the same thing over and over and hearing the same thing repeatedly.

Tina was my sponsor. I told her how I felt. She is a firm believer in "meeting makers make it," so she was not thrilled to hear my decision to stop attending meetings. We discussed it on her front porch one afternoon over glasses of iced tea. We finally came up with a solution, a compromise in a way, to keep me on track. We decided to call each other daily.

"Let's set some guidelines to these calls," she said, wanting me to know this was not just a place to shoot the breeze or whine about things.

The guidelines for our calls were simple:

- We would leave a message for each other in a three-minute time slot.
- We would discuss three good things we did for ourselves the day before.
- We would leave a list of what we are grateful for.

Like anything else, it took a while to master the calls. It was a new kind of relationship for both of us, and sometimes I would get overwhelmed by the events of the previous day and leave a long-winded message. But after ten years, it comes as naturally as breathing.

The most important thing I have found over the years is that gratitude has more weight when I say it out loud rather than just putting it in writing.

We both put our sobriety as number one on our daily list. Without it, I would not be writing this. I would be dead and buried in a potter's field with no mourners to grieve my drunken soul.

What we are grateful for does not usually include material possessions but includes:

- Family and friends
- A higher power
- The steps of AA
- Good health
- Our pets
- Each other — our daily calls and friendship
- Interests. For me, it is hiking and the outdoors, writing, and working with animals.

Of course, we are grateful for a roof over our head and a drivable car, but we know money cannot buy happiness. I remember different things to be grateful for, like not having any resentments taking up space in my head after going through a challenging period of acceptance.

It's tough to get this all in a three-minute time slot, so an extra call is allowed. There's nothing worse than pouring your soul out — only to be cut off by a beep.

These calls have given me a new outlook on life. No matter what bad stuff happens to either of us, we always seem to bounce back.

If I were to do a flowchart of one year, I would probably find fewer than ten days when life seemed not to be worth it. Once, I hit an all-time low over something. I can't even remember the incident but remember the hopeless feeling. I told Tina I didn't think I could call her anymore. She responded the next day that she needed my calls and she hoped I'd feel better.

Within a day, I was calling her again, licking my wounds and, if nothing else, grateful for sobriety. Within a few days, I returned to my more positive self. I also realized that these calls were helping me and just as crucial to Tina for her serenity.

We are a team, and when one of us falls, the other is always there to pick her up. I have put in that extra call and talk one-on-one when I am concerned about her. Tina does the same for me. I know I can count on her.

I feel like one of the luckiest people on Earth to have a support system like this.

— Carole Olsen —

Everyday Miracles

Beyond Butterflies

*Butterflies are nature's angels. They remind us
what a gift it is to be alive.*
~Robyn Nola

My husband Kevin and I were home inspectors in central Florida during the first decade of the 2000s. The housing bubble, undeterred by several hurricanes, kept us hopping every day of the week. Up early, lunch on the go, typing up and reviewing reports over dinner, off to bed to get up and go at it again the next day.

We worked together, ate together, slept together, and exercised together. We had the pleasure of meeting lots of different people over the years, each with their own story. There were many empty-nest couples who were downsizing to a small Florida house for their retirement. There were also a few couples who were upsizing so they could each have their own space, or to make room for children and grandchildren who would be visiting from out of state. And, of course, there were young people buying a starter home. Invariably, the one question they almost all asked us was, "How can you stand to be around each other 24/7?"

We'd laugh and say, "We're one of the few married couples who actually like one another!"

The houses that we inspected also ran the gamut, from brand-new houses, to older ones that the seller had carefully restored, to "tear-downs" — termite-ridden shacks on a canal that fetched a hefty price just for their location.

We had a system that helped to make us one of the best home-inspection teams in central Florida. Kevin would inspect the outside of the house, the roof, attic, garage, and occasional crawl space underneath. I would inspect the inside of the house, appliances, doors, windows, etc. Afterward, we would give a verbal rundown of our findings to those who had hired us, which was more often than not the prospective buyers of the house.

Once in a while, we would get to inspect a really nice house with few problems to report, which allowed us a bit of a respite in the middle of the day. On one such day, inspecting a very nice house in Palm Coast, Kevin had just emerged from the 130-degrees-Fahrenheit attic and headed for the back yard, where the previous homeowner had left a water hose. Since this was a rare occasion when no one else was present — no Realtors, buyers or sellers — he took the liberty of drenching himself with cool water from the hose, and I took a few minutes to enjoy the quiet beauty around me.

The house was on the outskirts of town, surrounded by vacant, wooded lots. I decided to head for the trees to find relief in the shade. As I approached the edge of the wooded lot, I noticed a few butterflies fluttering around the shrubs. Always intrigued by nature, I moved in for a closer look. The butterflies didn't seem to mind, and I got to see them in all their glory.

We packed up and continued to the third, and final, inspection of the day — a condo in Daytona Beach — which, to Kevin's relief, had no attic in which to swelter.

Upon completion of the condo inspection, we gave our verbal report to the buyer and the Realtor. While Kevin engaged in conversation about cars and airplanes, I excused myself to attempt to phone the buyer of the previous home in Palm Coast, whom I had been unable to reach earlier. I stepped out onto the balcony of the condo and enjoyed the onshore breeze while I dialed.

The buyer answered, "Hello?"

"Hello, this is Marsha. Is this Susan?" I asked.

"Yes," said the voice on the other end.

"Hi, Susan! My husband, Kevin, and I inspected your new home earlier today, and I just wanted to give you a rundown of our findings."

"Yes, I got your voicemail earlier. Sorry I missed your call," she said.

I proceeded to fill her in on our findings, which did not take very long, and then I asked for her e-mail address for the final report.

"That's it?" asked Susan, sounding relieved and excited.

"Yes, that's it," I said, "not much to share. It's a nice house that has been very well-maintained." Susan and I chatted a few more minutes. She was excited about her impending move to Florida where she and her husband would begin their retirement.

"Oh, I almost forgot!" I said before we said our goodbyes. "You should have lots of butterflies come spring."

There was silence on the other end of the line.

"Are you still there, Susan?" I asked.

More silence. "…Yes… What did you just say?" asked Susan.

"I said you should have lots of butterflies come spring. After we finished your home inspection today, I stepped outside and went over to the edge of the wooded lot next door to enjoy the shade. As I approached the tree line, I noticed a few butterflies fluttering around the shrubbery. I moved in for a closer look, figuring they would just fly away, but, to my surprise, they seemed oblivious to my presence.

"It was really magical. The butterflies were busy laying eggs on the leaves and branches, and I eased in between the shrubs. As I stood there, it was as though time stood still, and only the butterflies were in motion. They fluttered all around my head! One even fluttered so close to my face I could feel the breeze from its delicate wings on my cheek. I watched them in awe for several minutes. I've never experienced anything like that before. I just wanted to share it with you."

Again, there was silence on the line.

"Susan, are you still there?" I asked.

"Yes, I'm here," she said. I could hear the tears in her voice.

"Are you okay?" I asked gently.

"I lost my mother a year ago," said Susan. "She often said that, if she could, she'd come back as a butterfly and to watch for her."

I suddenly realized the potential meaning of my butterfly experience, for both myself and for Susan.

"Thank you," said Susan. "Thank you for telling me that." I could hear the smile in her voice.

"You are very welcome," I said, fighting back my own tears.

— Marsha Shepherd Whitt —

22

Look for the Rainbow

Magic exists. Who can doubt it, when there are
rainbows and wildflowers, the music of the wind
and the silence of the stars?
~Nora Roberts

Tooth-fairy nights were always filled with excitement and anticipation at our house. One such night, while my husband and I were watching a movie, our daughter informed us that, after much assistance, her wiggly tooth had finally come out.

"How exciting," we told her. "Don't forget to put it under your pillow so the tooth fairy will pay you a visit tonight."

We reminded ourselves to check for her tooth as soon as our movie was over. After all, we did not want her to miss out on the tooth fairy's surprise.

"Okay," our daughter agreed, and she skipped to her room, carefully guarding her newly acquired prized possession in a loose fist.

However, by the time the movie was over, we stumbled off to bed... completely forgetting our promise to each other.

Bright and early the next morning, we were awakened by squeals of joy coming from our daughter's room. "Mommy! Daddy! Come see what the tooth fairy brought me!"

Stunned, my husband and I exchanged confused glances. "Did you remember to check for her tooth before bed?" my husband asked.

"No... Did you?" I replied.

Quickly, we made our way to our daughter's room and found her sitting on her bed, looking out the window at a rainbow.

"Isn't it beautiful?" she asked, and her eyes shone with sheer appreciation.

As my daughter stared out the window at her prize in the sky, I reached under her pillow to "check for any other treasures that she may have overlooked."

"Are you sure you felt all around when checking for your prize?" I asked, and we watched as she carefully searched underneath her pillow.

"Wow! Two prizes!" she said, proudly waving the dollar bill she "must have overlooked" during her first treasure hunt.

I thought about all the different ways that scenario could have gone and found myself marveling at the reaction of my five-year-old upon failing to find a treasure under her pillow. How would I have reacted at that age? Would I have felt betrayed by the tooth fairy, or would I have looked for the treasure elsewhere?

Later, as I reflected upon the situation, I realized that the tooth fairy had left a hidden gift for me, as well: a reminder that when life rains on our carefully devised plans or even sends us unexpected storms, there are always treasures to be found. We just need to look for the rainbows.

— Cynthia Zayn —

23

Blessed Bloom

*There are always flowers for those
who want to see them.*
~Henri Matisse

Green thumbs run in my family, on my mother's side. It shouldn't be a surprise, I guess. Her father used to operate a greenhouse.

We kids grew up playing on lush green Ohio grass, lined with long, colorful rose and iris beds that separated the back yards in our neighborhood. When Mom planted something, it usually grew.

The acorns didn't fall far from that oak, and we children turned out to love the earth and growing things in it, too. As adults, we appreciate all our mom's labor-intensive gardening work, applaud each other's gardening successes, and commiserate about the frustrations of chipmunks that eat our strawberries or deer that strip our lilies.

All four of Mom's children are also remarkably healthy, just as she was. I have a theory that gardening is good for people. Working outside and putting our hands in the dirt to help plants thrive is therapeutic. Nurturing others (things and people) is symbiotic and, in turn, nurtures us. A vase of fresh daisies on the kitchen table, raised and picked right outside our door, is good for the soul.

I have always been the healthiest person I know, along with my mother. And grateful for it. While others come down with pneumonia or need knee surgery, I just get a light cold once every four or five years. I had perfect attendance at school and work most years.

That was until last year, when my good fortune hit a wall. A biopsy confirmed a small stage-1 lump. It was caught early and, luckily, removed in a lumpectomy (although it took two surgeries). But, to prevent it from coming back, the doctors recommended both chemotherapy and radiation. These kept me in treatments and drugs for six months and left me devoid of hair, white blood cells, and strength. But there was nothing to do but put one foot in front of the other, take one day at a time, and pray that it would all go away. I was well aware that millions of women have had to deal with the shock and trauma of breast cancer. You have to try to stay positive, even when it seems impossible, I decided.

But between the surgeries and the first chemo treatment, a sudden shocking diagnosis of type 2 diabetes landed me in the emergency room. I hadn't known much about diabetes but soon learned that I would need medicine the rest of my life. And that I could no longer eat most foods I like — or just two bites of them — or my blood sugar would soar.

That new development was exacerbated by the chemo treatments nearly shutting down my taste buds, so that even foods I have always loved didn't taste good and the mere smell of others — like fish cooking — set my stomach rolling. Queasiness from the chemo made eating tentative at best. And add to this the daily pricking of my fingers, bleeding myself to monitor my blood glucose.

With this double whammy of diabetes and chemotherapy, I quickly lost twenty-five pounds. I had no hair, and my bones were easily visible under my skin.

The doctors had predicted that I would come through it all fine, since I was such a healthy, active person to begin with. But they also warned me about fatigue. I hadn't worried about that too much, though, because of my normal energy and stamina. It was sick people who suffered from fatigue, I figured.

But the doctors were right. Even though my husband had taken over nearly every chore — grocery shopping, cooking dinner, cleaning up, laundry — I was exhausted by dinnertime and in bed by 8:00 P.M. wearing a soft, fleece sleep cap to keep my bald head warm. The diabetes kept me needing something to eat at least five times a day, so I was either hungry or queasy most of the time. Or both.

And depressed. How much I had lost astounded me, even though the surgery had been successful. My active life was gone. I had to leave volunteer activities and a part-time job and still didn't have enough energy to walk around a short block. I felt out of the loop and spent way too much time on the couch. And the doctor appointments! I typically saw the doctor once a year at my annual checkup. Like most healthy people, I suspect, I begrudged that time and hassle because I was always fine. In the eight months following the biopsy, though, I had surgery, a treatment, or a doctor's appointment fifty-five times. This was enough to keep a normally super-healthy person despondent nearly 24/7.

But one pleasure of my previous normal life did not disappear. Every morning, especially in the spring and summer, I like to walk around our yard and see how my flowers and crops are faring. Watching things grow is a tonic and helps reassure me that life goes on, no matter what.

When the daily radiation treatments were nearly finished, what was left of me was still standing, and I hoped that I had survived the worst of it. One Saturday on my morning perambulation, something new caught my eye. It was standing at the front corner of the garage where I couldn't miss it. An iris! One beautiful, blue-and-yellow iris was smiling at me. I had meant to plant irises for years because my mother had blue-and-yellow irises that I loved growing along our driveway when we were kids, but I hadn't gotten around to it.

This wondrous iris — that I had not planted — immediately brought my mom to me at this lowest point in my life, both physically and mentally. I knew she was there, and with tears rolling down my cheeks and a catch in my throat, I said, "Thanks, Mom. I'll be all right."

How to explain this sentimental, unplanted blossom appearing in my garden as if by magic? I like to think it was a message of blooming hope and strength from my mom up in heaven, watching over me with an "attagirl" smile. I could hear her voice saying, "You've survived. Many people don't. Think how lucky you are! No matter how hard things get, always be grateful for your blessings." And I am, especially for the one that's easy to take for granted: good health.

— Becky S. Tompkins —

24

Fifteen Dollars

Kindness can transform someone's
dark moment with a blaze of light.
~Amy Leigh Mercree

"Wake up, Mama!" I felt a chubby, little hand on my face and reluctantly opened my eyelids. There was my son, ready to start the day. I also heard my baby and toddler awake in the next room. Ready or not, the day had begun!

I loved being home with my little ones, but I felt the weight of the world on my shoulders. My husband and I had just bought a house, and some unexpected expenses made our budget tighter than it had ever been. I was weary of pinching pennies. We weren't foolish with our money. We worked hard. We were doing all the right things. But we had had one financial disappointment after another.

I dragged myself out of bed and pulled on my faded jeans and sneakers that had seen better days. I only had one task on the to-do list for the day. I was going to pick up my kids' photo portraits from the studio at the local mall. Despite our small budget, it was important to me to have pictures of my children as they were growing up. The previous week, I had found a coupon and used some change from the car to buy a $7.99 portrait package, and today was the day I was to pick up the portraits. Since we were going to the mall, I decided to make it an outing and packed some sandwiches for us to eat at the food court.

After breakfast, I bundled everyone into the car, and off we went. After we parked, I unfolded the double stroller, put in the youngest two kids, and gave the oldest his instructions to hold onto the stroller and not let go.

We wheeled into the portrait studio at the mall, and I approached the counter. The young woman smiled. "May I help you?"

"Yes, I'm here to pick up our photos."

The woman asked my name and squeaked open her large filing cabinet drawer. "Schmoyer… Schmoyer… Ah, yes, here they are. Aren't they just so adorable?" She fanned out the photos, and the smiling faces of my kids warmed my heart.

"Yes, they are great. Thank you," I said.

She scooped up the photos to place in an envelope for me. Then she spread out additional photos of my kids that I hadn't ordered. I knew what that meant. The upsell pitch was coming.

"Would you like to purchase these extra portraits? They are only fifteen dollars apiece!" she smiled sweetly.

My face hardened, and my heart turned cold. "I don't have fifteen dollars." I took the photo envelope and wheeled away, with my cheeks red after my curt reply.

Next, we stopped at the ride-on cars in the mall's food court. There weren't any other kids there, which was good because my kids still didn't know that the machines took quarters. They just climbed on them for some free, stationary fun.

After a while, I corralled them to a table and unwrapped our peanut-butter-and-jelly lunches that I had brought from home. It was early for lunch, but we were hungry and the food court was mostly empty.

After we bowed our heads to thank God for our food, I lifted up my eyes and was surprised to find a woman standing next to our table. She stretched out her hand and pressed something into mine. She said, "Here. Take your family out for ice cream after lunch." I was surprised. I managed to mumble "thank you" as she turned and walked away. Then I looked down at what she had given me.

The crumpled bills totaled fifteen dollars.

Tears rolled down my cheeks as I quietly finished my sandwich. The doubts in my heart melted away and my faith was renewed.

—Rachel Schmoyer—

25

Thank You, Mr. Truck Driver

There are only two ways to live your life.
One is as though nothing is a miracle.
The other is as though everything is a miracle.
~Albert Einstein

"Hurry up! We have to get going," I said to the kids. It was Tuesday morning, my busy day at work, and we always seemed to be running late.

We rushed out the door. I had a cup of coffee in one hand, a baby in the other arm, and some work papers tucked underneath my chin. I had already asked my ten-year-old daughter to grab my keys and phone. Somehow, with all the things I was carrying, I managed to reach in, lock the door and close it. Only then did I realize my daughter had my phone (which she was playing games on), but my keys were nowhere in sight.

"Where are my keys?" I asked, frustrated because I already knew the answer.

"Oops," she said.

Great, I thought, *now we are going to be really late.*

My daughter managed to find our spare rather quickly so it was only a twenty- or thirty-second delay, but getting locked out is just one of those frustrating things that always leads me to look up and whine, "Why, God, why? What is the point of this?" As if God has time to worry about me remembering to grab my keys or locking myself out of the house!

About twenty minutes later, we were almost to my parents' ranch, where I was going to drop off the kids so I could head to work. On a little farm-to-market road (the middle of nowhere), we had only seen three other vehicles. One of them was a big 18-wheeler headed in the opposite direction, which was about to pass us. Suddenly, his left front tire blew, and I saw it fly twenty feet into the air as the huge truck came barreling toward us. The truck swerved completely into our lane just a few car lengths in front of us.

In a split second, I had to decide if I should swerve to the left or to the right. Neither way seemed like it would end well at the speed we were going. I thought of my babies snuggled in the back seat.

By some miracle, the truck driver was able to pull that big rig back into his lane before he hit us or I made any drastic swerve, which would have surely rolled our vehicle. We passed him in what felt like slow motion as I realized the tragedy we had just avoided and wondered how that truck driver managed that impossible maneuver.

In my rearview mirror, I saw him pull over on the side of the road to fix his tire. I slowed down but continued on my way to my parents' house in a trance, with so many thoughts rushing through my head. I knew there was nothing I could do to help fix his tire, although I wished I could do something.

I pulled into my parents' driveway and came to a stop. I sat there for a minute, taking some deep breaths. I turned and looked at my babies. My son was snuggled happily in his car seat, and my beautiful daughter was playing with him and talking baby talk. I smiled and thanked God.

"I can't believe what just happened," I said out loud finally.

"What are you talking about?" my daughter replied.

They had been so busy playing that they apparently didn't see the big rig coming. I shook my head and went to turn off my ignition. When I reached for my keys, I cried happy, thankful tears again.

If we had been just a few seconds ahead of where we were on that road, if we hadn't gotten locked out of the house that morning, I don't think I'd be here to write this story today.

After I dropped off the kids, I stopped on the side of the road where the trucker sat, waiting for a wrecker to pull him to the tire shop. I didn't know what to say. Before I got out of my truck, I saw an unopened bottle of water sitting in my passenger seat. I grabbed it and walked up and handed it to him. It was a hot day and a kind gesture at least.

"I don't know how you pulled that truck back over into your lane so fast," I said.

"I don't either," he replied, shaking his head. "Was that you who was coming toward me?"

"Yes, me and my two babies," I replied.

Tears welled up in both of our eyes. This happened right in the middle of the COVID-19 pandemic, so we didn't shake hands or hug. As I drove off, headed to work once again, I almost turned around because what I had really wanted to say, although I was too choked up to find the words, was "Thank you, Mr. Truck Driver, for saving our lives." And thank you, God, for making me forget my keys!

— Kayleen Kitty Holder —

26

Shower-Curtain Liner

*Everything we need to fulfill our true destiny always
comes to us at the perfect time. But spiritual awareness
is required to recognize those gifts and opportunities.*
~Anthon St. Maarten

I am a morning person. By seven, I've eaten breakfast, had that second cup of coffee, washed the dishes, and taken my shower and put on make-up. Then, it's on to the household chores.

One early morning, I was scrubbing the bathtub and wiping down the shower curtain, as well as its liner, when it hit me. My budget was so limited that I was actually forced to scrub a two-dollar plastic liner because I didn't have a few extra dollars to buy a new one. I couldn't believe it! Grumbling isn't how I would normally choose to start the day, especially when the sun was shining.

To cheer up and continue the day a bit more optimistically, I left the chores for later and set out for my daily walk at the beach a little earlier than usual. The local shops had not yet opened. All was quiet, as the only other people nearby were dog walkers, joggers, and students on their bikes.

Along the way through the downtown area, something on the sidewalk caught my attention. From a distance, it appeared to be a package of some sort. I walked over and picked it up. Upon examination, it turned out to be a small brown paper bag with no markings. Had a name or address been on the bag, I could put it in front of the appropriate store for the owner to find and notify the customer.

However, without a name, there was absolutely no way to tell which store it had come from. The downtown stretched on for at least eight or nine blocks with stores, restaurants and coffee shops on both sides of the main street. Grocery stores, furniture shops, bakeries, hair salons, banks, churches, discount stores, home-goods stores, clothing shops and other businesses lined the street. And none of them had yet opened for business. It was too early.

All this meant that the item had most likely been purchased by someone the evening or day before. It would not be possible to figure out who they were or where they might be found. Since it was near the curb, I assumed someone must've dropped it, perhaps while loading other bags into their car.

There was nothing left to do but look inside the bag for more information. The item inside was wrapped in clear plastic with no writing on it. As it turned out, I was looking at the back of the package. So, I flipped it over to find any kind of identification on the front. No store name, but the brand marking on the front clearly specified what the product was. Believe it or not, it was a shower-curtain liner!

Speechless, I turned it over many times in my hands. It was a brand-new, unopened shower-curtain liner. I just happened to be the person who walked by and found the package on the sidewalk by the curb.

I don't know how someone else would've reacted in this situation. It even took me a few minutes to decide what to do next, not wanting to claim something that did not belong to me. Were it a more valuable item, I would've brought it to the police station right across the street, but I suspected the police might just share a good laugh over a two-dollar shower-curtain liner. I decided to keep the liner for myself.

But I was still stunned because, just a few minutes prior, I had been at home, complaining about this very same item. The worthless plastic liner that had needed scrubbing and inspired my grumbling and early morning walk had suddenly transformed itself into a gift left on the sidewalk for me! How that moment brightened my day. One could say it was an amazing coincidence. No argument there. It absolutely was. Likewise, one could say it was a blessing sent from

Heaven above. Again, no argument there. It absolutely was.

Having said that, I am certain of a few things. At home, inside the confines of my bathroom, my focus was exclusively on myself, my anxieties, my troubles, my needs, as well as my limits in being able to fix the problem. Once outside, thinking of the ocean and life across the horizon, I relaxed in the perspective of a much bigger picture, one that reached across the ocean and all the way up to Heaven. In so doing, my personal grumblings changed to thankfulness for the beauty that extended before my eyes and the manna from Heaven in the form of a brand-new shower-curtain liner. By the way, it matched perfectly with the color scheme and accessories in my bathroom!

—June E. Taylor—

27

Rock On

People appreciate and never forget that helping hand
especially when times are tough.
~Catherine Pulsifer

After a year of isolation due to COVID, my husband and I were looking forward to a few days away. We had talked about all the things we would do when life became normal again: dining out, traveling and seeing friends. We chose to travel to the shores of Lake Michigan. We both love being by the water, and I am an out-and-out rockhound. There is no place quite like the Michigan shoreline for beautiful rocks and fossils.

My husband is disabled, so I try to share as much of my adventures as possible. He is patient and enjoys seeing whatever I can share with him.

My long-time goal was to find a Petoskey stone, which is a fossilized coral. It is the state stone and only found in that area. But by day three, I was feeling that familiar disappointment. I had found an abundance of beautiful rocks for my collection but was missing the most important one.

I pulled out of one more roadside park on the shoreline and headed for the town of Petoskey. Surely, they would be plentiful there. If not, I would head home empty-handed one more time.

About a half-hour down the road, my cell phone rang, and someone asked if it was Carol. I hesitantly said yes. I was in no mood to be bothered by a telemarketer. The caller introduced herself as Connie and said she had found my suitcase in the middle of the highway. I could not believe it. I had not even labeled our luggage. I pulled over and walked to the back of my pickup. The tailgate was hanging wide open.

Not one other thing had fallen out except for the suitcase, which had not been disturbed since early morning when it was stowed and the tailgate firmly shut. Connie happened to find a three-year-old tag from a resort in Florida still hanging on the handle. We arranged to meet, and I thanked her profusely. It would have been a poor trip without clean clothes. The suitcase also contained my husband's wallet.

I offered Connie a reward, but she refused to take it. We made polite small talk. I explained that I was most likely distracted because I was on a mission to find a Petoskey stone, and I was failing miserably. She said she wanted to show me something and opened the trunk of her car. In an array of small buckets, she had various rocks and minerals, including Petoskey stones. I was in awe. She said if I wanted to find Petoskey stones, I should follow her.

About twenty minutes down the road, we pulled into another roadside drive and walked down to the shore. She quickly found a small Petoskey stone, and afterwards I kept finding those camouflaged fossils all on my own. Since that time, I have learned that Connie and I have much in common. We both love writing, family, and rock hunting.

Connie was being treated for cancer. Her outcome sounds promising. To get through the stress and treatments, much of her time is spent at the shore. I totally understand this. The sound of the waves and the beautiful blue waters have a way of taking the stress out to sea. I pray for Connie daily and hope that my support can repay her for her kindness.

I believe in divine intervention because none of this seems to have happened by accident. Everything happened for a reason. I found the secreted Petoskey stones thanks to Connie's help. My luggage fell out without explanation and was not damaged. It was returned thanks to a forgotten, old tag with my phone number. A kind and honest person was on that road at the right time and decided to stop and rescue the luggage rather than go on with her day.

The chance meeting of a special person, under the strangest of circumstances, was uplifting to both of us in different ways. Instead of remaining strangers, we found that we share common bonds, and that serving others in small acts of kindness brings us together in very big ways. When I see my Petoskey stones, they now mean so much more to me. I was truly gifted, and that's the only time before or since that my tailgate has opened without a struggle.

— Carol Anne Lake —

We Have Jalapeños!

If we experienced life through the eyes of a child,
everything would be magical and extraordinary.
Let our curiosity, adventure and
wonder of life never end.
~Akiane Kramarik

It's just a small garden in the back yard. I don't stoop down nearly as well as I once did, so a friend of mine helped me build four raised beds. It's more of a hobby than a food producer, with a few tomatoes, squash, banana peppers, bell peppers and jalapeños.

My son Billy was ten the first year we had the garden, and it didn't produce much. When we discussed the garden that fall, we decided we needed to "spruce up" the soil a bit. We added some manure in the winter — because what isn't improved with a little manure? — and then whatever we could find at Tractor Supply in early spring. So, with the "enhanced" soil, it was with great optimism that we planted the garden on Good Friday. My dad always planted his garden on Good Friday and had great success.

I'm an engineer for a software company, so when I'm not traveling, I work from home. On those days, when Billy got home from school we would go out to the garden and do an inspection to see what was new from the previous day. Billy doesn't care for tomatoes or squash, so it was only with an intellectual interest that he monitored the progress of those plants. He does like jalapeños, however, and it was with much anticipation that he approached his daily inspection duties in that section of the garden.

As spring moved into early summer, we began to get tomatoes, squash, and even bell peppers. The jalapeños, however, continued to be a no-show. The plants looked good — they were well-fertilized and staked — but they refused to sprout peppers.

In mid-summer, I was required to travel again, and I left instructions for Billy to keep an eye on the garden in my absence. I was meeting with our largest account, located in southern California, and it would be a long trip. It was not an easy place to reach by any means from northern Mississippi.

So, I was already tired and jet-lagged when the meeting started early the first morning. The customer was not happy, and though it had nothing to do with me or my department, I was the one sitting across the table. A morning of venting turned into an afternoon of yelling as they criticized my company, my clothes, and even the job my mother had done raising me. They were just getting into my questionable heritage when my phone rang.

My wife and I have a system for when I travel. I call her three times a day — morning, lunch, and evening. She doesn't call me unless she really needs me. If I'm busy, I return her call during the next break. However, if she *really* needs me, like an emergency, she will call me twice in a row.

When my wife called me twice, I knew it was an emergency. I stepped outside and quickly dialed home. It wasn't my wife who answered on the first ring but Billy, who loudly exclaimed, "We have jalapeños!" I was not feeling well because of the trip and the verbal abuse, but this simple statement gave me back some perspective.

I would endure the grilling and then make my way back to north Mississippi through the convoluted route dictated by Delta. There, I would find my wife, happy to see me home, and my son, thrilled to show off the little buds of jalapeños dotting the garden.

Billy is in seminary now and grows his own jalapeños on the balcony of his apartment. My wife and I don't eat them, but I grow one plant each year, just to remind me to keep everything in perspective. And should my wife or I ever lose that perspective and allow the troubles of life to begin sapping our joy, we just look the other in the eye and state, "We have jalapeños!"

— Marv Stone —

Wishing for a Blessing

Simple pleasures are the last healthy
refuge in a complex world.
~Oscar Wilde

I knew better than to start mending overalls, my most dreaded task, that late in the day. But that morning when my husband asked me to patch the torn knee of his otherwise perfect overalls, it seemed like a doable project. So, I promised him I would. That's what my cup of coffee did first thing this morning. It fooled me into thinking that the day was endless, and nothing was impossible.

So, late in the day, I slid the bib overalls onto the sewing machine's free-arm bed, stopping at the hand-basted knee patch. After lowering the presser foot, I pushed the start button. The machine beeped to life — sending the needle hopping left and right, creating a row of zigzag stitches. I raised the presser foot and rotated the overalls. Over the radio blaring in my sewing room, I said, "Side one is done." The second side was shorter and went quickly. But, by the time I got halfway down the third side, trouble was brewing. "You can do this," I said to my machine, now grinding under the strain. My words did not magically make any more room inside that narrow pant leg.

Patching a pant leg without cutting open the side seam is like walking a dog in a closet. Yet, opening a side seam can really make a machine growl when those same two pieces of heavy denim fabric must be stitched back together.

"It's getting late, and I still have to fix dinner," I complained aloud, while pulling, stitching, pulling, stitching the taut fabric. Much to my amazement, I managed to complete the third side.

As I got the needle into the correct position on the fourth side, I paused to listen. "Call the radio station," the lady DJ said, "and tell our listeners about something you've done for someone during the pandemic."

Hmm. Wonder if patching overalls counts, I thought.

After much more start-and-stop sewing, I finished the last row of stitching just in time to hear the voice of a female caller. "During this pandemic, people all over our country have been struggling with so many issues. I decided there must be something I could do for at least one family. The first person I heard about who needed help lived in another state, hundreds of miles away. I found a pizza place in the town where this woman lived and had pizzas delivered for her and her family. She was so happy that she contacted me, and we ended up becoming good friends. Each month after that, I found a struggling family in a different state and sent them pizzas."

"What? I wish someone would send *me* a pizza," I said aloud in disbelief. I leaned back against my chair and stared out the window. Green, rolling fields stretched on forever, except for that winding gravel road cutting around the edge. "But that's not going to happen out here in the middle of nowhere."

I shut my eyes and tried to imagine the doorbell ringing, and instead of hearing "UPS," I heard "Pizza delivery." *No, wait.* My eyes flew open. *The pizza I want doesn't even have a delivery service. It comes from Pilot Grove, and someone is going to have to drive fifteen miles to get it. And it won't just be any cheesy pizza. It will be a large supreme topped with all kinds of good stuff.*

Who would surprise me with a pizza that required that much effort? Not my husband, because he was too busy feeding cattle on a farm so remote that cell-phone service is iffy. I sighed and said aloud, "It hasn't happened in all these years, and it's not going to happen tonight."

I jumped up because it was 5:00, time to get dinner started. In the kitchen, I picked up my cell phone and listened to my husband's voicemail. He said he was going to be late, and I didn't need to… I didn't need to what? No idea. Of course, the call dropped at the most important part.

I was chopping spinach for our salads when I heard the basement door shutting, followed by the familiar sound of my husband's footsteps on the wooden staircase. He usually stops to pet the cat, who waits for him on the third step from the top, but I didn't hear him say anything to her tonight. I turned away from the sink to greet him as he opened the kitchen door. There he stood — the same man I'd seen almost every day for over fifty years. But nothing could prepare me for the sight of him that night. He held a large, flat box with a red-and-black design on top — a pizza box — from my favorite place in Pilot Grove.

"What?" I squealed in astonishment. "I don't believe this." I hurried over to him as he set the box on the kitchen table.

"Didn't you get my message? I told you that you didn't have to cook tonight."

"But," I sputtered, "you've never brought home a pizza before unless I called it in."

"I didn't have time to go get a pizza tonight," he said. "I had to fix a fence. But when I drove by Bud and Catherine's place, she called my phone and said to stop back by on my way home. I figured they wanted me to unload their animals' feed from the car. I didn't expect a pizza. They went to Pilot Grove to get one for themselves and decided to buy one for us."

I plopped down in the kitchen chair. "I am shocked," I said, aware of the fresh-baked pizza aroma wafting through the closed lid. "I wished for this pizza. I even said the words out loud."

He laughed. "You're always wishing for pizza."

"No, it was because of a story I heard on the radio." Then I told him the details.

When I unhooked the tabs on the cardboard lid, the large, supreme pizza nestled inside was a tapestry of red, green, black, white, tan and brown. How could something this common be so beautiful — a work of art? The first bite — a blend of vegetables and spicy sausage in gooey, cheesy pizza sauce — sent a burst of flavor to my taste buds. It tasted just like a miracle pizza should taste — perfect.

After savoring a large portion of the pizza, we saved the rest. I called Catherine and told her the entire story. She said Bud had mentioned buying us a pizza before, but that day just seemed like the right time. They had no idea what kind of pizza to get but guessed we would probably like a supreme. She said they had gone to get the pizza at 5:00 — right after the time I had said, "I wish someone would bring me a pizza."

I've often heard the expression, "Be careful what you wish for." But I never gave it much thought because blessings come to us whether wished for or not. And some create a memory to last a lifetime.

— Linda Kaullen Perkins —

30

Love Restored

Love makes your soul crawl out from its hiding place.
~Zora Neale Hurston

When I told my mother I was pregnant, she told me I had to leave town so no one would find out. She found a maternity home run by the Salvation Army in Omaha, Nebraska.

The drive to Nebraska was long, made even longer because my mother refused to talk to me about what she called "my situation." When we pulled up in front of the home, I remember thinking it looked so cold and foreboding. Once inside, an older woman came in and sat across from us. My mother answered her questions about me as if I wasn't there.

There was no talk of options. It was taken for granted that because of my actions, I was not fit to bring up a child, and the baby would have a better life without me.

After my mother left, I was shown to my room, which I would share with another girl. There were two beds and one chest of drawers. There were no mirrors or artwork on the walls.

We were assigned jobs ranging from cleaning toilets to clearing dishes from the tables in the dining hall.

One of the social workers told me about an opportunity to leave the home and live with a family until it was time for me to give birth. In exchange for looking after their three young children, cleaning, cooking, doing the laundry and ironing, I was given my own room and bath. I was much happier there than at the home. At night, I would lie in bed and talk to my baby. I'll never forget the first time I felt her move.

I was not prepared for labor, delivery or how I would feel emotionally. When the labor pains started, I was very scared. I had no idea what to expect, and the pain was intense. I remember lying on a gurney outside the delivery room. I was crying out, "I'm hurting so badly!"

A nurse came over to me and said, "Well, it serves you right."

The next thing I remember is waking up from the anesthesia and being told to sign the relinquishment papers on the clipboard in front of me. I asked to see my baby and was told I couldn't see her until I signed. Years later, I found out that was a lie.

On September 19, 1970, I saw my newborn daughter for the first time through the window of the hospital nursery. She was beautiful, and I wanted to etch that moment in my mind forever. Tears filled my eyes, as only minutes before a nurse had told me it would be the last time that I'd see her.

There was no counseling for unwed mothers back then. I was told that if I loved my baby, I should give her up so she would have two parents. The nurses told me I would get on with my life and forget the entire experience.

I left the hospital a totally different person than when I entered it. My heart was hardened, and a part of me was missing.

I always hoped that my daughter would contact me one day, but I never really thought it would happen. As much as I wanted to search for her, I never felt I had the right, and I was afraid to disrupt her life.

I never returned to New Jersey to live, even though all my family was back there. I moved to Denver two years later, attended the Paralegal Institute and worked as a paralegal for almost twenty years.

In September 1994, I received a letter from the Nebraska Children's Home that simply stated, "We have a matter of extreme importance to discuss with you," and provided a phone number. That call changed my life.

I was told that my daughter, Stacey, was looking for me and had asked if I wanted to be in touch with her. When I said yes, they proceeded to tell me all about her. My daughter was twenty-four, married and worked as a social worker. On October 3rd (my birthday), I received my first letter from her. It was a long letter, and she included her college picture. She told me all about her family. I'll never forget her exact words: "I've had a great life with wonderful parents, but I always wanted to find you just to say thank you for having me."

I called my mother in New Jersey and told her that my daughter had found me. She was very quiet, and as usual, I took her silence as shame. I could not hold it in anymore, and I told her, "I know you are ashamed of me, but I really need to talk to you about this."

Through her tears, I heard my mother say, "For twenty-four years, you thought I was ashamed of you? I was ashamed of myself for making you give up that baby."

My first phone call with my daughter lasted three hours. In January 1995, I flew to Nebraska. It was the most wonderful weekend of my life. I told her what I had held in my heart for so many years. I told her that I loved her, and I was sorry I had given her up. She told me, "You didn't give me up. You gave me a better life."

In 2001, Stacey was pregnant with her first child. I remember sitting with her and looking at baby books. She told me how much she loved being read to as a child. I told her how I missed having the chance to read to her. Stacey picked out a book, handed it to me and said, "It's never too late. Why don't you read a story now to me and my baby?" She stretched out on the couch and put her head in my lap. I read the book — through tears, of course!

Daniel Jacob was born on April 27, 2001. When D.J. was two months old, I flew to Nebraska to see him. Stacey asked if I wanted to hold him. Without hesitation, I reached out, and she placed him in my arms. As I held him close, I felt a warmth come over me that I had never before experienced, and I was transported back to that moment when I saw my baby for the first time. This time, however, I was given the chance to hold my grandchild.

Five years later, Stacey and her husband adopted a three-week-old baby girl. Her name is Kierstin, and I've been a part of her life, too. When I flew to Omaha to see her when she was just a few months old, Stacey greeted me at the airport. Standing alongside her was a woman holding my new granddaughter. Stacey introduced her. It was Kierstin's birth mother. It was a very special moment for all of us.

The first Mother's Day after Stacey found me, Stacey sent me a beautiful card and signed it, "Thank you for giving me the greatest gift — The Gift of Life."

—Jeannette E. Nott—

Live in the Moment

31

A Little Game of Checkers

*More and more, when I single out the person who
inspired me most, I go back to my grandfather.*
~James Earl Jones

I was eight years old the first time I played checkers. I've played about a thousand games since then, but none so memorable as that first one.

It was January in Kansas. That pretty much says everything right there. Windy, frigid, icy. That's Kansas in January. Yes, someone once wrote the words to a song, "I'm as Corny as Kansas in August," but no one ever wrote a song about January in Kansas because no one would want to hear it. And I'm from Kansas, so I would know.

But at eight years old, the cold is little more than an inconvenience. You don't have to scrape the car windows or shovel the walk. Those are Dad things. Poor guy.

But when THE storm hit — yes, capitalized — dumping three feet of snow and cutting off our power, the winter became more than an inconvenience if not a dangerous concern for everyone — even for me and my six-year-old brother.

It was around noon, and though it was technically still daylight, there was little to be had. We were plunged into darkness. No television, no heat, no light. No nothing.

This was back in the days when people relied on transistor radios in such compromising situations. Dad turned ours on. We learned that there was a snowstorm raging outside. Dad mumbled something about "a waste of batteries" and switched off the radio.

Granddad Charlie was staying with us at the time and was the only one in the household who seemed truly unimpressed about the whole situation. Methodically, he gathered up his winter coat, scarf and gloves, and headed for the back door. We watched in amazement as he disappeared into a whirling cloud of snow.

He was gone for several minutes and, when he returned, he was cradling a heap of wood. Glancing casually at my brother and me, he said, "C'mon, boys. Time to build a fire."

Being a seasoned Cub Scout, I had seen many a fire built. But not like this.

"To build a good fire, you've got to do it in stages," Grandpa C patiently explained. "Start with kindling, then tinder, then the logs. We're using hickory logs, which is a dense wood, great for long-lasting fires, which is something we'll need considering it's going to be our only heat."

Over the next several minutes, Grandpa C coaxed a tiny flame into a roaring fire. We were impressed.

But our enthusiasm for the fire wasn't enough to sustain the attention of two young boys, and we were soon badgering Grandpa C as to what was next. "There's no TV, Grandpa," I complained, stating the obvious. "What are we going to do?"

"Maybe," Grandpa C remarked, carefully considering the situation, "we could do something I used to do as a boy, before there was TV. Let's go camping."

My brothers and I looked at each other in amazement.

"Get your sleeping bags, pillows and stuffed animals, and meet me back here."

It took us only minutes to gather our sleeping gear. When we returned, Grandpa C had rearranged the furniture, clearing an open space in front of the fire. In short order, we had a fine campground.

"Now then," Grandpa C began, unfolding a strange-looking game board, "who's up for a little game of checkers?"

"What are checkers?" my brother and I asked simultaneously.

"Never played, eh? Well, it's time you boys learned. Set yourselves down, and let's give it a whirl."

For the next hour or so, Grandpa C coached us on the fine art of playing checkers, a gentleman's game as Grandpa C called it. I became a fair player after losing four games in a row. Then, remarkably, I beat Grandpa C. When I asked him if he had let me win, he merely winked and set the board up for the next game.

Checkers was soon followed up with hangman, the theme being "things associated with the summer" as Grandpa C said we shouldn't dwell on the obvious goings-on outside.

My mother, who had obviously experienced power outages before, had wisely salvaged food from our idle refrigerator and stashed it in the sub-freezing garage. It was there that she now went, throwing together what my brother and I determined to be the finest dinner a camper in the wilds could possibly have: ham-and-cheese sandwiches, potato chips, cold baked beans, and milk.

Afterward, Grandpa C retrieved his old, weathered guitar and sang us some authentic campfire songs, the words to which my brother and I did not know but to which we hummed along, nonetheless.

Even my resourceful father contributed to our festive camp by resurrecting an old propane tank and cooking stove from the basement and popping us some popcorn.

And then, in the midst of our camping escapade, something terrible happened.

The power came back on.

Mom and Dad gave a cheer, of course, being the pragmatic parents that they were. But for my brother and me, it was the end of a grand adventure. This was not how we wanted the night to end.

Grandpa C looked at us, smiled, and then slowly stood. He walked across the room to the light switch and turned it off.

"Oops, looks like another power outage, boys. Better hunker down for the night. Gonna be a long one."

And with that, our camping odyssey continued.

We played another game or two of checkers in the still-flickering light of the fireplace before bedding down. And there was Grandpa C right there with us, stretched out on the couch, his legs hanging over the edge.

In the morning, everything returned to normal: lights, television, heat. But my brother and I never forgot that special day. We were always grateful for the experience and played many a game of checkers in the years to come. But, most of all, we were grateful for my Grandpa C, who had known how to transform a cold, wintry day in Kansas into something memorable and magical.

— Dave Bachmann —

32

A Miraculous Journey

I'm not telling you it is going to be easy,
I'm telling you it's going to be worth it.
~Author Unknown

"My name is Christina, and I'm an alcoholic and an addict." It took me a long time to admit this fact. It's still difficult some days, but telling the truth is pivotal to beginning the road to recovery.

Besides, like many folks who struggle with addiction, I don't look the part. I'm the wife of a retired school administrator living in the suburbs, working as a freelance journalist. For decades, I've told other people's stories, but it's time to tell mine again in hopes it will encourage someone else.

My journey to sobriety might never have happened if it weren't for a caring lady I will refer to as "Mary" who passed away almost two decades ago. Like a second mother, this wonderful woman welcomed me into her family circle when I was a troubled teen. Mary and I would frequently sit at her kitchen table drinking coffee together while having deep discussions about how to solve the world's problems.

The thing is, I couldn't solve anybody's problems because, when I visited Mary, I was usually high on something. I abused prescription pills, marijuana, alcohol, and anything else that altered the state of the reality I didn't want to live in. I referred to my drug use as my "medication," enabling me to forget how overwhelmed I was by my circumstances.

During the early 1970s, growing up in a traumatic environment resulted in my battle with depression and low self-esteem, followed by a near-fatal suicide attempt as a high-school junior. I survived physically but gave up emotionally, losing hope that my situation could improve.

After spending a couple of months in a local psychiatric ward, I was committed to a state mental institution. This was before mental-health reform in Ohio, and the institution was a barren place that housed thousands of mentally ill individuals, along with society's other outcasts. I spent much of my senior year of high school there.

In the hospital and institution, I was first introduced to medication to control my depression and anxiety. When I took my "happy pills," life seemed much more tolerable, causing me to develop a dependence on sedatives, tranquilizers, sleeping pills, and whatever else was available.

Due to my addictive personality, after my release, instead of taking my medication as prescribed, I would recklessly increase the dosage to enhance the numbing oblivion the drugs produced. I would also dangerously combine the pills with alcohol and marijuana to further their effect. This was before the opioid epidemic, or I'm certain I would have been one more statistic in that group, too.

Back then, there wasn't much knowledge about substance abuse. My own mother felt that I could overcome addiction if only I would employ more self-control. In fairness to my late mom, experts were only beginning to realize that addiction was a disease, and those suffering didn't lack willpower. Rather, they had an illness and needed compassion and treatment, not condemnation and ostracism.

Mary had compassion for me, and she genuinely wanted to help. Yet, for a lot of years, she couldn't help herself because she was an alcoholic, too. I pretended not to notice her drinking while she overlooked my obvious drug-induced oblivion, understanding I was too buzzed to be accountable.

Anyway, that's what good addicts do. It's like an unwritten code. When we are using, we pretend we don't have a problem, and our loved ones who are hooked don't, either. We are adept at blaming others, our circumstances, or myriad nonsensical reasons for why we do what we do when it comes to our self-destructive habit, and we enable others trapped in the cycle as well.

Then Mary got sober. It wasn't a voluntary getting sober with a bottom-of-the-pit realization that her life was spinning out of control. Instead, it happened through an ugly confrontational intervention, when her family members decided they were fed up with how she was destroying herself. They committed her to a treatment center.

After Mary's release, she started faithfully attending Alcoholics Anonymous meetings. Even though she was twice my age, she was finally becoming the woman she had always dreamed of being.

We remained friends, sharing coffee at her kitchen table, but something had changed. Mary was sober, while my substance abuse continued. She was also wise and never tried to preach to me about sobriety. It wasn't time.

"Do you think you might have a problem?" Mary asked with concern one afternoon a few years later. I was in my early thirties by then and physically sick from abusing my body for so long. Even though I was holding down a job as a corporate sales representative, with a company car and a college degree, my life was a hot mess. I vomited green bile occasionally, smoked cigarettes and marijuana like a chimney, and was beginning to cough up blood. Mary had never questioned my behavior before, but I was in pretty bad shape that day, making it the right time.

"I like to party occasionally," I answered nonchalantly, trying to minimize my drug and alcohol use, fully aware that the word "party" didn't accurately describe my chaotic existence.

"I'll go to a meeting with you if you would like to go." Mary offered this option not in a self-righteous tone, but with the desperation of a mother helplessly watching her child die slowly.

Three decades ago, life got worse before it got better, as my deteriorating mental and physical health landed me on a psychiatric ward one final time. There, I began a personal relationship with the God who has walked beside me every step on this path to recovery.

Then I finally took Mary's advice and went to my first Alcoholics Anonymous meeting followed by Narcotics Anonymous. In the beginning, there were times when I attended two meetings a day to stay drug-free. Then I found even greater freedom in the recovery ministry of a local church.

My late mother became my biggest supporter, and our family bond was miraculously restored. I have even written Christian recovery books to assist others battling addiction, and spoken at seminars, conferences, church services, community meetings, TV interviews, 12-step meetings, and wherever else I was asked to tell my story of a transformed life. It hasn't been a perfect path — there has been failure and struggle along the way — but each new day is an opportunity to start over.

Long ago, Mary had the courage to confront me with the truth and support me in finding help. This empowered me to begin this miraculous journey of sobriety. Even though she's passed on, I will be forever grateful to her for the blessing of this beautiful, sober life I'm living "one day at a time."

— Christina Ryan Claypool —

33

Already There

Life is available only in the present moment.
If you abandon the present moment you cannot
live the moments of your daily life deeply.
~Thich Nhat Hanh

"What are you doing, Mommy?" asked my four-year-old.

"Thinking about what I need to get done," I said sadly, as I snuggled her baby brother and continued to sway in the hammock swing.

"Oh, Mommy, you're always worried about what needs to be done next," she said in her matter-of-fact four-year-old-going-on-at-least-fourteen voice. "Just enjoy now!"

I chuckled as I watched her run off to swing with her sister on the swing set. She was right, though. That girl at four years old would have life figured out before all the rest of us. I spent too much time worrying about what needed to be done next rather than basking in the blessings of now.

There was a time when it all felt like a mad rush to prove we could do it. Prove it to ourselves, to each other, to our families, to the naysayers. The imperative was to accomplish this and accomplish that. Always looking ahead to where we were going next. If one of us wasn't pushing for what was next, the other was.

That day, I looked around as I stood up to head down to the swing by the girls. I realized we were standing right where we were headed all along. We had the house, degrees, careers, savings, and now the family — things we had to struggle at times to get. There was no more need to rush. It would all come in time if it was meant to come. Even if it never did, we already had enough.

Standing there on that gorgeous spring day, I watched the girls and dog play in the back yard while my husband grilled our dinner. I breathed in the happiness of life that surrounded me. There was such joy in these little moments when we were all just simply being.

"Swing me, Mommy!" called my oldest excitedly as I approached the swing.

"Me, too!" cried my four-year-old.

I gave them each a little push as their childish legs pumped to keep them moving. With each little push, they climbed higher.

"More, Mommy! More, Mommy!" they cried in unison.

I balanced the baby with my one arm that was free from pushing the swing. "I think you're as high as you're going to go. Just keep on swinging and enjoy the view."

My husband waved down to all of us in the yard as he took a break from the grill. We were already where we were headed all along.

— Angela Williams Glenn —

34

In the Present

*The ability to be in the present moment
is a major component of mental wellness.*
~Abraham Maslow

I knocked on the apartment door knowing only that the lady I'd be meeting was a retired high-school English teacher in the early to middle stages of Alzheimer's. She was only in her sixties.

As her husband opened the door, Peggy stood beside him with bright, alert eyes and a hint of cautiousness. "Who are you?" she blurted out. That was a fair question, and one that I would answer freshly each time we met to take nature walks, work on iPad puzzles, read poetry aloud, dabble in water paints, eat lunch, or dance in her kitchen.

Peggy's husband hired me to be "a friend" to his wife a few days a week when he had chemotherapy, needed to go grocery shopping, or played an occasional round of golf with his brother. Otherwise, he was doing what he cherished most: caring for the love of his life.

Time plays devilish tricks on the minds of those challenged by Alzheimer's, so Peggy would ask about every half-hour, "Where's my husband?" Or, "Where's my father?" The notion of spouse and parent had begun to merge into one supporting role in her mind.

Each time she asked the question, I answered with the same calm tone, "Oh, Fred? Your husband is getting orange juice and bread from the store. He'll be back soon. Look at these cool pencils. Do you want to color the rainbow with the blue one or the pink one?" Or I'd open the iPad to a kaleidoscope-drawing app and gently guide her hand until her fingers magically triggered bursts of vibrant shapes. I saved her creations and texted them to Fred, knowing it would make him smile.

The repetition of assurance and the redirection toward an activity put Peggy at ease. Even when she'd say in a panic, "I want to go home. My parents will be worried," I'd gently reassure her that they knew we were together having fun, and she would be home soon. Past and present were merging for Peggy. The challenge for me was to choose words and a tone that would soothe her "child within," while always honoring the adult woman who quickly became my friend.

Peggy's response to her surroundings was akin to the curiosity with which a child experiences the wonders of the world for the first time. During our walks, she'd stop and watch the gentle movement of wind through the boughs of trees and exclaim, "She's dancing. Isn't she beautiful?" Her senses seemed heightened, and the inanimate became animate. Or, maybe, Peggy became one with the weeping willows, daffodils and swallowtails. She observed keenly and with such appreciation for the mere presence of natural life forms. These moments were spontaneous meditations that taught me to still my racing thoughts and live in the moment.

After lunch, a group of residents in Peggy and Fred's apartment building would congregate in front of the fireplace in the lobby for a sing-along. A retired elementary-school teacher would strum a ukulele that she had been playing for decades. What I had not expected was that Peggy spontaneously sang along, often with the correct words and other times carrying the melody with sounds. Her anxiety disappeared completely when we were singing.

As the year passed, Peggy's medical needs grew greater, and so did Fred's. He made the difficult decision to transition Peggy to a memory-care community close to where he lived so that she would receive specialized care and he could see her most days.

I continued to visit Peggy, but her skills for puzzles, reading and speaking were declining. What could I do that would make a difference? The answer was, at first, daunting. Play the ukulele. But wasn't I too old to learn a musical instrument? Well, the only way to know for sure was to try.

First, I needed to buy one. Who knew ukuleles came in so many shapes, colors and sounds? After strumming a simple C chord on half of the inventory, I chose a Martin soprano. Now for the challenging part: hours upon hours of practice, practice and more practice. By the time I had learned to play and sing my first few songs, I was convinced that my husband would never leave me. Or was he secretly putting in earplugs? But the true test came when I brought my ukulele with me to see Peggy.

One of her favorite songs was from the musical, *Oklahoma*. My strumming was clumsy, but Peggy didn't mind at all. Together, our voices filled the air. Peggy was everything you could want in a friend. Although she had seen dozens of Broadway musicals throughout her life, she didn't point out the flaws in my playing. Instead, she did what a true friend would do and just sang right along. Nothing else mattered during those moments we shared.

The COVID pandemic has separated many of us from loved ones in the most heartbreaking ways. After over a year, Fred was finally able to hold hands with his sweetheart once again in her room. He called me and asked if I'd like to talk to Peggy. I quickly switched to speakerphone, picked up my ukulele and began singing her favorite tune: "Oh, What a Beautiful Morning." It surely was.

— Rosemarie Zannino Law —

35

Our Big Little Blessing

We can only be said to be alive in those moments
when our hearts are conscious of our treasures.
~Thornton Wilder

The baby was crying. The phone was ringing. My blood pressure was rising. The house was a mess, and I sat there, in the midst of the chaos, trying to breathe and make sense of all that had taken place in recent months.

After caring for, and losing, both my parents within a year of each other, I was sure my caregiving days were behind me. I could finally come up for air and get back to my life.

But barely two weeks after my dad's death, I received a call from a caseworker that would change everything. A relative of mine was in the hospital and on her way to a drug-rehab program once again. Would I be willing to serve as a "kinship foster parent" to her child while she was in treatment?

The caseworker told me I had to make a decision that day. She also said that if I didn't take her, the baby would be put "into the system" and placed with strangers. My heart was sinking as I said yes, knowing that this was not going to be a short-term commitment.

Once again, I would be thrust into the role of caregiver, and my life would be placed on hold. I looked at my calendar. I'd have to cancel my long-anticipated lunch dates with friends, my overdue doctor appointments, and my plans to take some time to travel, read and write. But I couldn't say no.

I sat there crying almost as loud as the baby. The phone continued to ring. I reached over and picked it up, trying to compose myself enough to say hello. When I did, a woman with a kind voice introduced herself and said she represented an outreach ministry I had supported. She was calling to ask if there was anything I'd like her to pray about.

The poor woman. I went on to pour out my story to her. She listened quietly and then began to pray that God would help me and bless me with strength, peace, hope and joy. As she prayed, I felt as if a blanket of warmth was wrapped around me. By the time I got off the phone, I sensed a reassurance that, somehow, everything was going to work out.

Fast forward two years. My husband and I found ourselves in the middle of a pandemic, sheltering in place with a toddler who talked nonstop, woke us up early every morning, and required full-time attention until she'd go to sleep at night. While my husband tried to work from a makeshift home office, I was tripping over toys, cleaning up potty accidents, preparing meals and snacks, doing loads of laundry, and playing endless rounds of hide-and-seek and Candy Land.

The days were long, and I was often exhausted and frustrated, longing for some time to myself. I desperately wanted the situation to change. But there was no light at the end of the tunnel.

And now here we are — almost two years later. My husband and I are in our mid-sixties. Retirement is not an option at this point. Our little one is in kindergarten. Her mother is still floundering.

There has been a lot of change. But it hasn't been in my situation. It's been in my heart. These difficult years have shaped and molded me. I'm complaining less these days and focusing more on the many blessings in my life.

This little girl has won our hearts. Her presence has enriched our lives in ways I never thought possible. She's filled with promise, life and joy — and it's contagious. She still talks nonstop and wakes us up early in the morning. She comes bounding onto our bed, ready and eager to see what the new day will bring. She brings me dandelions and makes silly jokes that don't make any sense. Our refrigerator is covered with her happy artwork.

Our home is loud and chaotic and wonderful. And I'm grateful. I've come to believe and accept that I am exactly in the place I'm meant to be. My life is not on hold. This *is* my life. John Lennon wasn't kidding when he wrote, "Life is what happens to you while you're busy making other plans."

We still don't know how this story will end. Legally, this living arrangement is not permanent. I've been told it can only end in heartbreak. Maybe so. Maybe that's the price of loving someone. I can't worry or dwell on that. All I know is every day is as much a blessing as it is a challenge. Even more so.

I often think back to that telephone call from the woman who prayed with me. I believe God assured me that day that it would all work out. I'm still holding on to that promise and watching as, every day, it unfolds a little more.

— Geri D'Alessio —

36

Renaissance of the Ordinary

Engage yourself in the Living Present.
The Future will take care of itself.
~Ramana Maharshi

My eleven-year-old daughter stared sadly at her stack of "Bobcat Bucks" — a sort of pseudo-currency that her elementary-school teachers gave to their students as rewards. She had earned her Bucks over the school year and had made the decision to save them all despite the tempting items the kids could "purchase" each Friday.

It was the peak of the 2020 pandemic, and she had been cooped up at home for three months. As she carefully counted her Bucks, she mentioned, "I really wanted the dog keychain that the teacher was selling the last Friday of school being in session. But I didn't get it because I didn't want to spend two Bobcat Bucks."

"Why?" I asked.

"I thought I'd save them all for the year-end auction," she said. "But now there won't be any opportunity to use them."

Typically, at the end of the school year the teachers held an auction, and the children could bid on exciting goodies such as a dozen donuts to share with their friends, the chance to pick a kid-friendly movie to watch with their class, or a five-dollar Starbucks gift card.

Since she was transitioning from elementary to middle school this year, her Bobcat stash was essentially just paper. That was the reason for the heaviness in her heart.

We both took a deep breath and locked eyes. In that moment, at our different levels of understanding, we shared one of life's lessons: Tomorrow is not guaranteed. Take advantage of every opportunity.

I reflected upon my own hoarding and habits. Too often, I was guilty of not valuing each day enough. I never unwrapped the good china. (It was for special guests.) I barely wore my beloved, glittering diamond ring. (I was waiting for a dazzling occasion.)

We don't have to blow our whole savings at once, but we don't have to postpone the little indulgences. That stack of unspent currency taught us both a valuable lesson.

That night we used the fancy silverware at dinner. It was a perfectly ordinary, special evening.

— Amita Jagannath —

It's a Day!

Let the winds of enthusiasm sweep through you.
Live today with gusto.
~Dale Carnegie

At sixty-seven, I am a big believer in being grateful for what I've got rather than dwelling on what I don't have. The first thing I do when I wake up each day is shout out loud, "It's a day! Hurrah! Yippee! I've got a day!"

After which I usually add, "I sure hope that I'll get a whole day!" And? So far, so good.

The fact that I live alone makes this practice easier, of course. Back when I had a partner, I couldn't start the day by shouting. That would be rude. The fact that I can currently wake up and shout all I want is a silver lining.

I'm one of those people who find silver linings.

Every morning, I pause to savor the fact that God or Luck or the Universe has granted me a brand-new day to enjoy. And I do enjoy my days. I'm old enough to realize that even a day filled with running errands or dental work is a day to be grateful for.

And grateful is what I am.

I know too many people who didn't get to make it to sixty-seven. I am happy to have done so. With any luck, I'll make it to sixty-eight and beyond.

It's also true that, after celebrating the fact that I have been gifted with another day, I'll usually lie in bed and ask myself, "What hurts?"

I know I'm not the only senior who takes a quick survey of their aches and pains each morning.

Just in case you're wondering, the current answer to that question is:

(1) My right shoulder aches from carrying around my twenty-three-pound, one-year-old grandson.

(2) My tailbone has hurt ever since I shot down the slide three weeks ago with my three-year-old grandson in my lap, slid off the end and landed — blam! — on the ground, right on my poor tailbone. (He loved that and wanted to do it again.)

(3) I had a tooth pulled months ago, but the gap where it used to be continues to ache, even though the tooth is gone. (Why? I have no idea. I'm a retired librarian, not a dentist.)

Once I've cataloged my aches and pains, I go downstairs and make myself a cup of coffee, a small daily blessing that I never fail to appreciate. The first cup of coffee of the day makes life worthwhile.

So do a lot of other things. I lead a quiet existence, and the days are packed with simple pleasures. Writing an essay. Playing the piano. Working with my clients as a writing coach. Walking to my sister's house to have tea. Enjoying a swim. And the best blessing of all? Grandchildren!

When I was a child, I woke up happy, took the many days ahead of me for granted, and suffered no aches and pains. I bounced out of bed with a smile each morning, ready to enjoy my day.

At some point, though, it occurs to us that the days ahead aren't endless. If we have any sense, we begin to be grateful for each one. When I think about my life, I don't dwell on the fact that I have a chronic illness, that I'm slowly going deaf, or that a relationship I thought would last forever went kaput after two decades.

The only thing that matters is that I've got a day! And I'm going to enjoy it.

— Roz Warren —

38

My Mother Shouldn't Be Alive

*Life is a great and wondrous mystery, and the only
thing we know that we have for sure is what is right
here right now. Don't miss it.*

~Leo Buscaglia

One of my first memories is my mother telling me I was her best friend. You can imagine how it felt for three-year-old me to be told, "Hey, you know your favorite person in the whole world? Well, guess what, you're her favorite person, too."

It was like having my own personal sun — warm and familiar, with an unexplainable light wrapped around me at all times.

There are a lot of things that people admire about my mother: her beauty, her kindness, her feisty Italian flair. But my favorite thing about her is her ability to live completely in the moment and appreciate all that she has.

"I don't like to waste time," she often says. "Why put off until tomorrow what you can do today? Tomorrow isn't promised."

I never knew why my mother was so fixated on living in the moment, but it's something I've always admired. Then, she sat me down one day and explained, "The reason why I live every day like I don't have a tomorrow is because I almost didn't."

It happened in 1982. She was seventeen years old and in her final semester of high school. Her boyfriend at the time was driving through an intersection when, without warning, a garbage truck smashed into the passenger side — where my mother was sitting.

After an ear-shattering bang, everything went black. It stayed black for twenty-seven days, she tells me.

The doctors told my nonna (grandmother, in Italian) that the chances of my mother waking up from her coma were slim. If she did wake up, they said she might never walk or talk the same way again, if at all.

Since you're reading this, you probably guessed that the doctors were wrong. Thankfully, they were wrong on all accounts.

As my mother told me her story, I sat in awe and slight confusion. How could my mother — my strong, fearless, you-better-clean-your-room-Mariann mother — have been lying in a hospital bed for weeks when she always had breakfast ready before anyone else woke up? How could she have not remembered any of her family or friends when she remembered every detail about how she convinced me I was Barbie as a child? How could she have spent months in a rehabilitation center learning how to talk, walk and become herself again when she taught me how to speak my mind, stand my ground and discover who I am?

Day by day, fragment by fragment, she was forced to glue herself back together. Now, she shows me the importance of building myself up and appreciating every piece of life that I am given — even the pieces I'm not always fond of.

"The past will never change, and things in the future aren't yet within your grasp, no matter how much you scratch and pull in either direction. All we have is the present, so you might as well live in it," she often tells me.

As an adult, I still carry my mother's lesson with me. Sometimes, the only thing that keeps my life in perspective is remembering how quickly it can be snatched out of my hands, and I owe that to her.

My mother shouldn't be alive. Therefore, neither should I. But we both are, and if my mother has taught me anything, it's how to appreciate the life I have right now.

— Mariann Roberts —

39

The Laugh Dance

There are shortcuts to happiness,
and dancing is one of them.
~Vicki Baum

My daughter loves to dance and is quite a good dancer. She inherited her dancing ability from my wife Angela.

Angela encouraged Marissa to dance from a very early age. I recall fondly how she would swing our daughter around the living room over and over to the song "Dancing Queen." The two of them filled our living room with laughter and joy each time they danced together. Because of that, our daughter has always loved all types of dance, and she took classes in Irish dance, hip-hop, jazz and more.

I love music, and I will dance occasionally, but my dancing is — how do I put this? — awful! Every time I try to "get my groove on," two things get in the way: my feet.

A couple of years ago, Marissa was a bridesmaid in a wedding that my wife and I attended. It was a beautiful wedding on a gorgeous spring day. At the reception, my daughter was dancing away. I was sitting at a table minding my own business when she coaxed me into dancing with her. That means she begged me to get off my chair and out on the dance floor.

When we got out on the floor, the DJ's music took over my body. The problem was that it missed my hips and feet. I tried my best. As I began moving to the beat, I gave myself a silent pep talk. I thought of that famous phrase: "Dance like no one is watching." That didn't work… Everyone was watching. My brother-in-law was laughing so hard that I thought he would fall off his chair.

I tried my best to keep up with my daughter's moves. Unfortunately, I was always at least two steps behind. She was busting a move, and I was just a bust! Her "Hips Don't Lie," and my hips didn't even know what to say. If she was the dancing queen, then I would have been the court jester. I think you get the picture.

We danced to a medley the DJ put together, and, despite my poor dance moves, we had a blast. We had so much fun and were laughing so hard that tears streamed down our faces. We laughed almost as hard as the people who were watching me. (It must have been like watching the world's funniest train wreck for them.) They must have been puzzled that my daughter could dance so well, and I danced so poorly.

I walked off the dance floor feeling proud of my daughter and her dance moves. I also left the floor with a tremendous feeling of happiness because I had chosen to dance with her despite my inability to dance.

Life only gives us so many smiles, so many magic moments, and so many chances to dance! Dance with your kid (whether they're five or twenty-five). Dance with your spouse. In fact, if anyone asks you to dance, stand up, give it your all, and dance like there's no tomorrow. It's far better to dance like a fool than to sit there with regrets when the music's over.

— David Warren —

40

Premature Baby

*As we express our gratitude, we must never forget
that the highest appreciation is not to utter words,
but to live by them.*
~John F. Kennedy

When I was four years old, my mother told me the story of my birth. "If you were there," she said, "you would have noticed the furrow between your brows, suggesting you were trying hard to breathe and stay alive."

When I remained unresponsive for two minutes, however, everyone thought that hope was lost. My father completely lost it, my mother was too numb to react, while my grandmother was already calling a priest to administer the last rites.

Born prematurely at twenty-six weeks gestation, I came out as a three-pound very weak and sickly infant. I had a weak heart, poor lungs, and only a ten-percent chance of survival.

My mother's doctor thought that I would die. After all, two other preterm infants born on the same day at the same hospital did.

"But you were brave," my mother told me. "You held on to dear life."

We would both smile. She'd tell me that I was a good fighter and a brave child. I grew up listening to her stories and believing that I was Hermione Granger, Wonder Woman and Ultra Violet rolled into one.

I admired Mulan and Pocahontas more than Princess Aurora and Snow White. I joined all the competitions that I could — swimming, chess, impromptu speaking contests — and even made competitions of my own simply because I was determined to show my strength and bravery to everyone. And, through it all, my mother supported and cheered me on.

Behind her optimism, however, I knew she was sorry sometimes. She was sorry for the infirmities caused by my premature birth, for the things I could never do.

I saw it in her eyes when I would have asthma attacks in the middle of the night. I heard her say it when she explained why it was harder for me to master the alphabet, which my younger sister had already mastered at the time.

Perhaps this was why my mother told me the story of my birth in the first place. She gave me a story that made me see my condition not as a setback but as a blessing. She gave me a story to hold onto when I was six as I battled severe pneumonia and once again fought for dear life, or perhaps when I was frustrated over my first homework, ready to give up.

I would remember the story, and a voice would reassure me, saying, "You can do this, Leah."

I believed in that voice. And I persevered.

That voice pushed me to keep working as I spent every summer reviewing my schoolwork in advance so I would not lag behind my full-term counterparts. That voice kept me breathing even when it was hard.

I may not remember what I thought of my story when I first heard it fourteen years ago, but now I know that it is more than a miracle.

Over the years, it has unconsciously become my "why" — my fuel — in life.

My story instilled in me the conviction that if I was given this chance to live, I must be meant to do something good — both big and small things in life.

I still believe that I can be as wickedly smart and gutsy as Hermione Granger, or perhaps as kick-ass and daring as Wonder Woman. But somewhere along the way, I've also learned to be sweet and demure like Aurora and Snow White — at least, I think I have.

I've learned to forget the rat race and my self-imposed competitions and appreciate and celebrate the little things in life. A stranger's smile. The air I breathe. Breakfast.

With my parents' guidance and my miracle giving me a reason to be better each day, I lived my way into who I am now. My story forged and molded me, and now I know that I would not change it.

I embrace that part of me even if it means having a lifetime of rhinitis and being the smallest in our family. I will persevere even when everyone thinks I can't. I will persevere just like I did the day of my birth. And I will persevere throughout my life.

It is an ideal that I — an always-on-the-go, five-foot-tall, Filipino idealist — hope to live for and achieve. And it is one that I hope I will bring with me until the day I die.

— Leah Angela Cioco —

The Right Words

41

Logical

Love as powerful as your mother's
for you leaves its own mark.
~J.K. Rowling

I blink away the tears as the two of us walk through the parking lot. The afternoon sun warms the blacktop around us, making the cool autumn air seem not so bad.

But the news I just received is bad. Really bad. Well, not like somebody-is-dying bad. Or even my-boyfriend-dumped-me bad. I should keep that in mind.

But still. My social life is as good as dead. And my boyfriend will probably dump me. So, there's that.

Our green minivan is still several spaces away. Mom told me to park there, away from the other cars, when we arrived before the appointment. Logical. After all, I've only had my permit for a few months and haven't exactly mastered parking yet.

But, right now, I hate the remote-parking logic. I just want to get inside that beast of a car, sink into the gray upholstery, and have a good, illogical cry. There is no good reason for these tears. They make no sense. I know that, but I don't care.

Mom cares a lot about logic. She's an accountant. She has a certain way of doing things. A logical way. A way that makes sense. Mom always has a good reason for what she does.

So, I hide these stupid tears from Mom. She won't understand.

We're halfway there. The outline of the minivan swirls in my vision.

It's no use. I'm not gonna make it. A single tear slips down my cheek.

Mom fumbles for the keys in her purse. "You should drive. We have to stop at the bagel place off the highway. It'll be good experience." She taps the keys softly against my left arm. "Here."

My left hand carries my school bag, so I pivot to grab the keys with my right hand. I say nothing. I can't, not with this gigantic lump in my throat.

As I turn, Mom gets a glimpse of my face. I look down at the pavement, so maybe she won't notice my red, watery eyes.

No such luck. Mom stops and puts her hand on my arm again to stop me, too.

"What's wrong?" she asks.

I lift my chin, but there's literally no way for me to get out the answer.

Her brows furrow, and her lips frown. Here comes a well-deserved, perfectly logical perspective check.

She's gonna tell me the truth: My jaw is out of alignment. My teeth don't line up. I get headaches every day, and when I sleep, I don't sleep deeply, so I'm tired all the time.

She's gonna tell me what the orthodontist had told me: I need to wear headgear all day, every day, for the next few months. That's the only way to fix the problem.

And she's gonna be right.

I sniffle a bit, look at the ground, and wait. She's gonna say a bunch of things that make sense: This is for the best; it's only a few months; it's not the end of the world. She's gonna say what I need to hear. I take a deep, rattly breath and ready myself.

Only… I'm wrong.

Mom doesn't say a word. Instead, she pulls me close, wrapping me in a fierce hug.

And she starts to cry.

But that doesn't make sense. My mom doesn't cry illogical tears in parking lots. She doesn't get emotional over stupid stuff like obviously needed orthodontic procedures.

Does she?

Her sniffles let my sobs loose. Together, we cry and hug, right there, three spaces away from our ugly green minivan.

After a minute or two, I say, "This is dumb, I know."

"No, it's not," Mom says.

"It's not?"

She smiles. "I was fifteen once, you know. I understand."

She does?

"I'll tell the orthodontist to find another way." She shrugs. "Or we'll get another orthodontist. Don't worry."

"Really?"

"Really." Mom holds out her hand. "But maybe I should drive this time."

Logical. After all, I've only had my permit for a few months, and I'm not allowed to drive with a friend in the car.

— Melissa Richeson —

42

You're That for Me

I think gratitude is a big thing. It puts you in a place
where you're humble.
~Andra Day

L ife once provided me with a stressful trifecta of challenges. The day after my mother had emergency surgery, my brother had emergency surgery in another hospital upstate. Before the end of that week, my stepfather fell and broke his hip, necessitating yet another emergency surgery in yet another hospital.

For several weeks, I found myself traveling between three different hospitals, trying to stay outwardly positive and cheerful. It wasn't easy, and I felt sorry for myself on a daily basis. I was tiring fast.

One afternoon, I took a break from visiting Mom and walked up to the terrace on the fourth floor of the hospital to get some fresh air. The area offered an outside patio where patients and visitors could sit in the sun.

I spotted a woman sitting in a wheelchair who seemed to be watching what my mother calls the "human parade." Such a person is more than content to be wherever they are, in no hurry to move along, and somehow exudes complacency in the simple process of observing others. Mom loved observing the "human parade."

For whatever reason, I struck up a conversation with the woman in the wheelchair. She seemed eager to talk. I thought I was doing her a favor. She enjoyed talking to me; that much was obvious.

Eventually, the conversation turned to physical conditions. She said she had been in the hospital for twenty-eight days and probably wouldn't get out anytime soon. I took that to mean that her condition was very serious, yet she seemed quite at peace about it. When she asked me why I happened to be there, I told her how scary it was when we almost lost Mom, then about my brother's surgery the following day, and my stepfather's subsequent fall and surgery.

The woman listened attentively, providing appropriate nods. At the end, she sat back in her chair and said, "Well, then, you're that for me." Then she smiled appreciatively.

I didn't understand. I asked her what she had said, and she was kind enough to repeat it.

"I said you're that for me."

I asked her to explain what she meant.

"You see," she began, "everybody's got problems."

I knew that and waited for her to go on.

"And we all think our problems are the biggest problems in the world."

I could definitely agree with that.

"So, when I get to a point where I feel like I can't take it any longer, it always happens that someone comes along and offers me a sadder story than my own. I can find someone every single day. And that's how I get from one day to the next. Today, you're that for me."

I leaned back, taking this in, trying to figure out if it was a good thing or not. I was glad that she was comforted by the fact that I had a dilemma that, for the moment at least, was bigger than hers. But did I want to be "that" for anyone?

We talked a while longer, and when I finally went back to see Mom, I thought long and hard about what that woman had said. I was never to see her again, but I would take her words with me wherever I went.

The following day when I was home, I heard about the daughter of a childhood friend who had been in a terrible car accident. The top of her car had literally been torn off in a collision with a tractor-trailer. The girl was in a coma. I could not imagine what my friend was going through and prayed that somehow a miracle would happen and her daughter would recover.

As I signed the card to her mother, I had a realization: "You're that for me."

This human parade has its share of music, laughter and good times marching down the street of life, but it also has its share of sadness and tragedy. Perhaps it is a worthy goal to simply be thankful on a daily basis that we are not "that" for someone.

As it turns out, the woman I met at the hospital that day did me the favor. She truly altered my attitude. She taught me that time spent feeling sorry for myself is surely time wasted. What really matters is getting to the next minute of our lives as unscathed as possible.

The hope, then, is to be as cheerful as possible when things are going well, to appreciate the good moments, no matter how insignificant they seem, and to be grateful for the wonder and peace of each and every breath we take. Perhaps to capture such moments, we might think the word "thank" as we inhale and exhale the word "you," gratefully praying we're not "that" for anyone right now.

—Pat Dickinson—

43

The Woman by the Side of the Road

We rise by lifting others.
~Robert Ingersoll

It was a blistering hot, summer day. The temperature hovered near 100 degrees, and with the humidity the heat index was more like 105. It was windy, too, a dangerous mix of conditions for the scores of cyclists pedaling the hilly, sixty-mile course.

It was a benefit for the Oklahoma City homeless shelter, a worthy cause, and I thought the challenging course would be a good test of my endurance and strength. We left downtown Oklahoma City as the sun broke through the clouds early that morning and made our way to the nearby college town of Norman, with its scenic, rolling country roads.

The first twenty miles passed smoothly, and I stopped at the second rest stop to fill my two water bottles with an icy mix of water and Gatorade. It was my first year of cycling, but I figured I could make it safely to the forty-mile rest stop with no problem. I hopped back on my bike to pedal the toughest part of the course.

The sun began to bear down as the course made loners of everyone, weeding out the great packs of riders as each tried to establish a bearable pace. As I drained the final swig of liquid from my water bottle, I noticed it had been a long time since I had last seen any other cyclists.

Several miles back, I had passed a cyclist who was walking his bike. As I went by, he yelled, "I think I have heat exhaustion." I yelled back that I would send someone to get him from the next rest stop, trying to sound more confident than I felt.

The encounter now seemed longer ago than it was, and I began to wonder if I was on the right course. It was not clearly marked, and all the roads looked the same — big, rolling hills with no signs of life, cyclists, cars, or houses. There was nothing around but increasing heat, wind, and relentlessly steep hills.

I began to panic and silently berated myself for misjudging the distance between rest stops. I tried not to think about how thirsty I had become. The best thing was to just keep pedaling. My speedometer indicated the next rest stop should only be four miles away, but all I could see ahead were more steep hills.

The course was directly into the wind for the rest of the ride, and I suddenly felt so demoralized that I almost cried. *Keep going,* I thought. *Surely, you are on the right course. Just keep pedaling. It will all be okay.*

The next hill brought me up out of the saddle again to pedal against the incline. As I looked up, I thought I saw the outline of a woman on the right side of the road near the top of the hill. I was relieved to see any sign of life and continued watching her as I climbed, hoping she was real and not a mirage.

As I reached the top, I could hear her yelling and see her dancing up and down, clapping her hands and cheering wildly.

Maybe she has mistaken me for someone else, I thought. One would think it was the Olympics, and she was cheering her daughter to a world cycling record. Our eyes met as I passed, and she yelled, "Come on! You can do it! We are so proud of you all. Come on, keep going! Don't quit, you're almost there. You can do it!"

I smiled and yelled, "Thanks!" as I passed. A surge of energy overtook me and pumped into my legs. My spirits lifted as I realized I was on the right course. I was going to make it! The next stop was just around the corner.

Oh, thank you, lady! I thought. *Thank you so much. You will never, ever know what you have done for me this day.* How amazing for her to walk all the way up to the street on such a blistering hot day just to clap and cheer for a lonely rider she would never see again.

What she gave me in that moment was something I needed more than water, for it was life to me — power, energy and encouragement. It was hope.

I went on to finish the course, sent help back for the stranded cyclist, and spent the rest of the day pondering this stranger who had come out on such a brutal day to cheer me wildly in the middle of nowhere. She made all the difference that day.

—Dorian Leigh Quillen—

44

Stuck in Kazakhstan

*When we focus on our gratitude, the tide of disappointment
goes out and the tide of love rushes in.*
~Kristin Armstrong

After two years of volunteering in Kazakhstan, I was getting burned out. I'd spent months planning our English as a Second Language summer camps up in the mountains, only to find out that everything was canceled. No horseback-riding. No rock-climbing. No art classes where our students make dream catchers and slime. Nothing.

It was a huge blow. I had come to this country to make a difference, to help the kids here learn English and apply to study-abroad programs. Now, I had to do Zoom classes and deal with the constantly spotty Wi-Fi. This was not what I had signed up for, and I wanted to leave.

I'd written my letter of resignation but continued with some of the online lessons. I struggled, and I think the students could tell. My heart just wasn't in it anymore. Like most teachers, I always put on a happy face before my lessons, but I figured they could see that the magic just wasn't there.

I planned to talk with my boss on Friday, to thank him for this opportunity and wish him the best before I flew back home to America. That day, I'd learned that all flights were canceled and, no matter what I wanted, I was stuck.

I had some free time (well, a *lot* of free time), so I decided to put all my efforts into my online lessons. I planned virtual writing competitions and even helped some of my students get published! I created an online escape room for some of the higher-level students. It wasn't the same as rock-climbing in the mountains, but it was the best I could do in a difficult situation.

When it was announced that flights had finally reopened, I went online to book a ticket. That same day, I had a class of fourth graders. They had an extremely low level of English, and I always struggled to get them to turn on their cameras and participate. I would not miss this class when I went back to America.

I was teaching them about adverbs, and because most of them couldn't turn on their microphones, I asked everyone to write an example sentence in the chat. I got some fairly standard responses:

"The dog is really fat."

"Monkeys are usually funny."

"My mom is definitely loud."

There were ten sentences in total, but the last one caught my eye: "Mr. Evan is extremely cool."

I had to laugh. Students never think that adults are cool. Besides, I was probably the least cool person they knew. I asked the student why I was cool. In her broken English, she said, "Because games." And another student said, "Because jokes." And another student, the smartest in the class, said, "Because you help us."

That was the moment I decided to cancel my flight, delete my resignation letter, and stay where I was. Even though my experience in Kazakhstan had turned into something I hadn't expected, I was still doing what I love: helping kids.

Maybe the next summer, I'd get to have my rock-climbing, horseback-riding experience, but for now, I was happy with what I had. Every student is a gift, and every class is an opportunity to make a difference. It didn't matter whether I was in a classroom or in front of an old laptop struggling to connect. I'm a teacher, and this is where I was supposed to be.

— Evan Purcell —

45

Bounty of Blessings

A good laugh heals a lot of hurts.
~Madeleine L'Engle

"A re you almost ready?" my husband yelled from downstairs. It was my first time out in public since I'd lost my hair. It was a simple brunch date with my husband and two young daughters and an attempt to forget that I was a thirty-year-old, breast-cancer patient.

Autumn in England can be quite chilly, so despite my determination to be the most boss bald gal around, I found myself needing to cover my head quite often. Hats and beanies were my go-to, but they often made an outfit appear dressed-down. Feeling really well after the latest round of chemo, I wanted to look as good as I felt. The local cancer center where I sought treatment provided wonderful courses on everything cancer-related, and I felt particularly empowered after a recent scarf-tying class, so I decided that I would wear one for this special outing.

Now, I don't pretend to be a fashionista, but black seems to pair with everything, so it's the scarf color I chose. Versatile and practical, yet chic. At least, that's what I thought.

"Almost," I answered. "I just have to put on my scarf."

Here it was, the big moment. I folded the scarf into a triangle before wrapping it around my head and tying the double knot behind my neck and over the triangle point. I adjusted, tightened and tucked. In our small bathroom, I did a quick rundown of my outfit. Cute black heels, check. Slimming red pants, check. Favorite black sweater and gold hoop earrings, check. Beautifully tied black scarf, check, check, check. My outfit complete, I stepped to the full-length mirror in my room to assess myself.

And then I saw it: my mistake. An error in judgment that was now so obvious. Panic started to set in. I didn't have time to change. No, no, no. No one had mentioned this in the scarf class, forgetting somehow to tell me that black would look like…

"Hey, hon, are you ready? Both girls are in their coats. I don't want to miss the reservation." He was coming upstairs. I jumped back in the bathroom and slammed the door.

"I'm not going!" I yelled.

"Wait, what? Where are you?" He was outside the bathroom. "What's going on in there? Are you feeling okay?" He tried to turn the doorknob, but I pushed it shut. "Babe, open the door. Are you okay?"

"Yes, yes, I'm fine. I don't want you to see me like this." I tried to make my voice sound calm.

"Like what? Seriously, are you okay? Are you sick?" There was panic in his voice.

"No, I promise, I'm fine. It's just, I look… I just don't want to go."

I could hear the shift in his tone from concern for my health to a more traditional husband-waiting-for-wife impatience. "I'm sure you look amazing." He tried to turn the knob again, but I continued to hold the door shut, my entire body pressed against it, and my hand locked on the knob for dear life.

"No, I don't."

Frustration built in his voice. "Yes, I'm sure you do. We are going to miss our reserva—"

"I look like a pirate." The words came out fast and loud. The tension on the door stopped. There was silence. I waited for his response.

His voice was softer and confused. "Did you say… that you look like… a pirate?"

I rested my head against the door and let out a loud breath. "Yes."

"A pirate, like of the Caribbean?"

"YES! A pirate. Wooden leg, parrot, whatever. I look like A PIRATE!"

More silence. I knew he was still there, contemplating what to say next. I stepped away from the door, twisting the knob to unlock it. He gave it a soft push, and we were there, staring at each other. I watched as he took in my outfit before meeting my gaze, his eyes widening as he pursed his lips, sounding out words in a slow manner. "You. Do. Not. Look. Like. A... Pirate." His voice cracked on the last word, betraying him.

"You're trying not to laugh," I said, feeling a smile form as I started giving him light slaps.

"Don't you mean that 'you *arrrrrrrgh* trying not to laugh'?" He grinned as he dodged my blows. We could no longer suppress our laughter.

I stepped around him and threw myself on the bed, trying to pout through my laughs. "It's not funny. I'm not going."

He lay on the bed next to me, propping his head up to look at me. "Seriously, though, you look beautiful, like you always do. I don't think you look like a pirate. If you did, you'd be the most gorgeous pirate ever."

"I don't want to look like a pirate, though." There was a stinging behind my eyes and, before I knew it, the laughter had turned to tears. "I want my hair back. I don't want to look sick. I don't want people to look at me and feel sorry for me because I have cancer."

"Oh, baby, I'm so sorry." He pulled me in and kissed my head, holding me tight. "We don't have to go to brunch. I'll make something for us here."

"But that's the thing. I was really looking forward to brunch. I wanted to look nice for this, so I took that class and got this scarf, and now I look like Halloween."

He lifted my face to look at him. "No, darling, you do not. If you hadn't said it, I wouldn't have noticed anything. And neither will anyone else. You know what they will see? The same thing I see every day: a woman with the confidence to go out there and show the world that cancer is not going to keep her down or take anything else from her. Someone who shows her daughters that being comfortable in your own skin has nothing to do with hair. Now, you don't have to be her today if you don't want. But, if you do, I'd love to take that woman to brunch."

No, cancer was not a blessing, but it did bless my life in that it opened my eyes to the gifts in front of me: a husband prepared to make me laugh, hold me when I cried, and walk me through the times when I couldn't see my own strength.

I reached the top of the stairs with my hand locked in my husband's as we prepared to leave for brunch. I looked down at my two beautiful children and appreciated the wonderful family I had.

"Wow, Mommy, you look like a pirate!"

Okay, I'm also grateful that kids find pirates to be so darn cool.

— Margaret Johnston —

46

Believe

Thousands of candles can be lit from a single candle,
and the life of the candle will not be shortened.
Happiness never decreases by being shared.
~Buddha

My hands gripped the steering wheel, and my stomach tightened as I turned into the parking lot. This building had become all too familiar over the past several months. "You're here for a Christmas party. Happy times," I reminded myself.

I shifted my car into Park and looked down at the square box that held the ornament I had brought for our ornament-exchange gift. I had chosen a glass globe that had the word BELIEVE in red script. I'm sure it was created in the spirit of Christmas and Santa. But, for me, that word was a beacon of hope along this journey. I hoped it would be for someone else, too.

Once inside, relief that I wasn't the only one to show settled over me. About twelve women filled the waiting room, drinking hot chocolate and making small talk. A large Christmas tree brightened the corner, and several small square boxes sat underneath. I placed my gift alongside the others and made my way to the hot-chocolate counter.

The host encouraged us to sit in one of the chairs forming a circle around the room. She told us her story and why she had started hosting ornament-exchange parties for the clients of Dr. A.

I looked around at the other women sitting before me, and for the first time in my infertility journey, I felt like I was surrounded by people who understood the pain.

One by one, we shared our journey of trying to conceive. The first woman was twenty-four weeks' pregnant with twins and felt guilty about coming to the party. She knew how much it sucked to be trying to conceive and see pregnant women. But she came because she was hoping to provide support and show that a happy story was possible. She went on to tell us how this was her third in-vitro fertilization (IVF) treatment and the first one that worked. She worried every day that something might happen to one or both of her babies, and she'd miscarry.

Another lady had one son and felt like maybe she shouldn't have come because she already had a child, and most of us would have done anything just to have one. Another woman was on round 6 of IVF and frozen embryo transfer. She talked about how this would likely be her last chance because money was running out.

I shared my story next. I spoke of trying to conceive for eight years with my husband. We'd never been successful but hadn't been able to afford infertility treatments until now. We were still early in the process. We had been getting tests done and had more appointments scheduled. I'd come that night because I wanted to be able to talk about it openly with like-minded people. It's a subject that often feels taboo with family and friends who often express pity or give unwarranted advice. It felt reassuring to hear the other women agree with my feelings.

Then another woman, a teacher, shared her story of anger. Several young teachers in her building had become pregnant, and she had to participate in all the baby showers. She just couldn't take it anymore. It wasn't fair. Most of us murmured our agreement. We all knew what it was like to attend gender announcements and baby showers while we kept seeing that negative line on our own pregnancy tests.

Suddenly, a woman said, "Ladies, I heard something that has really helped me along my journey, and I want to pass it on to you. 'Their blessing isn't taking away yours.' I hope it will help you guys find the same peace it has helped me find."

The words sank into my soul as if God had placed them there

himself. It was a pivotal turning point for me. I could now hear somebody announce a pregnancy and be happy for them. I could think, *My time's coming. It just hasn't happened yet.* It all routed back to that word: believe. After all, I had to believe that my journey would end in a positive pregnancy and live birth. Doubting and being angry at others wasn't helping my blessing come any faster and it didn't change the facts.

From that night forward, I went through my fertility treatments and procedures with more confidence and hope. I believed that my blessing would come, and it did. I now have two amazing boys who are two years apart in age. My struggles with infertility and my journey with IVF seem so long ago.

But those words, "Their blessing isn't taking away yours," have stuck with me for years. When I run into hardships and see others flourishing, those words still guide me.

— Heather Hartmann —

47

The Best Poker Hand of All

There has never been, nor will there ever be,
anything quite so special as the love
between the mother and a son.
~Author Unknown

Life is like a poker game. It is impossible to change the cards that we are dealt, but what really counts is how the hand is played. In 1989, I received a hand that I had absolutely no idea how to play. My adorable, spunky, two-year old son, with his trademark spiky, blond hair, had just been diagnosed with a form of autism. I was devastated.

We also found that little Zachary was nonverbal, which added a unique twist to his autism. Imagine not being able to express your needs, wants or emotions. The frustration must be monumental! It was even impossible for Zack to tell us when he was in pain.

We kept trying to find a communication method that would work, but he was unable to focus long enough on any technique. After all, he was just a toddler exploring his environment, which was filled with many sights, sounds and adventures. His exasperation grew along with my desperation to make his world coexist comfortably with ours.

Eventually, I began losing touch with the little things that used to make a difference: reading a favorite book, taking a long walk, driving with the top down on my Jeep. Instead, I found solace in climbing into bed at night, hiding under the sheets and forgetting about this poker hand that I was not playing very well.

Time marched on. As Zack trudged through the terrible twos, he struggled to find ways to make himself understood. Dragging family members by the hand offered limited possibilities at best. We tried to keep pace with him. Current technology didn't interest him.

When all else failed, my creative, industrious son drew upon his quirky problem-solving strategies. Finding him perched on top of the refrigerator or sitting on the top shelf of a bookcase were not unusual occurrences in our household. He was fast and furious, small yet mighty, requiring twenty-four-hour surveillance. Occasionally, though, his aggravation would become overwhelming. Screeching at the top of his lungs or throwing things resulted. It broke my heart.

We had definitely entered a "new normal." A couple of years later, Zack was in a special-needs preschool that he enjoyed, and many adjustments had been made to accommodate his autism. Life was moving along, but it was never quite the same. I seemed to have lost a piece of myself. The sounds of young children talking to their moms made me envious. Hearing Zack's voice would mean the world to me!

One beautiful morning in May, I gave Zack a big hug when the school bus dropped him off. I told him that I would get a snack ready. But something was amiss. He wasn't interested in eating. Instead, there was a look of determination on his face. He had a mission!

Keeping careful watch over him, I stood in the kitchen as he walked over to a wooden shelving unit in the dining room where I kept a collection of fragile Precious Moments figurines. He picked up one of them, turned it upside down, and examined the bottom of it. Part of me wanted to say, "Please put that down, Zack!" But the words got stuck. Something told me to remain silent.

As he put down the statue and picked up another one, following the same process, I realized that he was looking for something. This went on for a few minutes. Suddenly, he turned around, clutching his newfound treasure. Gazing at me with those beautiful brown eyes, a small smile briefly appeared on his face as he offered the piece to me. Then he quickly scooted off to watch *Sesame Street*.

Puzzled, I found myself looking at an adorable image of a little boy with big brown eyes. He was holding a flower. I peeked at the bottom, just as Zack had been doing. Tears welled up in my eyes as I read the words that I thought I would never hear: "Mommy, I Love You!"

In one brief moment, my nonverbal four-year-old son said it all! A little boy who had to struggle to make himself heard came through loud and clear. It suddenly occurred to me how much I had been missing in the past two years. What had I been thinking? All I had to do was look around to be appreciative of all the wonderful blessings in my life. So often I had neglected to give thanks. Whispering a soft "Thanks, God," I walked over to my son and gave him a warm, snuggly hug. "I love you, too, Zack."

Thirty years later, I still recall the morning that a loving, silent message taught me to count my blessings daily, fill my heart with gratitude, and learn to play my cards like a pro!

— Gail Gabrielle —

48

Finding Meaning in Suffering

If you really want to receive joy and happiness,
then serve others with all your heart. Lift their burden,
and your own burden will be lighter.
~Ezra Taft Benson

I had my son in October 2017. It was early, and after two miscarriages and his sister's pre-term birth, I was anxious about what could happen. Luckily, just like his beautiful sister, he came out perfect and just needed a week in the NICU.

The NICU was difficult for me because I had never been away from my two-year-old daughter. I also missed being able to hold my newborn son. And to make matters worse, I was hooked up to a magnesium IV to keep from having seizures, uncomfortably swollen, and sleep deprived.

Thankfully, the nurses in the NICU were great at caring for us exhausted moms. One night, one of the nurses and I began chatting, and she told me that she was newly back to work from bereavement leave. She had found her twenty-year-old son deceased in his room earlier that year. She was starting to function again and was fighting to find a new routine. I was crushed as I listened to her. I had seen this situation firsthand with my own parents. Fourteen years ago, we had lost my older brother in a tragic car accident and had been learning to live through the tears ever since.

I started to open up about my own experience for the first time in a long time. We began telling our stories to each other through sobs and holding hands. She told me that she had four other children, and her youngest, who was fourteen, seemed to be handling it the worst. She was acting out and being mean. Because she had been so close to her brother and idolized him, she was clearly lost since his passing. She didn't know how to help her daughter and was afraid she was losing another child.

For a moment, it felt like the entire world stood still… and then suddenly I comprehended what she had just said. I had been in the exact situation that her daughter was in.

I looked right at her and said, "I can help! I *was* your daughter. I *am* your daughter. My brother died when I was thirteen, he was nineteen, and I thought he was the coolest person on Earth. I can tell you some things that could help her and you."

She hugged me and wept. This was the strongest my voice had ever been in my whole life. Right then, I knew that no one could help this grieving mother and her hurting daughter as much as I could. It wasn't because I had some fancy letters behind my name or an expensive college degree in counseling. It was because I was probably one of the very few people that would cross this woman's path who had lost an older brother at such a confusing and impressionable age. I knew I could give her some insight on where it went so wrong for me and what could have helped.

I spilled my soul to this new friend, who was listening without judgment or pity to my every word. Looking back, I see how therapeutic this was for me as well. Here I was trying to help her with her "baby," while she was helping me take care of mine. I think they call that collateral beauty.

Fast forward a year. It was the annual memorial 5K for my brother. My dad was giving a speech, just like he has for all of them. He recited this famous quote from Friedrich Nietzsche. "To live is to suffer, to survive is to find meaning in the suffering." He was referring to his grandchildren (my sweet babies), who have eased so much of his suffering. But even with that sweet reference, I thought to myself, *Well, geez, that's a negative way to look at it!*

Months later, I realized that what my dad had quoted really did have meaning. On February 13th, my brother's now heavenly birthday, I found myself silently sobbing into a pillow, alone in my living room, while my children napped. It always seems that these days really bring out the tears.

For the first time since coming home from the NICU, I thought back to that nurse and realized, *There it was! There was the meaning to my suffering. That's what he meant by surviving.* Right then, I realized that I might have saved her and her daughter so much extra trauma and hurt by telling her *my* story, sharing *my* experience. As much as I do not believe that everything happens for a reason, I am a little more at peace thinking that helping her fourteen-year-old daughter could be the small glimmer of a silver lining in all my heartbreak.

The darkest and messiest parts of my life had exposed the biggest message. I learned that if I continue to be brave enough to use my voice and share my story, I can keep finding my purpose and the meaning in the suffering.

— Taylor Reau —

49

Nursing-Home Blues

*When you look into your mother's eyes, you know that
is the purest love you can find on this earth.*
~Mitch Albom

"Oh, you mustn't cry," my mother said as she held me tightly. We were standing in the lobby of the nursing home where my brother had placed her the week before. Mom had been living with me for a year after we realized her dementia was worse than we originally thought.

We'd sold our house in the country so that we could move into town to be closer to doctors for Mom. Before we found another house, my husband decided to do a two-week consulting job in another city. Since we had a motorhome, he thought it would be an adventure for the three of us — Mom, Paul, and me — to travel together in a 36-foot motorhome.

When my brother David learned of this, he insisted on Mom staying with him for two weeks. I thought it was a better idea than the motorhome, so she went to Oklahoma to visit him. Nothing had prepared David for Mom's inability to remember anything. He quickly learned that he couldn't even go into his back yard for five minutes and leave her alone. When he came back in the house, he found Mom in a state of panic. She had no idea where she was or who she was

To his credit, he realized what I had been living with for the past year.

"I don't know how you do it, Sis," he said. "I don't have one minute to myself."

Then, he reluctantly told me that she had said she didn't want to come back to my house. She was afraid of me. I admit that it hurt to hear him say that. I had fixed up my spare bedroom with her things. I had rearranged my life to take care of her, but many days she came into the kitchen and didn't know who I was.

I had taken her out of her familiar surroundings so my house was strange to her. We had also taken her car. She would get angry with me when I insisted she take a shower or eat a meal. I was no longer her daughter; I was a stranger.

So, in my heart, I knew David had done the right thing by finding a nursing facility in her hometown. He explained to me that when they visited Country Trails Care Home, several of the staff members had grown up going to church with Mom. She had fed them streusel and Dr. Pepper after church many times. As they gathered around her and began hugging her and telling her how happy they were to see her, she relaxed and began talking and smiling. When the visit was over, she told David that she wanted to stay there with her friends.

Still, it was hard to let her go. I didn't mind taking care of her, as difficult as she could be at times. I enjoyed sitting on the porch in the afternoons with her. I enjoyed shopping with her. She could out-walk me at the mall.

David got her settled in the next week, and Paul finished his job that Friday. We headed straight to the nursing home Saturday morning. After a few hours' visit, David and his family said their goodbyes and headed out. I stayed behind to have a few moments alone with her. I could tell she was happy and felt like she was home. So, I didn't feel remorse at leaving her there. I did harbor a little anger at David because he had done it without telling me. But I knew it was the right thing to do, and I loved him for that.

I don't know why the tears came as I hugged her goodbye. I was trying to be discreet, but she felt me tremble. Pushing me back, she saw tears filling my eyes.

That's when she told me I wasn't to cry. She was fine. Her eyes twinkled with merriment as she reminded me that she didn't have to cook, clean, or wash clothes.

"I get three good meals every day, and I get up from the table and leave the dirty dishes for them to clean," she laughed.

So, I wasn't allowed to shed tears for her. At least, not in her presence. When I got in the car, I bawled. Not because of where she was physically, but because she was still concerned about me.

"Oh, you mustn't cry. You go live your life with your husband. Take care of him. I'm fine." Those were the words from a loving mother to a grateful daughter.

—Darlene Carpenter Herring—

50

Chicken Soup
for the Soul

Gentle Persuasion

No duty is more urgent than giving thanks.
~James Allen

Joe Barone was the contractor everyone wanted. He was repu-
table. He was reasonable. He was reliable. Reachable?

He was not. We were warned by our neighbor, whose home
he had completed with detailed perfection.

"If you are willing to be patient, Joe Barone is worth the wait. He
lives in our town, and he works from his home. Just leave a message
on his machine. Be persistent and call at least once a week. When he
is ready, he will return your call," he advised.

We decided to persist and wait patiently.

On Monday evening after dinner, and every Monday evening
thereafter for an entire year, my husband left the following message
on the answering machine of Joe Barone:

"Hello, Joe? This is Mr. Baghsarian at 648 Arizona Avenue. My
phone number is 555-4365. Please return my call at your earliest
convenience."

I decided to take matters into my own hands.

I found the home address of Joe Barone in the telephone directory.
The following Monday at around 5:00 P.M., I called the local Italian
pizzeria and made them an offer they couldn't refuse.

"Please send a pizza with everything on it to the following address
with this note: 'Hello, Joe? This is Mr. Baghsarian at 648 Arizona
Avenue. My phone number is 555-4365. Please return my call at your

earliest convenience.'"

The pizza was delivered at 5:55 P.M. At 6:00, my phone rang. It was Mrs. Joe Barone. I could hear her children's laughter and excitement in the background. She, too, found it hard to contain her emotions.

"I was just on my way out to pick up a pizza for dinner when I saw the delivery man walking toward my house!" she explained. "But I hadn't ordered a pizza, so I called Angelo's. 'Someone else ordered it for you,' they told me. Then I read the note."

Three things happened that Monday evening. The Barone family enjoyed a pizza with everything on it, compliments of the Baghsarian family. Mrs. Barone admonished her husband for "making these nice people wait so long." And Joe Barone finally returned our call just as we were finishing our dinner. This time, it was our turn to show excitement and laughter as I know his family could hear our voices in the background.

"You really got to me!" said the phantom contractor whose voice we had waited to hear for the past twelve months. "When can we sit down and talk?"

Joe Barone lived up to his impeccable reputation as a builder. He began work on our home and fulfilled his contract by the promised date. His six-man crew was courteous, respectful, and professional. They did not miss a day of work and accepted no other jobs until our home was completed. In return, we provided fresh bagels and coffee every morning and homemade subs for lunch. They even savored age-old village recipes from "Joanna's Kitchen" and experienced Armenian and Greek hospitality at its best when they dined at our table. For the next two months, we became their extended family.

The story does not end there.

One hot summer day, Joe and his crew were on their next job site in upstate New York. They were on their lunch break, sitting in their truck, eating store-bought sandwiches. Thirsty, they asked the owner for a drink.

"The hose is in the back yard!" they were told.

Later that day, I received a phone call from Joe.

"The boys are homesick, and we want to come home!" Joe jested.

"Come back any time, Joe. There is always a place for all of you at our table."

—Joanna Baghsarian—

Simple Pleasures

51

The Dream House

Some of God's greatest gifts are unanswered prayers.
~Garth Brooks

When I discovered the house on the side of the mountain, I knew it was perfect. Surrounded by pine trees, it had an amazing view and was just how I imagined living in Montana.

We were a young couple with two small children, ages two and four. We wanted to get out of our hectic California lifestyle and raise our girls in a healthier environment. The romance of the western lifestyle had enticed us to make the move.

Leasing a place for a while seemed like a good way to get familiar with the area. Perusing the paper, we'd narrowed it down to two possibilities. One seemed like an average house, located in a small neighborhood by a pond. It didn't thrill either of us.

But the other one I'd found? It was more like what I'd pictured. The house was picturesque. It looked like something from a movie I'd seen as a child — a home tucked in the mountainside. It captured my imagination, and I was smitten. My husband was back in California with the kids, and I was supposed to get things lined up. I contacted the owner and discussed the one-year lease he wanted. I agreed to meet him and move forward, depending on resolving a few remaining details.

My husband was as enthusiastic as I was. Since he couldn't come out and see it for himself, the final decision was mine.

The day I set out to meet with the man about the mountain

house, I stopped by the office of the agent representing the house by the pond to let her know I wasn't interested anymore. We had put in an offer to rent that house with an option to buy. Because I wanted the other house, I had taken a hard line on the terms, figuring they would refuse, and that would be the end of it.

"Good news!" the agent greeted me. "They've accepted your conditions. The house is yours."

Oops. I was stunned. My mind was recalculating like the car's guidance system does when I take a wrong turn. What about the mountain fantasy? Mentally, I had us already settled. Instead, it seemed we'd be living in a standard two-bedroom house instead of one with a spectacular view and wildlife at the door.

Feeling defeated, I signed the papers, wondering how I'd break the news to my other half. After I left, I notified the other party that I wouldn't be coming and resigned myself to mediocrity.

A few months later, we moved in, and I was still feeling I'd settled for less than what I'd hoped for. But the reality was otherwise.

The pass where the mountain home was located was a miserable road during the winter, and winter in Montana can last nine months. The wind whipped through there with ferocity, making the biting cold even more bitter. A trip to the grocery store in January would have been an ordeal. Living with toddlers, isolated on a mountainside, would have been brutal.

What had I been thinking?

You might be wondering how it worked out, having to settle for an unglamorous, if not more practical, housing choice.

In a word: wonderful.

The neighborhood, consisting of about ten homes, was lovely. There were other children, friendly neighbors, and pleasant surroundings. The homes circled a pond where the girls could fish and float in a rubber boat in the summer and ice skate and sled in the winter. The drive to town was easy, and we were just far enough out to feel like country folk.

There were ducks, geese, and the occasional osprey to amuse us. I could sit at the living room window and watch the fish jump and the birds frolic in the water.

After experiencing our first winter, I realized it was likely we wouldn't have lasted the year if we'd lived in the pass, and we would have been forced to return to California with our hopes dashed.

Instead, I've been here forty years. My daughters grew up in a wonderful environment. They married amazing Montana men, and I have precious grandchildren, who I see often. My roots are firmly planted.

Every day, I count my blessings, grateful that, in this case, I did not get what I'd wished for. The alternative proved to be so much better, surpassing even my wildest dreams.

—Lynn Kinnaman—

52

Disco Saves the Day

*Don't think about tomorrow; don't think about
yesterday: think about exactly what you're doing right
now and live it and dance it and breath it and be it.*
~Wendy Whelan, American ballet dancer

During the pandemic, it was nearly impossible for kids to let loose at school and just be kids. Due to COVID-19 restrictions, they'd missed out on beloved traditions such as field trips, dances, and athletics.

As a middle-school teacher, I'd been searching for ways to lift the students' spirits and create a sense of normalcy. Then, an unforeseen solution appeared in the form of an often-maligned, cultural and dance-music phenomenon from my own childhood: disco.

I work with seventh graders in a rural Georgia school district. I love them, but twelve-year-olds are probably the weirdest humans by far. Against the backdrop of puberty, they fluctuate wildly from joy to tears to rage, sometimes in the span of a few moments. They routinely fight, lie, bully, fart, share heartwarming personal stories, and yearn for as much attention as anyone is willing to give.

Above all, a seventh grader needs constant adult supervision. Granting even a little freedom can lead to disaster.

In November 2021, I worried what might lie ahead when our assistant principal and two of our seventh-grade teachers had to miss school because of a student disciplinary hearing off-campus. When a substitute teacher failed to show, leaving us short-staffed, we expected the worst, especially since it was the Friday before the week-long Thanksgiving break. The students were already revved up and unfocused.

The first part of the school day passed without incident, but the real test would happen around noon, the moment when almost 200 seventh graders assembled for the cacophony of gossiping, arguing, and open-mouthed chewing known as lunch. Lunch is when seventh graders tend to forget impulse control.

I led my kids into the cafeteria, caught off-guard by the reverberations of a bass riff. Our school was in the midst of a two-week fundraiser, and for some reason, the company conducting the event decided a Friday before a holiday was a good time to bring in a DJ to motivate the students.

My colleagues and I were on edge, not looking forward to the next thirty minutes of crowd control or possible anarchy.

But I found myself captivated by the memories blaring from the speakers — a collection of classics from the '60s, '70s, and '80s. I'm a fifty-six-year-old. This was my music. These were some of the very songs I listened to on AM radio when I attended middle school. I couldn't resist singing along to "My Girl" by The Temptations.

Out of the corner of my eye, I noticed one of my students laughing and mouthing to a friend, "Look at Mr. D." This was the first time since the pandemic began that I was enjoying music with others, and I wasn't going to let the moment pass, even if children were giggling at me.

The DJ switched to disco, and suddenly, amazingly, the kids were singing, too.

How did they know the words?

In the late 1970s, disco was the most popular music in the United States, but that ended on July 12, 1979, during a Major League Baseball promotion at Comiskey Park in Chicago. Spectators were admitted to the double header for 98 cents if they brought a disco record. Between games, organizers blew up the records on the field, leading to a riot and cancellation of the second game. Shortly thereafter, cries of "disco sucks" swept the country, and disco was officially dead.

More than forty years later, disco experienced a revival in 2020, the same year the coronavirus shut down the globe. Fans couldn't gather to dance. Most clubs were closed, and yet people wanted to — needed to — move to the hypnotic disco beat.

The singing in the cafeteria escalated. I wondered if we should tell the kids to quiet down. Would this get out of hand?

We teachers decided to go with it. And then a girl tentatively approached the teachers' table. "Would it be okay if a couple of us got up and danced?" she asked.

Without hesitation, my middle-aged colleague replied, "Sure!"

A few of the braver kids wasted no time in showing off their moves. I admired their courage. Even though seventh graders are crazy, they never want to stand out from the pack for fear of being devoured.

I didn't possess such gumption at that age, and with my lack of rhythm, I'm still uncomfortable getting on the dance floor. However, I cast aside decades of awkwardness the second I heard that iconic trumpet fanfare beckoning me. It was an unforgettable tune from 1978, my eighth-grade year, a song that topped charts around the world and is still a mainstay at weddings and karaoke bars from New York to New Zealand — "Y.M.C.A." by the Village People.

I turned to my friend Amy.

"What do you think?" I asked.

"I'm in," she responded.

We grooved with gusto, throwing out our arms to form the famous four letters in the chorus: "It's fun to stay at the Y.M.C.A."

Our lack of expertise and limberness didn't matter. The group of five or so student dancers swelled to fifty or sixty, along with almost every teacher, prompting a cheeky student to exclaim to an instructor, "Miss, it looks like you've spent a lot of time at the clubs!"

Normally, by this point, a kid would have shoved a classmate or thrown a milk carton, but on this magical Friday, all was well.

The half-hour lunch period stretched to thirty-five minutes, forty minutes, but no one wanted it to end, not even the cafeteria workers waiting to clean up for the day.

Finally, the DJ settled the matter by shutting off the sound system, resulting in a chorus of teenage "Awwws!" That was the sole objection. The kids tidied up the tables quickly, and willingly walked back to class, reveling in the fact that their usual, rule-laden lunch break had metamorphosized into an impromptu dance fest.

I've seen a lot during twenty years of teaching, stretching across three continents and all age groups, but I can't recall an experience more satisfying than cutting a rug in the cafeteria that day. And those teenagers have a story to hang onto for life — about the day their teachers crossed over to the dark side.

— Mark Dickinson —

53

French Fries

*Our brothers and sisters bring us face to face
with our former selves and remind us how
intricately bound up we are in each other's lives.*
~Jane Mersky Leder

For a few years, my brother and I grew up in a Norman Rockwell household. Mom, Dad, my brother, and me. We lived in a two-story tract home in Palmdale. We attended the local schools, church, and youth group. Just your ordinary, average family. We enjoyed eating out, playing sports, shopping at the mall, and going to movies.

It was a nice upbringing. Until it wasn't. My parents decided to divorce.

After my parents separated, my brother and I moved to a new town with our mom. New schools, new schedules, new friends — all things that come with moving. To any outsider, we still looked like a typical family. We had a roof over our heads and clean clothes to wear. My mom had a car.

But, during my parents' divorce, what we didn't have was money. Like, no money. The roof over our heads belonged to a family friend who was gracious enough to let us live there temporarily until we could find our footing. Our clothing came from friends and family. Our car was old but ran.

After not having worked in several years, Mom had trouble finding a job. Our parents' divorce was long and contentious. We eventually ran out of savings. At times, we had no food. At our lowest point, my brother and I had to recycle cans so we could afford to buy bread. No one ever enjoyed bread as much as we did on those nights.

One day, my brother came home with a fast-food coupon good for one order of small French fries. There was a photo of those golden, crispy fries on the front of the coupon and no expiration date on the back. Those fries looked delicious! My brother and I kept meaning to use it but never made it to the restaurant. Eventually, we lost the coupon.

Luckily, things eventually turned around. Mom and I both got jobs. We could afford to pay rent, and we could afford to eat!

A couple of years afterward, I moved out on my own while my brother continued to live with Mom. As an apartment-warming gift, my brother gave me a beautiful card with the French-fry coupon, which he had found, inside it! He thought that was hilarious, and so did I. Now that we were back to being more comfortable, we could look back and laugh.

And I kept that coupon. Thirty-three years later, living in a beautiful home with my husband and son, I have that coupon on my vanity mirror. It's a daily reminder to me to be grateful for how far I've come and how much I have.

But if things ever get that bad, I may cash in the coupon. I love fries.

— Crescent LoMonaco —

54

The Kindness of Strangers

Sometimes it takes only one act of kindness
and caring to change a person's life.
~Jackie Chan

Sweat rolls down my back. The noise of the crowd fights with the music, forcing me to shout at the customer across the counter. The checkout line curves around the room. I force my face to maintain its smile.

"Hi!"

"Welcome!"

"Is this your first time in?"

My god, what am I doing here? I should not be working retail at a place with no air conditioning on a summer Saturday in Texas. I hold an MBA. I'm a trainer, an instructional designer. I was good at both. By now, I should have a real job again.

***

I wish I could say that my layoff came out of the blue, but I don't think it actually did. When the Director of Human Resources called me at exactly 1:00 in the afternoon, I knew. My heart didn't sink. I didn't panic. I walked down the hall in a state of absolute calm and managed the meeting without tears. It was only when I returned to my office that I became enraged.

Two copy-paper boxes were enough to hold my belongings. I had enough severance and savings to get me through for a few months. I could freelance and look for another job. I would show them.

* * *

"I'm so proud of you, honey," Mom says. "You're staying so positive through all this. I thought for sure you'd find your dream job by now."

Me too, Mom. Me too, I think.

My attitude has spiraled downward for weeks, although I apparently hide it well. That's a first. I'm the person whose every emotion paints itself across her face.

I apply for jobs and work on my portfolio and say all the right things to the right people. Dishes pile up in the sink, and I cry after I cancel my CrossFit membership. At home, I crawl into bed as soon as I return home from work.

"I'm going to be okay," I whisper to the ceiling in the dark, believing it less each time I say it.

* * *

"I'm so excited that the bakery is open!"

I look, really look, at the two women. Something in the brunette's voice strikes a chord.

"It's so cute. You're going to love it," I assure them.

"What do you get there? We want to make sure to get the best thing they have!"

I think for a minute. "I like the cupcakes with the white icing because it's not as sweet as the chocolate. I don't like super sweet icing, if you can believe that."

The woman with highlights has a smile that lights her face. "I'm the same way," she says. "Is there anything other than cupcakes?"

"The cheddar-bacon biscuit is one of the best things I've ever eaten. I mean, come on. Cheddar and bacon in a biscuit? Am I right? And I've heard the cinnamon roll is even better, but it's been sold out every time I've made it over there." I hand the women their bags. They could be sisters; they look so much alike.

"Thank you so much!"

I wave them off, glad to have met them. They brightened my day, and I hope they enjoy the rest of theirs.

***

I lose all sense of time at the register. Perhaps it is the way the heat settles over me like a damp weight. Perhaps it is the endless greetings to the endless line of people.

"Having fun?"

"Find everything okay?"

"Hi, there!"

In my peripheral vision, I sense a mild commotion, but I focus on the guest at my register. He wears a pressed gingham shirt with khaki pants. Everything about the man screams "Southern gentleman." He is very concerned about whether he chose the best gift for his wife.

"I'm sure she'll love it, sir." I carefully fold the T-shirt and place it in the bag. "Have a great day!"

I use the short lull between customers to take a swig of water. Hot, tired, and wishing I were anywhere else on a Saturday, I turn back to my register.

It takes a moment to understand what is happening. First, I see a plain brown box held up like an offering. Behind it, two women radiate excitement.

"They still had one left!"

I catch up in a flash. It is the two women who'd asked me about the bakery. "A cinnamon roll? That's great! You'll have to tell me if it's as good as everyone says."

"No! It's for you!" The brunette thrusts the box toward me again. "Take it! We got it for you."

Before I can get another word out, they are gone.

***

Over a year later, I stand in a line filled with excited tourists. A woman turns to me with a printed order form clutched to her chest.

"Have you been to the bakery before?" she asks.

I smile and nod. "So many times." I didn't say it was because I worked next door.

"Is it really worth all this?" The woman waves a vague hand toward the line that curves around the corner of the building and to the front door.

"Oh, yes. It's worth it."

I glance next door to the store, the place that had been a quick detour in my life. I never imagined how much I'd miss it now that I've moved on.

"Get the cinnamon roll," I add. "It'll change your life."

— Michelle Hanley —

55

Finding Myself

Life is full of beauty. Notice it. Notice the bumble bee,
the small child, and the smiling faces.
Smell the rain, and feel the wind.
~Ashley Smith

My business card had the title Vice President written just below my name. For many years, my work had defined me, and this was confirmation that I was valued. If someone thought I was good, then I was good.

Until one day, my spirit and self-esteem shattered with the simple phrase, "Your position is being eliminated."

How could this be? What became of my sacrifices that had contributed to the company's bottom line?

I slept around the clock for two weeks after my termination, barely eating.

Then, one morning, I woke up with an unsettled feeling and went in search of my husband. As is his habit, he was having coffee in the wooded area near the stream behind our home. He calmly acknowledged my presence by pouring coffee into the extra cup he had waiting. I was not surprised to find that this man, who understood me as no one else did, had patiently waited for me to rejoin the world.

We sipped our coffee in silence as we watched the hazy dawn burst into a glorious sunrise. The birds provided a canopy of sweet sounds. I gasped in delight as two deer came to the edge of the creek, stopping to drink. The spotted fawn eyed us curiously and came over to visit. Startled, the mother deer lifted her leg, signaling the availability of nourishment. The fawn rushed back to its mother, who then fled to the safety of the woods followed by her hungry baby.

Weeks turned into months as we continued this morning ritual. It became my time to reflect. We connected on topics other than work and whose turn it was to pick up the dry cleaning.

I had long desired a flower garden but never seemed to find the time for it due to my hectic work schedule. When I shared my simple dream, my patient husband began to teach me how to turn the earth, plant the flowers, fertilize with just the right amount, and water them before they were too dry. Immersing my fingers in the richness of the damp soil and inhaling the earthy fragrance were newfound sensual experiences.

Imagine my excitement in discovering that, through that garden, our love and commitment to each other were also nurtured. The morning glories, sparkling with dew in the sun, provided inspiration. The roses attracted hummingbirds that never seemed to tire as they flitted flower to flower, relishing the life-sustaining nectar. The yellow daisies were home to myriad butterflies. My favorites were the ferns that, even without showy blossoms, provided solid dignity to the garden. I learned that the loving care I gave to the garden returned love and peace in kind.

I found myself chatting with my children more often. I shamelessly began to get all caught up in their lives. Surprisingly, they were delighted. "I really like the unemployed mom because you're so funny," my daughter said.

"Good stuff, Mom," my son agreed. "Your face is happy, and your eyes sparkle like they used to when we were younger."

Also, during this time, my best friend, a wise and patient woman, needed me. I sat by her side at the hospice for two weeks as her life ebbed away. Her voice took on strength as she told me to value all the dimensions of life. I was there, in the moment, truly with her as she shared memories of her life.

I thanked her for helping me understand the role of working wife and mother while I strove to be a decent human being. I told her I was humbled by her unconditional kindness and love. Smiling through my tears, I reminded her, "I love you, Mom."

Amazingly during this time, I also learned to care for myself. The cortisol level that was creating havoc with my waistline reduced, and suddenly my waist reappeared.

"So, that's where you've been hiding," I said to my reflection in the mirror one morning as I turned this way and that way, viewing my reclaimed body shape.

I finally started a new job and have come perilously close to reverting to my workaholic pattern. This realization came the first week when I said to a co-worker, "Hurry and get me trained so I can start adding value."

He smiled and said, "You already are. Your calming presence makes this chaos around here easier to handle."

This simple epiphany came to me: Life is multi-dimensional. Cherishing my husband, laughing with my children, being there for my mother, relishing the sunshine, feeling dirt through my fingers, and caring for myself are equally important. My life now includes so much more than a title on a business card. And, with a grateful heart, I will not lose myself or my value again.

—Linda B. Breeden—

56

A Tale of Two Turkeys

Live in the sunshine, swim in the sea,
drink the wild air.
~Ralph Waldo Emerson

When the COVID-19 pandemic struck in early March 2020, our lives, like everyone else's, ground to a halt. Our family of five settled into a long stretch of days hunkered down in our log home in the Appalachian Mountains of Virginia. I was already set up to work from home, but my husband Paul joined me, and we struggled to adjust to working together from home as well as overseeing online school for our three boys.

Soon enough, we settled into a routine, and the boys started doing their schoolwork in the mornings, leaving the afternoons open. We live on a farm of about seventy acres, and the boys would take to the fields and mountains when the weather was nice. News stories hit social media about how much children were suffering from the effects of the quarantine, but as a new look of fulfillment settled over the faces of my children, I realized all the time spent outside in nature was beneficial to them.

Soon, the boys filled our evenings with their tales of treasures and adventures. They had never spent so much time outdoors. They found long-abandoned tires and barrels, parts of an ancient wagon, and bottles dug up from beneath a tree. They dragged those treasures down the mountain behind our house. One day, Cort spent the entire day learning how to walk on an old barrel. He amused us that evening with his circus tricks.

Our two-year-old Australian Cattle Dog, Owen Meany, accompanied them on each adventure, and we saw a contentment in him that we had never seen before. He stopped chewing up shoes, pencils, and the side of the house, coming home from his romps with the boys to lie on the floor exhausted, occasionally letting out a groan.

With each day that passed, the boys deepened their appreciation for nature. Reid decided to go barefoot. He began walking a mile, then two, then three barefoot on the old logging roads around our property. On one particularly warm day, the boys accidentally stirred up a rattlesnake when walking through the woods, but Owen Meany intervened and chased it into a log. Our oldest son, Pierce, began to build a tiny cabin on the top of our mountain by our usual camping spot, and soon online orders were placed for tools to peel bark and saw boards.

On a mild day in April, Cort and Reid were out hunting for highly coveted morel mushrooms when they discovered the nest of turkey eggs. They accidentally flushed out the mother turkey, and she didn't end up returning over the following days. After checking to make sure there weren't any regulations against doing so in our state, Cort and Reid brought down eight speckled eggs and set them up in our incubator. That spirit of nature that my children had learned to embrace was crossing the threshold and moving into the house.

Over the following twenty-eight days, I didn't expect much from the eggs. The weather had been poor at times, with heavy rains and winds, and twice we lost power. Once was for a period of twelve hours, and I thought the loss of the heat lamp in the incubator would surely kill any viable eggs. But then around Day 26, some of the eggs started to look like they were wiggling and wobbling. By Day 27, we started hearing peeps coming from the eggs.

Cort and Reid were glued to the window in the incubator at this point, waiting impatiently to see their turkeys. We thought that three of the eggs were viable. They began rocking and peeping more vigorously on Day 28, and little chips of egg began coming off. Unfortunately, the first turkey was born with a prolapse, and he didn't make it very long. Three other turkeys hatched, but one had a deformed foot. Although it seemed to be doing well, it died unexpectedly in the first week. That left two.

Once it was clear that the two turkeys were healthy and adjusted to humans, they were showered in attention and named Homer and Marge. Cort and Reid always seemed to have a baby turkey perched on a shoulder. The babies would make happy, little chirping noises while hiding in the boys' hair while they were watching television.

All the attention backfired a bit in the evenings when Cort and Reid went to bed as the turkeys would call and call and call. No one in the house was getting much sleep at this point. We were surprised by how much racket a tiny turkey can make. Finally, it occurred to me that they might just miss hearing the voices of the house. I dug up an old weather radio from the basement and placed it next to their cage. The weather was stormy that night, and the turkeys happily listened to all the monotone emergency weather broadcasts while the rest of us fell into a deep sleep.

Around this time, my work hours were cut in half, so I decided to try something new with my time. I had never played an instrument, but the boys had a ukulele, and I thought that I would try to take a few beginner lessons on YouTube. Trying to learn an instrument at midlife isn't the easiest of tasks, and while I told my fingers what to do, they didn't always listen. Still, I practiced. One day, as I was working on the chords to "House of the Rising Sun," I realized that the turkeys were calling to me in the rhythm of the song. Six bars. They were way off-key, but they had the cadence correct.

Eventually, Homer and Marge had enough feathers to start flying. This proved slightly problematic. One moment they might be sitting on a shoulder, and the next they would be zooming through the air around the house. They were still too small to be moved to our chicken coop outside, so we had to keep an eye on them when they weren't in their cage.

I'm amazed that the raising of two turkeys could bring such joy to our family during the quarantine. Learning to care for them gave my children additional purpose, especially when it was too cold and rainy to venture outdoors. Once Homer and Marge finally reached maturity, they were able to join our three chickens and guinea in the chicken coop, where they seem to be getting along without their emergency weather radio. Although, I must admit, I haven't yet asked our chickens if they are getting much sleep.

—Lisa R. Workman—

Flying Solo

Let us be grateful to the people who make us happy;
they are the charming gardeners
who make our souls blossom.
~Marcel Proust

I was slightly miffed when my daughter, Sara, arrived at 10:00 on my birthday morning. My big plan for the day had been to sleep in so there would be less of the day to deal with. I mean, why not? It was my second wedding anniversary since my husband had passed away. And I was quarantining.

Sara set a bouquet of fresh lavender on my dresser and announced, far too cheerfully for her not-a-morning-person mother, that she was going to make me a cup of tea. I was asleep before she reached the kitchen. But then I was rudely awakened by the doorbell, and I wondered who would be stopping by at this ungodly hour. Certainly not anyone who knew me well.

Sara reappeared with a bouquet so elaborate it could have been the centerpiece at a wedding reception.

"Wow, look at these flowers that just arrived," she exclaimed.

"Must have left them at the wrong house," I grumbled.

"Read the card, Mom."

They were from a friend whose husband had passed away a few months after mine.

"Birthday hugs. Thank you for your love and support," she had written.

The day changed tone.

An inviting smell was coming from the kitchen.

Sara brought in a tray with breakfast and a pile of cards. For just a moment, I felt a twinge. No anniversary cards. Not this year. Not last year. Not next year.

The cat joined me on the bed.

The phone rang. Linda was calling from Virginia. As she has done every year since we were college roommates, she sang "Happy Birthday." And, as we do every year, we fell into laughter.

Sara handed me a small box that held bright pink nail polish.

"Pedicure time," she said. An hour later, I walked my fancy feet into the living room where I found a cake with icing that matched my toes and a bottle of pink champagne.

I was pampered in pink! And loving it — even the part where she made me put my pedicured foot on the ottoman next to the cake so she could take a photo.

That evening, as she was getting ready to leave, I asked her for the name of the nail polish. When she turned over the bottle to read the name, her face flushed in astonishment.

"Oh, Mom, it's called Flying Solo."

I am indeed flying solo these days. But I'm not alone.

—Patricia Bunin—

58

Discovering Glory in the Ordinary

Gratitude opens the door to the power, the wisdom,
the creativity of the universe. You open the door
through gratitude.
~Deepak Chopra

Spice cake with caramel frosting. Bright green Matcha lattes. Sunsets on a cold winter day. These are the miniscule moments in life that I've come to love the most.

I started a joy journal three years ago. It was a period when joy, for the first time, didn't seem to come naturally to me.

My grandmother had passed away a month prior, and everything felt topsy-turvy. Empty boxes that once held her belongings were strewn around our home, still smelling of peppermint and leather — just like her. I felt her absence in the air, thick and heavy. All I could think about was the sound of her laughter, the way she danced when ABBA came on, and the way she made me smile when I felt like crying.

As I was cleaning out my drawers to make room for some of her things, I found a pocket-sized leather journal with my name stamped on the front. The words "Joy Journal" were scrawled across the first page, reminding me of a plan I had made months earlier to keep a joy journal. A plan that never came to be.

I sat down and took out a pen to write down ten moments of joy that I had experienced that day. It was a challenge that should have been easy.

Finally, I finished my list:

- The tingling after a strong cup of coffee.
- Ingrid Michaelson's music.
- The smooth feeling of my teeth after biting an apple.
- Laughter.
- The crunch of freshly baked bread.
- Warm weather.
- Flowers.
- Hugs.
- Sunlight.
- Friends who will sit with you in sadness.

That first attempt at a joy list took me a long time. But, after that day, I set an intention to journal ten items a day for a month. Days turned into weeks, weeks turned into months, and eventually joy journaling transformed into a habit.

My lists grew in size, along with my appreciation for life. I discovered a joy independent of grief or happiness, successes or failures, while leafing through those pages. This joy lived, instead, in the smell of mint picked fresh from the garden, sunrise picnics with friends, and banana pancakes on a gloomy day.

After years of searching for a joyful life, one that was all sunshine and rose petals and glittering lights by the sea, I realized I had overlooked the greatest joy of all — the joy of everyday miracles. No matter my circumstance or situation, these tiny blessings taught me that the glory of life exists in the most ordinary moments of our everyday experiences.

I write a joy journal not because I am always joyful and perfect but because even in the darkest moments, I know that joy can still be found.

— Dana Drosdick —

59

Maximizing Minimalism

We are not what we own; we are what we do, what we
think and who we love.
~*Francine Jay,* The Joy of Less, A Minimalist Living Guide

Two years ago, I woke up to the oddest sound. It sounded like we were next to a rushing river.

I wasn't prepared for what I saw when I looked outside. There was no longer a street. Or a sidewalk. Or porch steps. All of it had been replaced by rushing, muddy water several feet high.

We lost our chest freezers, laundry machines, and almost everything in our basement. The things we held onto never worked the same again, including our cars. Still, most were replaceable. We thought it was a financial hit that we'd survive.

But when the insurance agent came through, we learned the worst part: Our house had depreciated to the point where we were upside down on our mortgage. We owed the bank more than half of what the house was worth.

We had to decide: Did we stay in a money pit, needing a ton of work in a town quickly going downhill and unsafe for our children? Or did we lose everything we had already put into it — a decade of paying our mortgage — to try to find somewhere better and start all over? It was terrifying to abruptly face a no-win decision that would change the course of our lives and the lives of our children.

We chose to take the leap. My mother found a wonderful town that we fell in love with when visiting her. We instantly knew we wanted to raise our children there, but it was in Indiana. We were fourteen hours away in Pennsylvania. Going there would mean uprooting our children, leaving the rest of our family members, moving to a place we only saw for a total of five days, and spending all our savings.

I was scared to move somewhere new. I mourned the idea of leaving the home we had our children in, the only home they ever knew. Could I give up walking through the nursery and pointing to the exact spot I was sitting in when I felt my daughter move for the first time while her daddy sat next to me, building her crib? I was heartsick over the situation, and I wasn't one who knew how to take chances. I liked detailed plans, security, and assurances. We had none of those.

Despite it all, we jumped. We put our house up for sale, found an apartment a mile from my mother, and scheduled a moving truck. We tried unsuccessfully to get my husband a job before we moved. Everyone said to interview when we got to Indiana, which meant we were making a huge move to a completely new state with no financial security.

We prayed every night that this would work. We took comfort in little signs that this was meant to be, that the calling in our hearts to go meant everything would work out. For months, we lived on faith alone. We repeated to ourselves that family was most important. As long as we had each other, everything would fall into place.

The move was riddled with sacrifice for all of us — not only to lose the home we loved but to downsize. Drastically. We were leaving an 1,800-square-foot home for an apartment that was only 1,000 square feet. The moving truck could only fit so much. It meant parting with half of everything we owned. It was a lot of sacrifice for the chance at a better life. But we pushed on.

My husband and I both expected to dislike the tiny apartment — an in-between until we could find a new home. However, we instantly fell in love with the small place. We spent the first three days with no furniture, sleeping as a family in sleeping bags on the floor, and realized how good it felt to not be surrounded by so much stuff.

We felt a little sad when the moving truck arrived. Starting fresh felt good. Minimalizing everything was like a deep breath of the country air outside our window. Suddenly, we were thrilled to have gotten rid of so many items we had clung to before. Living in a place that had open space and was easy to keep clean felt better than anything we had parted with. We got a storage unit and moved half of the items from the moving truck to it.

It took weeks for my husband to find work while we watched the number in our bank account dwindle. We were learning to love living with less, but we were afraid of how much less we'd have to live without if he didn't find a job soon. Right in the middle of COVID many places were shut down, everyone was struggling, and assistance programs were already wiped out. I stressed. I prayed. I hoped that since everything here felt so right, it had to be the correct move to come here. But the weeks stretched out without many callbacks, and people hiring were often out of the office due to positive COVID tests.

In the meantime, between finding a new job and learning to be minimalists, we noticed more. Without so many toys, the kids wanted to spend time with us and chat more. We played board games every night. We went on bike rides to explore the new town up close. We took extra time to make little moments into teaching moments.

We did free things like fishing, cooking outdoors, catching fireflies, playing outside, and reading together as a family. We started our new life by becoming closer as a family with more time to spare now that we had fewer things in our new environment. Without the clutter, there was room to be grateful for each thing we had and to count our every blessing.

Those habits stuck. Even after my husband found the exact job we hoped for, and our children made lots of new friends, and we got more involved in our community, we continued to put family time first. Every weekend, we have one-on-one play dates where my husband takes one child and I take the other, and we do whatever they want. We do family dates. We started playing more board games and getting better at the old ones.

We lost a lot in the flood and more in the move. But we gained so much more.

—Jill Keller—

Dragged into Paradise

Wherever my travels may lead,
paradise is where I am.
~Voltaire

I am standing on one of eight Tellico Village pickleball courts on a hilltop overlooking Tellico Lake and the mist-shrouded Smoky Mountain peaks receding to the horizon. The early morning sun is rising. I hold a yellow plastic ball in my hand and prepare to serve. I look across the net at two of my pickleball friends. I glance to my left at my doubles partner. A thought hits me. There is nowhere on Earth I would rather be at this moment than exactly where I am, doing exactly what I am doing. This is paradise.

As much as I would like to take credit for moving to this retirement community in eastern Tennessee, I can't. The truth is that my wife Carolyn dragged me here kicking and screaming.

Three years earlier, we were living in Vero Beach, Florida, helping Carolyn's mother, Marian, care for her father, Rowland, who was suffering from Alzheimer's. We worked with a lawyer to finance Rowland's nursing-home care while protecting Marian's assets. We worked with a Realtor to sell their condo. We found an independent-living facility nearby and helped Marian move in. We comforted her when Rowland grew abusive during the later stages of the disease. When he passed, Marian found herself in a new home, supported by friends and financially secure. Mission accomplished.

Now, it was time for Carolyn and me to take care of ourselves.

We were sixty-eight years old and without a place to spend our golden years. Settling in Florida was not an option. We longed for mountains, lakes, and four seasons. We decided to relocate somewhere between Vero Beach and Albany, New York, where our daughter lives. We wanted to be within a day's drive of each location. Six weeks before our lease expired, we gave notice that we would not renew.

Carolyn found two retirement communities of interest halfway between New York and Florida. I resisted. I wanted to *do* things in my retirement, not just sit around. But these were *active* retirement communities.

Carolyn enjoys meeting new people and socializing. But for an introvert like me, the mere thought of moving into a community of seniors was terrifying, exacerbated by my inability to view myself as a senior. Carolyn tried to reassure me.

"Wouldn't you like to live where you could play tennis, work out in a fitness center, hike, bike, and join clubs?" she asked.

"Not with strangers."

"You'll make friends."

Ironically, this conversation reminded me of one we had with our daughter thirty years earlier when we were moving to a new school district. I finally understood her fear.

Carolyn booked us two nights in a private home in Tellico Village. I was not pleased with this arrangement. I like my own space.

"Why don't we stay in a motel?" I asked.

"There are none nearby. Besides, we'll be staying right in the community with a resident so we can learn firsthand what it is like to live there."

A week later, we were driving to a place we had never been to stay with someone we had never met. Fortunately, our visit to "the village" (as the locals call it) convinced us that this might be the community, facilities, and setting we had been looking for. I was pleased to learn the village was not age-restricted. Non-seniors (and seniors in denial) were welcome.

We "test-drove" our new community by renting for a year—a year of discovery. We discovered pickleball rather than tennis was the game of choice and learned to play. The daily fun and camaraderie were contagious. Hearing friends shout out our names when we arrive at the courts reminded us of the welcome Norm receives on the TV series *Cheers* where "everybody knows your name."

We discover kayaking. We purchased two kayaks and joined the Soggy Bottoms kayaking club and explored local waterways. In June, we expanded our horizons by traveling to Washington State and kayaking the Lewis and Clark trail on the Columbia River. Who knew kayaking could be so much fun and educational?

Throughout the year, we added activities. We joined the Muddy Boots hiking club and explored the Smoky Mountains. We biked the greenways in Tennessee and neighboring states. We played bridge and mahjong. We rented a plot in the community garden and enjoyed fresh vegetables.

When our year's lease was up, we purchased a home and cemented our commitment to our community through volunteer work. Carolyn volunteers in the local library, and I volunteer as a pickleball trainer. When someone is sick or injured, we, along with others, provide a card, kind word, visit, or meal.

Now at seventy-one (almost a senior), I admit that although I was reluctant to move to a retirement community, it turns out to be the best idea I never had.

— D.E. Brigham —

Eye-Openers

61

The Blessing of a Smile

Peace begins with a smile.
~Mother Teresa

Every muscle in my neck and shoulders ached as I drove to the paint store. The stress was weighing me down: my recent divorce; the anger of my stepchildren, whom I dearly loved; and the fraying of several friendships over polarizing political differences.

Plus, I'd purchased a fixer-upper house. It was affordable because of its condition, but it demanded an unexpected amount of time, expense, and a skillset I lacked. Recently retired, I had the time. But I'd used all my money on the down payment, and I had no experience with anything requiring the use of tools. I was wholly dependent on the goodwill of friends to teach me the simplest of tasks as I fumbled through projects in every room.

I found it more and more difficult to climb out of bed in the morning. Luckily, my dog Gracie's cold nose reminded me that, despite my woes, she needed her kibble, walks, and cuddles. And whether I wanted to or not, I had a house to fix up. I'd imposed on friends who had lent me their rental house long enough.

Still, how could I get through another day?

Steeped in these thoughts, I gripped the steering wheel and began to make a right turn, not noticing two men in the crosswalk until I was almost upon them.

I braked, shouting, "Sorry, sorry!" Then I dropped my head into my hands. I could have seriously hurt one of them! If a police officer had been nearby, he or she would already be filling out a well-deserved ticket. How angry the two men must be. I'd read of incidents like this where a handgun is pulled. Frightened and ashamed, I waited for them to at least hurl obscenities or pound on the hood of my car.

I lifted my head in time to see one of the men — dark-haired, mid-thirties, the burlier of the two — step around to the driver's side of my car. He knocked on the window, his brown eyes searching mine. My heart pounded, and my breath caught in my throat as I opened it. Stupid? Maybe. Scenes of violence from TV shows and movies flooded my mind. But complying with his unspoken request seemed, in the moment, to be the right thing to do.

"I'm so sorry. I should have paid better attention," I apologized again.

He studied my face.

I waited, silent.

He smiled. A warm, generous smile. "Has anyone told you yet this morning what lovely eyes you have?" he asked.

Shocked, I couldn't utter a word.

"Beautiful eyes. And those freckles. If no one has told you lately, I'm telling you now. You are stunning. Have a good day."

"Thank you," I managed to mumble.

With a slight nod, he stepped away from the car to join his friend, and they finished walking across the street.

I sat dazed for a moment longer and then inhaled a deeper breath than I had in months. The man I had nearly run over had smiled at me! In the times we were living, that smile felt like a gift from God.

I said a prayer of thanksgiving. The muscles in my neck softened. My jaw relaxed. I finished my turn, pulled into a parking spot, and sat, reliving the moment. The depression that had been haunting me, painting the world gray, magically lifted. I awakened to the world around me.

Now, I noticed sunshine pouring through trees, showcasing new buds and warming my cheeks — the ones with freckles. Tulips and daisies filled the front yard of a sweet, white cottage across the street.

Next door sat a cream-colored Craftsman with a wide, wrap-around porch much like the one where I'd been raised. Down the street was a warm gray house, similar to the house I'd just purchased and was once again excited to work on.

Because of an unexpected smile, the world around me had changed. I had changed.

When my Good Samaritan looked into the car, he could have seen an older woman with nothing special about her eyes, whose freckles might easily be mistaken for age spots. But he had stood at my window with a deliberate intent to spread goodwill, to change the world one gracious encounter at a time.

I drove on to the paint store, parked, and checked my face in my rearview mirror. Same ordinary eyes, but there was a sparkle in them that I hadn't seen in a long time. "Wait 'til I tell my family and friends about the power in a stranger's smile," I told myself.

Gratitude bubbled up inside me. Now I could see how many other blessings I had. I owned my own home. I had friends who were volunteering their time and energy to teach me handyman skills. I had Gracie, my canine buddy, to cheer me on. I had food, heat, a good car — things easily taken for granted that would be luxuries in many countries.

As optimism replaced my despair, I realized that a new life awaited my creation. I would find ways to rebuild my relationships with my stepchildren and focus on common ground with friends who had different political views. And I would join my Good Samaritan in his effort to change the world one smile at a time.

— Samantha Ducloux Waltz —

62

The Break-In

When you are grateful, fear disappears
and abundance appears.
~Anthony Robbins

My two kids and I had just returned home from an afternoon soccer practice and a brief stop at the grocery store. I was still unpacking groceries when my seven-year-old called attention to the wide-open door at the front of our house. It was a door we rarely used since our back door was more convenient. I quickly scanned the dining and living areas and saw evidence that someone had gone through one of our cupboards.

"Hurry," I called to my kids. "We need to get out of here."

I called 911 from our locked van, and a police cruiser pulled up in the driveway within minutes. The officer told us to wait in the van while he checked the house to make sure the intruder was gone. After searching every corner and closet, he gave us the green light. His manner was kind, and he reassured my seven- and nine-year-olds that our intruder had likely been looking for something easy to steal to make a quick buck, and it was highly unlikely he or she would return.

I was still feeling a little shaky when my husband arrived home from work, but together we took an inventory of the house. In the end, it appeared we'd lost just two laptops: one that was old and almost worthless, and my work laptop.

Given that our home had just been violated, I expected to feel extreme anxiety. Instead, I found myself mentally compiling a gratitude list. During a painful season three years earlier, I'd clung to gratitude as a way to survive. The exercises I'd adopted during that season had become so ingrained that I automatically fell back on them whenever life got stressful. And a break-in was certainly a stressful event!

But, instead of anxiety, I felt remarkably calm. There was so much to be grateful for: That the intruder had waited until our house was empty. That I had backed up my laptop on an external hard drive recently. That the police had arrived so quickly and had been so kind and reassuring.

And there was still more to be thankful for in the days to come. I received an outpouring of support from friends and neighbours when they heard what had happened, and an excellent deal on a new laptop from our small-town computer store.

But as I reflected on the break-in, I felt an even deeper gratitude. Friends expressed all kinds of outrage about the criminal who'd invaded our home. But I'd seen someone pass our property earlier that day who might have been the intruder — someone who clearly had not had the opportunities and privileges that I'd enjoyed. Like the police officer told my children, I don't believe he wished us harm; I believe he wanted to make a quick buck, likely to pay for his next drug fix. While a drug addiction or an unhappy life don't excuse criminal activity, I could certainly feel compassion.

But in the aftermath of our break-in, I had something even bigger to be grateful for. For much of my adult life, I'd struggled with fear and anxiety about all kinds of potential threats. There was even a period during my twenties when I'd stacked cans next to my townhouse doors as a cheap alarm system. But, in my forties, I'd started tackling my fears and phobias one by one. The break-in was a perfect test of my progress.

A stranger had been in my house, right in my bedroom, which was where I'd left my laptop. A few years earlier, that violation would have left me a basket case. Now, I felt calm, even grateful!

My gratitude and the peace that came with it never wavered. And my children picked up on that peace; none of us had difficulty sleeping that night or the nights that followed. It was a small miracle.

We've since fixed our front door to make it more secure, and I store my laptop out of sight when I leave the house. But we don't live in fear — and I count that as a blessing!

— Rachel Dunstan Muller —

63

Different Strokes...

Be curious, not judgemental.
~Walt Whitman

I still had a few minutes before my next class, so I swung into the cafeteria to grab a coffee. That's when I spotted him: a menacing-looking punk rocker with razor-sharp, twelve-inch mohawk spikes. He had some kind of safety pin embedded in his face and wore a studded dog collar that matched his biker leathers and black leather boots.

Honestly, he scared me, so I clutched my coffee and quickly ducked out the side door. I preferred to walk a little farther if it meant avoiding a potential confrontation.

It was 1989, and I was a "mature" journalism student, heading to my favorite elective: Sociology — A Study in Deviant Behavior. The class was eye-opening and provocative, and our gray-haired professor was a straight shooter. He told us he didn't care if we came to class. He never took attendance and said our final grade would be based on three things: the mid-term, a final exam, and one classroom presentation. He didn't give extensions and didn't want excuses. "So, learn — or don't learn. I'm getting paid either way."

We all signed up for a presentation time slot and worked in small groups to bring in a guest speaker who represented "deviance." We understood that deviance didn't necessarily mean "bad." It was a description of someone who didn't fit the norm. That gave us a wide range, and it made for some interesting speakers.

Our guest speakers included an exotic dancer who was studying to become an accountant, a tarot-card reader who took herself extremely seriously, a gay couple who talked about the discrimination they were facing, and the leader of a local chapter of a white supremacist organization (who was booed and evicted after spewing several minutes of hate-filled rhetoric).

I was curious to see who our guest speaker was going to be that day, and I guess I shouldn't have been so surprised when "Mr. Mohawk" walked into the class. His group got up and introduced him, and our wide eyes watched his every move.

He started to talk in a very calm, soft-spoken voice and told us he was a university student on a full scholarship. He lived with his grandma because she wasn't doing very well, and the doctors told the family that if someone didn't stay with her, she would need to go into a nursing home, which she didn't want to do.

So, he moved in with her and helped with the cooking and shopping, cleaning and laundry. He made sure she took her meds and tried to make her laugh at least once a day. He described it as a "win-win" for both of them, but I suspect that it was a lot tougher than he made it sound.

"I know I look kinda scary," he confessed. "But, honestly, I'm actually a nice guy. I don't drink, smoke, or do drugs. In fact, the only thing I do that could be considered deviant is to look like this."

We were captivated as he continued, "I get good grades, I enjoy reading, and I go to concerts or movies whenever I can afford to. I have a few really good friends, and we like to get together to talk and play music."

And then he said the words that have stayed with me for more than thirty years: "I just figure if you don't want to get to know me because of the way I look, then we haven't wasted each other's time."

Wow. Just wow.

He filled in some of the gaps by adding, "I don't believe in violence, I volunteer and enjoy helping people, and I'm happy to be here today to talk about my lifestyle." Then he asked if we had any questions. Well, of course, we did!

So, he explained how he managed to get his hair so tall and spiky. It took a handful of gel, a large comb and a blow dryer, all while hanging his head off the end of the bed and then dousing the finished style with hairspray. He said it took at least an hour to get it to look like that, and when he told us we could touch it, we lined up. It was stiff and poky, sort of how you'd expect a porcupine to feel.

I was really impressed with him — and ashamed of my reaction when I first spotted him in the cafeteria. Here was a smart, young man who loved his family, got good grades, helped people, and was very kind and articulate. I thought of my own two boys, who were six and eight years old at the time. Would it really be so bad if they turned out to be like him?

"Hey, it's just hair and clothing," he said. "I don't plan to look this way forever, but for now I like it, and it makes me feel good."

Every so often, I think about that young man. He'd be about fifty now, and I hope he realizes what an impact he made on me. Because of his visit to the classroom, my kids were allowed to wear whatever they wanted — as long as it was relatively clean and not morally offensive.

The boys made their own decisions about hairstyles, resulting in one teenager bleaching his brown hair California-blond and both boys experimenting with various lengths and styles. As long as they kept it clean, it was their choice.

We still set boundaries when they were growing up, like asking them to wait until they were eighteen before getting any piercings or tattoos. And the fifteen-year-old who was adamant that he'd get his eyebrow pierced the day he turned eighteen never did. But it was his choice either way, thanks to the wise words of a very unlikely role model.

— Lori Kempf Bosko —

64

Reflections of a Septuagenarian

I can be changed by what happens to me.
But I refuse to be reduced by it.
~Maya Angelou

"Ma, why are you so glad to turn seventy?"
Child, seventy years is what the good Lord promised us, eighty if
 we're strong.
The Bible is true, even the part that says the years are full of trouble
 and sorrow.
Life is soon over, and we are gone. Then there's no more tomorrow.
Many tomorrows have come and gone before I reached this birthday.
My mother, father, brothers, and sisters are gone, and yet I'm still here
 is what I say.
I've got a stack of obituaries for grownups, teens and babies, too.
Most were younger than I, so I'm delighted to be right here with you.
That means no person, bullet, accident, disaster, or disease,
Nor any other dreadful happening succeeded in snuffing out my life.
Celebrating birthdays is a matter of survival.
Each year I have a personal revival.
I like to take time out and share,
And challenge others to rejoice in each moment if they'll accept a dare.
You young folks tend to enjoy whatever you have today
Because people in my generation helped to pave the way.
I survived segregation and Jim Crow laws, and made sure I stayed
 out of jail.

I helped Mama clean up white folks' houses all day to earn a dollar.

I learned firsthand why Marvin Gaye sang "Make Me Wanna Holler."

I went upstairs to the movie theaters through the side entrance for colored only.

I learned how to hold my urine without wetting my panties

'Cause we couldn't use public restrooms unless our job was to clean them.

I didn't slap anybody's face, cry, or hide in disgrace.

Neither did I pull a trigger when called a black n-----.

My Black teachers told us what to expect and gave us hope.

They said education was the way out of oppression, not getting high on dope.

I made a fire to cook after gathering wood all year 'round.

I never knew if a snake might bite me as I picked up sticks off the ground.

I survived the stench from outhouses and thank God never fell through that seat.

I read by kerosene lamp and carried many cans of that stuff home for heat.

I walked long, dusty roads because no city bus drove down our street.

I washed clothes on a scrub board and graduated to a wringer washer.

I drew buckets of water from a well and later learned to use a dishwasher.

That's progress, my child. That's progress.

I escaped the Vietnam War because I was a female,

But I witnessed the killings of our fathers, sons, uncles and bro-ers — Black men.

It's no coincidence that many Black women never had a husband or children.

Genocide, mass incarceration and such took them away.

Heroin destroyed many as sleeping men stood on sidewalks like frozen trees.

Crack cocaine and the AIDS epidemic spread like a wildfire in our community.

I'm so glad that STD didn't appear when I was messing around.

By that time, I'd quit playing church and was firmly planted on solid ground.

Like so many women, my heart was broken during the sexual revolution.

But the peace and hope I found in salvation made me happy with my solution.

"Wake Up Everybody" and teach the children, Teddy Pendergrass sang.

I learned that war is not the answer, but love is a wonderful thang.

So, I've entered a new era in my life.

I look back and wonder why all the bickering, turmoil and strife.

Everybody receives the same twenty-four hours each day brings.

But the Lord determines how much we keep and how much He'll take away.

The game of life is kind of like spending time in arcades.

Choose wisely, play safe, and pray that you, too, can have decades.

I must confess, at times, gang wars and race riots worked my nerves for sure.

Advancements and promotions followed setbacks and helped me to mature.

Child, you are listening to a grateful woman who has seen her children grow up.

A cancer survivor who chooses to bless rather than hate those who persecute me.

I'm a happy septuagenarian who eats meat and does not condemn the vegetarian.

I'm glad to be an American who respects both the African and Hungarian.

Life is a precious gift given by God alone.

Some suffer for a season, suffer long, or suffer not.

It is not man but God who determines our lot.

And, whatever my lot, he has taught me to say, God is good and, in the end,

He is the one who will vindicate me.

Child, stay humble so God can use you.

And when you turn seventy, take time to reflect on all He has brought you through.

— Gloria Shell Mitchell —

65

A Jar Full of Blessings

Gratitude is a powerful catalyst for happiness.
It's the spark that lights a fire of joy in your soul.
~Amy Collette

I'll never forget the day I realized my husband had finally reached the end of his rope. During other difficult times, I'd always been able to lift his spirits and help him find the light in the darkness, but this time I felt like a failure.

Layers of bad luck had settled upon our family. As a part-owner in his business, my husband had gone a long while without a paycheck, which had thrown our family deep into debt. Eventually, the truth came out that his business couldn't support two owners, so he stepped aside.

Throughout his life, my husband had tried to work at something that brought meaning and satisfaction to his life. But, at his age, the only job he could find was selling shoes at a store located an hour away — a job he loathed. To add to our troubles, I'd lost my job and hadn't found another one yet.

It broke my heart to know that if my husband quit his sales job, it would make a huge difference in the quality of his life, but it would also plunge us into greater debt. With all that had happened, he already felt as if his world had crashed, crushing his hopes and dreams.

While my husband felt grateful for the many blessings he had, his hardships had multiplied to such a magnitude that he believed the negative far outnumbered the positive in his life. It was as if he could no longer find the bright side in this dark situation.

One day as I sat thinking about what else I could do to help, a silly idea shot through my head. I glanced at the clock and figured I had plenty of time to work on my nifty plan before my husband arrived home from work.

In the pantry, I found a medium-sized glass jar with a screw-on lid, washed it in soapy water, and dried it until it shined. While rummaging through my craft studio, a colorful ribbon caught my eye, which I wrapped around the neck of the jar and fastened in a bow. At last, I glued a label on the jar and placed it in our bedroom.

That evening when my husband arrived home from work, I told him I had a surprise for him and led him downstairs.

After one glance at the jar, he looked at me as if I'd lost my mind. "What's this for?"

I grabbed the jar and held it in my hands. "It's a blessing jar."

"I can read the label, but what is it for?"

"It's a jar to put your blessings in."

I pointed to the stack of brightly colored peel-off notes I'd placed next to a pen. "When you get home each night, I want you to write one thing you are grateful for and put it in the jar. That way, when you feel like your troubles outnumber your blessings, you can see how many blessings you have."

He shrugged his shoulders. "Right now, I can't think of anything I'm grateful for. It's been a long, horrible day and a long drive home."

I ripped off a bright turquoise slip of paper, grabbed the pen and put them in his hand. "See, you found your first blessing. You're grateful you're finally home."

My task wasn't easy. It took a lot of pleading to get my husband to commit to doing this. But as time flew by, the jar looked bright and beautiful filled with its colorful notes, a reminder to my husband that he still had much to feel grateful for.

Did the blessing jar make everything better? No, it honestly didn't.

But what it did do was force my husband to change his attitude. For a short time each evening, he had to concentrate on his blessings and go through the motion of feeling grateful. During those precious moments, he got a break from the troubles that had held his mind hostage all day. No matter how slight, this tiny attitude change was a fresh start and sprinkled us with hope as we continued to wade through those rough waters together.

—Jill Burns—

66

The Bluest Sky

I concluded that gratitude makes optimism sustainable.
~Michael J. Fox

I came to with a start and realized I was bloody and wet. My husband was frantically calling my name.

We were spending the weekend in a hotel while visiting family. I remember yelling to my husband to be careful because the bathtub was slippery. Soon after, I was the one who fell, hitting the back of my head on a granite ledge, twisting my ankle, bruising my forearms, and cutting both elbows. An ambulance was immediately called to the scene.

I was diagnosed with a traumatic brain injury. I had absolutely no idea what all that entailed, but I was about to get a down-and-dirty lesson. I would lose a large percentage of my vocabulary and the ability to complete my sentences. I would experience headaches so severe that I lay in bed for days crying, unable to go about my daily activities and function normally. For a time, I would not be able to recall my mailing address, phone number, or employee identification number, along with other basic information that I normally knew by rote.

One of my favorite pastimes had been sitting outside on the patio in the sun. Now, I hid from the sun because I could not tolerate bright light of any kind. I had trouble seeing for the first twelve months after the accident. I also had excruciating neck pain. And worst of all, the medication I was prescribed for my severe headaches resulted in extreme side effects, including a deep depression.

I missed more than a month of work and was afraid of losing my job, because my company was doing layoffs. I also had to spend a lot of time going to doctor's appointments for that first year after.

However, the old adage that all good and bad things come to an end proved true. My fall changed another kind of vision for me—not my physical vision but my "gratitude vision." There is absolutely nothing like an injury that threatens your life, or your life as you know it, to give you clarity and an appreciation for everything that you hold dear. Every morning, I thank God for one more day. I thank him for my wonderful husband Sidney and my two girls, Veronica and Brittany, my dog Missy, my dear friends, some good doctors, and two great pharmacists. I am grateful that I have a second chance to communicate with my family and friends from an enhanced place of love and gratitude.

Three years after my fall, I won't say that all my symptoms have totally abated, but they are significantly improved. After seeing two different neurologists, my headaches have become considerably less frequent. My vocabulary is probably 75–80 percent restored. My memory is constantly improving. I took myself off that horrific medication that practically had me howling at the moon and felt immediately better. My vision slowly returned to normal. I came to be able to tolerate bright light again. The neck pain, sustained because of whiplash from the fall, has significantly improved after months of physical therapy. In short, I am feeling much better.

Before I was injured, I appreciated life but I took living for granted, not as the privilege it is but as my right. Today, I celebrate life. I so appreciate every one of its offerings, great or small.

Believe it or not, I would not change one minute of my slip-and-fall experience. The lessons I learned and the insight I gained were invaluable. I appreciate the simple things around me differently. Now, when I look up, I relish the bluest sky. It is as if I now see everything in vivid, vibrant colors. I'm grateful for every sunrise and every sunset.

—Gwen Mulkey—

67

Sticky Notes from a Bouncy Unicorn

Blessings cannot be computed or counted,
for the true blessings of life are the treasures
hidden in the reservoirs of the human heart.
~T. D. Jakes, Can You Stand to be Blessed?

I am on an emotional journey right now. My ten-year-old, Sienna, has sickle cell disease. She has also had four strokes, receives monthly blood transfusions, and was recently diagnosed with and had brain surgery for moyamoya disease.

As a mom, I am on the verge of having to make some very difficult decisions regarding Sienna's healthcare. I have quietly struggled for the past week. There have been nights when I have not slept at all. There have been nights when I have cried myself to sleep. I have swallowed at least a gallon of water in the shower trying not to scream. And I have sat in the same chair for hours, too physically, mentally, and emotionally exhausted to move.

Today, Sienna and I talked about her health and wellbeing. We moved on to chatting about her behavior and the things that drive us crazy about each other. We rounded out our chat by discussing things we could do to help us do life together more seamlessly. Most of the time was spent with her being intentional about making sure I knew she had very valid concerns. Having had a good, hearty chat, we went our own ways in the house.

This evening, I left the house to get food. When I returned, Sienna had left sticky notes on my bathroom and bedroom mirrors. These little sentiments both broke and healed my heart at the same time. There was one particular note that stood out. It simply read, "Don't Forget Me." That made me cry for hours. Tears are still occasionally flowing from my eyes and the depths of my heart as I type this. It felt as if Sienna knew and had made peace with her mortality, which a child her age should not even be concerned about.

As I processed Sienna's message, a comfort came over me. I realized her words were not morbid at all. They, along with several other notes, were reassurances about all the things that had been troubling me. The other notes read:

"You're the best."

"You're amazing."

"I love you."

"Thanks for taking me to school every day."

"Thank you for everything. I love you so much."

"I hope you love me as much as I do."

"I love you. You will stay on my heart forever. I hope you know that."

"You are the last piece of my life."

"I'll be your shoulder to cry on."

As if by magic, my tears were suddenly replaced with smiles. Yeah, that's it. Magic.

This little girl is absolute magic. She is both unicorn and bucking bronco. She is sunshine and thunder. She is firefly and hornet. She is sometimes all these on the same day. And me? I am just grateful that God chose me as her mommy. It is a privilege to love such a beautifully spirited little person.

Sienna still faces several medical challenges, but there is a blessing even in her simple daily activities, like speaking without a slur, walking, having a lively personality, and still recreating who she is as a person. I look at her romping about like she doesn't have a care in the world. In that moment, I realize that each fit of laughter is a fresh reminder of grace. Each made-up song yelled at the top of her lungs is an example of mercy. Each clumsy, careless bounce is a tangible blessing. And, some days, I am content to just count them one by one.

—Suzettra L. Walker—

68

Chicken Soup for the Soul

Meaningful

When I started counting my blessings
my whole life turned around.
~Willie Nelson

I was the social worker in a long-term-care facility. In theory, my work should have been meaningful, but much of my time was spent fielding complaints.

Recently, a woman said, "When I moved Dad in here, he had ten pairs of matching socks. Now he has three! Where are the rest?"

If only I had an answer.

When I started working at the facility, I'd been enthusiastic about my job. I wanted to make a difference in people's lives, not search for lost socks.

Besides looking for lost clothing, I was frequently paged to calm an angry or confused resident. One day, the first-floor nurse called me. "Mr. Hartley is going off on everyone. His favorite sweater is not in his room, and he's cursing and screaming. We need you to talk to him."

"Lost sweaters, socks, shirts—I hate this job," I groused as I trundled down to Mr. Hartley's room and knocked on the door.

"Come in," he yelled.

I managed to keep the impatience out of my voice when I approached the elderly resident. "Hello, Mr. Hartley. I'm Diana Walters, one of the social workers. I understand you have a problem."

He waved his arms and swore at me. "You people lose my stuff all the time! I'm not going to stand for this. I need that sweater, and

I need it right now!"

"I want to find it for you. Would you describe your sweater?"

"It's bright blue and has a pattern across the front, like zigzags. You people lost it, and you better find it. I need it when I leave in half an hour."

"I'm going to look for it right now, Mr. Hartley. It sounds as if this particular sweater is important to you."

"It's the heaviest one I have," he explained in a calmer tone.

"So, you need a really heavy sweater when you go out."

"Yes, I get my chemotherapy today, and it's freezing in that room. It's the only sweater that's warm enough."

"Can I look in your closet and drawers?"

"They've looked there! It's not in this room!" He was shouting again.

I scurried to the ground floor and searched the laundry and Lost and Found. There were six women's sweaters and five men's, but none that fit the description. There was a bulky cable-knit sweater that zipped up the front, however.

Back in Mr. Hartley's room, I sat next to him. "Mr. Hartley, I haven't located your sweater yet, but I'll keep looking, and I know it will turn up. But I found this really heavy sweater that may do the trick for today. I would be happy for you to wear it. What do you think?" I held my breath while he fingered the material.

After a moment, he nodded and smiled. "This should work." With tears in his eyes, he added, "You truly are an angel of mercy. I won't be cold with this on." He leaned over to kiss my cheek.

It was like I'd given him a bag of gold instead of an old sweater. Frail, thin, and cancer-ridden, all he wanted was to be warm when he received his treatment. I was glad I'd been able to make him happy, at least for the moment.

But Mr. Hartley had given me something more valuable than a sweater. He'd reminded me that my work mattered.

It mattered when I comforted an upset family member. It mattered when I helped the staff calm a confused resident with sundowner's. It even mattered when I found a warm sweater for an angry, old man who was scared of being cold but was also scared of dying.

A Bible verse says, "Enjoy your work and accept your lot in life — this is indeed a gift from God (Ecclesiastes 5:19 NLT)."

I had often prayed for meaningful work. That day I was reminded that God had already blessed me with a job that made a big difference. It was time I thanked Him for the gift.

— Diana L. Walters —

69

When My World Turned and Righted Itself

Minds, nevertheless, are not conquered by arms,
but by love and generosity.
~Baruch Spinoza

I was one of the most depressing people to be around, always blaming others for my woes and bemoaning my fate. Even when I got married to a loving husband and had a lovely daughter I was still depressed and focused on the negative. For example, my father and my father-in-law were busy doctors, both working well into their nineties. Instead of being proud of them, I complained that they had no time for me.

My mother-in-law was an energetic and independent woman, carrying on her household duties to her full capacity. Instead of appreciating her help, I was always lamenting her sharp tongue.

My husband and daughter were not spared. I complained my husband was not earning enough. I complained my daughter was not appreciative enough. I always blamed my mother, too, because I thought she was never on my side.

Soon, however, things came to a head. My mother realized my depressing attitude was making everyone around me unhappy. Especially my daughter! A gifted, talented girl, she was soon to be married and would be moving to the far-off USA. My mother realized that her granddaughter would be leaving home with the burden of her mother's depression still hanging over her. Immediate action was called for!

My mother asked me to meet with her. She said she had a surprise for me. For once, I was excited and quickly made my way to her place. But once I was there, my feelings turned to dismay as I found her in tears. This was something new for me because I was the one usually crying, and she was the one always comforting me. When I asked what was wrong, she said that she would only reply if I promised to agree to her wish. By this time, I was desperate enough to agree to anything!

Slowly, she took out a white envelope from her purse and handed it to me. I opened it and saw it was stuffed with money. When I asked her about it, she replied, "Your father and I have been saving this for a long time, and now we want you to do something for us."

"What do you want me to do?" I asked.

"Go to the 'Pilgrimage of the Walk.' You know we won't be able to go, so you do it for us."

How could I refuse? I agreed, albeit with a lot of apprehension. The pilgrimage was three months away and entailed a 90-kilometer desert walk to be completed in three days.

Soon, I found myself in training! It seemed my whole family had joined forces to get me ready for the pilgrimage. My husband prodded me out of bed in the morning to train. My daughter got me new shoes. Even my in-laws adjusted their schedule so that I would not miss my daily walk.

Something magical happened and the cloud of depression that hung over me started to lift. I had always heard stories about the "Pilgrimage of the Walk," where prayers were answered. But it seemed as if I was already receiving the blessings.

The day of my departure arrived, and my whole family came to see me off. The next day, I sat outside my tent gazing at the golden sand dotted with green date trees. It was cool now but soon the sun would start blazing down.

I was apprehensive. Would I be able to accomplish my mission? A 90-kilometer walk in three days!

I came out of my reverie as I walked toward the large breakfast tent. As I entered, I found it lined with food-laden tables and people bustling about filling up their plates. I did the same as I knew this was the one certain meal of the day.

Soon, it was time to start "The Walk," so I laced up my shoes, slung my backpack over my shoulder, and headed down to the trail.

As I started walking, I looked ahead and noticed an old man several paces ahead of me. His back was bent, and he held a walking stick in one hand. He leaned heavily on the stick as he shuffled along.

As I overtook him, I realized his clothes were dusty and worn. His feet were clad in cheap sandals unfit for walking such a long distance. But then I happened to glance at his face, and I was taken aback. There was no sign of discomfort in his eyes, no misery, no complaint; they were bright and focused. His gaze was expectant and reverent as he gazed ahead.

As I came abreast of him, I smiled and gave him a nod. He waved at me and smiled back. It was a wrinkled and cracked smile but beautiful.

He signaled me to stop, and as we paused in our walk, he thrust his hand inside his frayed coat pocket and took out a handful of candies, which he generously offered to me. I attempted to refuse, but the old man insisted.

I took them and started walking. As I walked on, my thoughts kept going back to the old man's generosity. He had so little, but he chose to give. On the other hand, I had several packets of biscuits and dry fruits in my backpack, but I hadn't thought to offer him something in return. How I wished I had!

Something stirred inside me, and I felt myself change. I felt more gratitude and became more aware of my surroundings.

After walking for a couple of hours, I was ready for a break. The sun was now right overhead. I sat down to rest my aching feet in the shade of a date tree. I reached for my water bottle, but it was empty. Too tired to look around for some water, I just closed my eyes and tried to ignore my thirst.

Something fluttered against my hand, and I thought it was a bird. I opened my eyes and gazed into the loveliest, most innocent face. A small girl was holding a water glass and offering me a drink. She was dressed in shabby clothes and was obviously poor. But with her smile, she looked like a princess.

She was so small and had so little, but she had so much to give. This time, I remembered the biscuits in my backpack and offered one to her. She gratefully took one and, as I watched, crossed the road and gave half of the packet to a couple of very hungry-looking boys.

By the end of the day, all the goodies in my backpack were gone. I kept finding people to share with, and I enjoyed the smiles I got in return.

The second day of "The Walk" dawned, and I found I was no longer apprehensive about what lay ahead. I stopped at a roadside stall and bought more biscuits and candies, some for myself but most of them to give away.

As I walked along, I saw more and more instances of selfless generosity. Dirt-poor people offering home-cooked food or water to the walkers amazed me all over again.

By late evening, I was ready to wind up my walk for the day and was looking for a place to settle down for the night. The sunset and the darkness of the desert wrapped around me like a cloak. Little points of light signaled the presence of tents that were erected by locals for the walkers. Soon, to my dismay, I realized all the tents were full, and there was no extra mattress available. I resigned myself to sleeping on the rough sand.

As I stretched myself out on the ground and tried to sleep, a shadow loomed over me. It was the old man again. He smiled and took my hand to pull me up. He gestured to an empty mattress and signaled for me to use it. I thought I must have missed it in the darkness and was happy to make it my own. I thanked the man and, in no time at all, I was fast asleep.

I woke up refreshed as the gray light of dawn crept across the sky. As I looked around, I saw a bundle of clothes lying on the sand. Then the bundle moved, and I realized it was the old man. He had given up his mattress for me!

I walked across and shook the old man awake. He looked at me with tired, blurry eyes and smiled.

As I neared the end of "The Walk" on the third day, I noticed a subtle change in my fellow walkers. They, too, seemed to be treading with a lighter step as if their hearts were lighter. Had they been touched by miracles, too?

I completed my pilgrimage and returned home to the welcoming arms of my loving family. They all remarked on how I glowed, and I replied, "This glow comes from a heart filled with gratitude. This is the glow from having encountered endless generosity and the joy of giving. Thank you for giving me this life-changing experience."

My world had turned and righted itself.

—Shaista Fazal—

70

The Pedestrian Overpass

*Be the reason someone smiles. Be the reason someone
feels loved and believes in the goodness in people.*
~Roy T. Bennett, The Light in the Heart

I tried to remain solemn. That was my mood as I started off on a Saturday afternoon walk, and I had no desire to change it. As I sauntered toward the campus of a local community college, the thin cloud cover and the freezing temperatures reflected my mood. I was deep in thought about small things: little aches and pains, little irritants that were sandpapering the edges of my life.

Two children, laughing, ran past me. That was rude of them. They had no business interrupting my gloom.

Soon, I came to a major thoroughfare on the other side of the campus, and I decided to go north on it. There was a pedestrian overpass just ahead. I decided it would be somewhat interesting to climb that pedestrian overpass and observe the traffic. I could watch the cars go under me. Each held a driver and maybe passengers, all living their separate lives, all going to their separate places, all doing all their separate things. I could get even more contemplative and withdrawn, which was attractive to me at that moment.

Traffic roared under me, and I was sure that the people in those cars and trucks were completely unconcerned with my solitary observation of them. So, what if some clown was up on the pedestrian overpass watching them? What difference would it make to them? What interest could they possibly have in me?

As I watched the traffic flow, I began to stare into the private worlds of the people's vehicles. But then, unexpectedly, one person waved to me. It caught me off-guard. What was happening? Then, in another car, two more people waved at me. Suddenly, most of the people in the cars below were waving and smiling.

I was shocked at first. This wasn't supposed to happen! This wasn't part of my plan. I had determined that I was going to have a solemn, isolated moment on this cold afternoon on the pedestrian overpass. But, as if by magic, I was catapulted into a different state of mind. It was a conspiracy, I'm positive. My gloom lifted. Something welled up within me that was making me feel, well, joyous.

I waved at those who waved at me, and other people in cars and trucks going under the overpass responded. I had been singled out and zapped by a wave of love from random drivers and passengers on the street below. There was nothing I could do to stop their assault. I was defeated in my attempt to remain introspective. I smiled, laughed and waved at the parade of humanity, who may not have known the depth to which they touched me in their travels that day.

— Vic Zarley —

Saying Thanks

71

Practicing Gratitude

Acknowledging the good that you already have in your
life is the foundation for all abundance.
~Eckhart Tolle

Being grateful doesn't come easily to me. I usually notice what's lacking before I appreciate what's already there. One time when I broke a glass in the kitchen during dinner, all I could see at first were the shards and tiny glittering specks strewn across the floor. It took me several minutes to appreciate that no one was hurt. This is how I approach most things, but I didn't realize how difficult it was to live with that mindset and maintain my happiness.

In December 2019, my husband was laid off from work. I struggled not to panic. My husband, in contrast, is especially good at finding a bright side. He reminded me that we'd have extra family time around the holiday season. Plus, we had financial security due to some stringent budgeting.

Five months later, as the pandemic brought stay-at-home orders, my husband was still unemployed. I felt myself sinking. The thoughts running through my brain were a chorus of problems that I didn't know how to fix: unemployment, shrinking bank account balances, remote learning, juggling the needs of three children, and the daunting prospect of what full-time jobs, if any, I might find in my own job search. With seven years of stay-at-home mothering on my résumé, coupled with a few years of freelance writing, I didn't feel like anyone's top choice for anything. I wasn't even my *own* top choice.

Pre-pandemic, I always took some joy in looking put together before leaving the house. Now, I was taking my kids for walks in the neighborhood in my old sorority sweatpants. One time, I didn't brush my hair for a week. It stayed in a messy ponytail, the hair tangling around the elastic.

As my self-care became non-care, my children began to suffer the effects of my mental state, too. Laundry? Not done until my oldest child asked me to wash her clothes. I found keeping track of homework and virtual meetings truly overwhelming.

Then I remembered my planner. I used to use one every day. With multiple schedules to keep track of, I needed to get organized. So, I invested in a new planner.

Writing in it was a joy. Organizing my life felt like I was picking up the pieces of myself and putting them back together, although the puzzle looked different now.

My planner included daily space to list three things I was thankful for. Each morning, I made myself think of three things and write them down.

Thursday 8/20/20: Coffee. Coffee. Coffee.

That was the best I could come up with on the mornings when I was particularly grouchy and sleep deprived. A more reflective and grateful me would include my husband, my children, and coffee, in that order. Coffee almost always made the list.

Monday 9/14/20: Coffee. Fun colored pens. Baths the kids got last night.

I began to notice I was grateful for past actions that served my future self. Whenever I did laundry, I was grateful for clean clothes the next day. When I remembered to run the dishwasher at night, I was thankful for clean dishes in the morning.

Monday 10/19/20: Feeling my baby nestle into my shoulder with her tiny hands around my neck. My parents and brother living only a few minutes away. Coffee.

Recognizing little things to be thankful for was getting a little easier, but I was still struggling with my self-worth and anxiety. I applied for jobs and got turned down. I participated in a virtual, freelance portfolio showcase and came away with no new clients.

I felt frustrated. And sad. I questioned my value with every rejection, and then I had to build up the courage to try again. I wanted to celebrate the steps I'd taken but felt unable to because I hadn't gotten the results I wanted.

I made myself write down the attempts as accomplishments anyway.

Wednesday 11/18/20: Adding to my portfolio. Reading to my boy. Coffee.

It seemed important to be grateful for the experience. At the very least, I had a complete portfolio now, and my résumé was in great shape. It had to be progress.

Friday 12/11/20: Finding time to write yesterday. Holding hands with my seven-year-old on our walk last night. Coffee.

As Christmas approached, with no change for us in sight, I reminded myself even more to be thankful for the little things: setting up the Christmas tree, decorating it with the children, and resisting the urge to rearrange the ornaments when they all ended up on the same branch.

I baked cookies with the kids and tried to focus not on the mess we were making but on the way they took turns mixing the dough and using the cookie cutters.

The local farmstead had a free light display, and I found some affordable Christmas crafts. My kids were having a blast. We were pulling off one of the toughest holiday seasons we'd experienced!

I ended the year being thankful for the most basic, necessary, and profound things. I was thankful for my children, who reminded me every day to live in the moment; my husband, who supported me in my quest to be happier; our home; and, lastly, my health.

On Christmas Eve, I woke up feeling sick, with most of the symptoms of COVID-19: sore throat, congestion, fever, body aches, and chills. I drove to five different locations, trying to find a place where I could take a COVID test. It felt like I could barely swallow around a huge rock in my throat, and I was longing to go back to bed. Finally, I found a clinic with availability right before they closed.

My COVID test was negative. I was never happier to learn that I had a bad cold. I lost my voice but felt much better by Christmas

Day. I was truly thankful for my health, my family's health, and having access to a coronavirus test when I needed one. It could have been much worse. Reflecting on that gave me a genuine sense of joy.

It would be nice to wrap this in a bow and say that my husband or I found full-time employment, my anxiety abated, or my attitude completely changed. The truth is that I still struggle. Some days, I do feel joyful for the little things we have. I find myself noticing something small, like how easily and genuinely my youngest child laughs when we play peek-a-boo. Other days, I feel like I'm going through the motions. On those days, I try to be gentle with myself. I still have a desire to be thankful, and I think that's important, too.

Monday 1/4/21: Cozy robe. My oldest child turning eight. Coffee.

—Rebecca Schier-Akamelu—

72

Never Too Late

*I awoke this morning with devout thanksgiving
for my friends, the old and the new.*
~Ralph Waldo Emerson

Blinking under the bright lighting, I surveyed my surroundings upon waking from a disturbed sleep. The intensive care unit was loud and busy. An aide was tending to my feeding tube. I glanced down at my arms, supine and propped on pillows. I tried to lift one, but it didn't respond.

Memories of the car accident came flooding back. I'd never lost consciousness after my best friend lost control of her SUV and we flipped. I didn't feel any pain, I noticed with relief, but when I attempted to free my body from the wreckage, it didn't respond at all.

In the helicopter flight to the city, tears I couldn't wipe poured down my face. I knew then what a surgeon soon confirmed: I'd broken my neck, and I was permanently paralyzed.

Now, the tears began again, the loss hit me in crashing waves. Just days ago, I had been a strong, athletic, independent woman. I was a proud single mom. I'd grown up in a small town and gotten pregnant in high school, but then I moved to the city and had become a traveling tradeswoman at twenty-one.

These hands that couldn't move an inch to scratch my nose used to weld and operate heavy machinery and climb iron. I thought of the hundreds of things my hands would never do again: dress me, feed me, braid my thirteen-year-old daughter's hair.

I thought about swimming in the ocean and riding roller coasters, road trips, romances — everything I was going to miss — and then I started to realize something: I hadn't truly appreciated what I had. I hadn't sat back in my shoes, looked around and marveled. I felt my heart soar with gratitude like it would if I could have that all back.

It's true. I didn't really know how to appreciate anything until almost everything was taken from me that summer night six years ago.

Even as I cried about my fate, another realization hit me, this one a soothing balm over an angry wound: Everything that really and truly mattered, I still had right there.

As if on cue, they entered then: my brother with his coffee and that worn copy of Marcus Aurelius's *Meditations* he was reading to me; Daddy with his blue eyes, gentle and full of love; Mama with her own ailments, so strong for me now; and my baby — my baby! That's everything right there!

What mattered most in life had never been clearer to me.

It wasn't my career I took pride in, new cars, or a perfect figure. It was the people in my life whom I loved.

My mom dried my tears, and my brother made me smile. When my daughter pressed her head against mine like a cub with her lioness mommy, I knew I still had everything that mattered.

***

This morning, I woke to my caregivers drawing my curtains and asking how I slept. They were two of my favorites and were sure to share some laughs while they got me ready. I had a class at 10:00.

We joked around while they did my passive stretching and got me dressed.

In the years that have followed, my disability (I am a complete quadriplegic, permanently paralyzed from the chest down) has made life far from easy.

Maintaining appreciation can be difficult at times but not as much as my able-bodied peers might imagine. Humans are far more resilient and adaptable to change than we give ourselves credit for.

Yes, for a while, depression darker than I'd known could exist pulled me in. I didn't want to see anyone with an able body. I wasn't interested in communicating with people with disabilities, either, as if that would make me more disabled or something.

I couldn't wallow in misery forever, though. No matter how close I'd come, I hadn't died, so living was in order.

I got a dog, a van and a haircut. I got out of bed every day (with lots of help) and took charge of my life again. I wrote and published a book about it.

I learned to be grateful for things I would have never acknowledged before.

I appreciate a nice, long hair scrub, and thank my caregivers over and over for cooking my meals, cleaning my room, and brushing my teeth.

I can't meet my body's needs anymore, so I live life in this constant state of gratitude toward the people who act as my hands and feet.

Gratitude is good for us. Gratitude helps people feel more positive emotions, relish good experiences, improve their health, deal with adversity, and build strong relationships.

I am grateful to be alive, foremost. To come that close to death definitely fosters some appreciation for life. I have gratitude for my loved ones, including my latest blessing — a precious grandson! And I have so much gratitude for my caregivers.

For my daughter, who sacrificed much of her adolescence to make sure I was taken care of: dressing, eating, transferring, bathing, hours of physical therapy. Her love and devotion got me through not only physically, but emotionally.

Each caregiver who shows up for a shift is a blessing. They help me keep my life running smoothly. I'm now a busy freelance writer (typing with a mouth stick!), and I'm in grad school to teach high-school language arts.

I tell my caregivers they are like links in this unbroken chain. One by one, they keep up my quality of life. I do try to bless their lives in return with affirmations, validations and anecdotal wisdom. Whether they perform my care for wages or not, they bless my life with their care, especially the kind and patient ones.

Looking back on my life on legs, I know I didn't truly appreciate everything. I remember complaining, blaming, and feeling entitled. I wasn't a bad person; I just didn't have much perspective.

I know now that one second can take so much away. If I could go back, I would have taken more pictures and cared less about what I looked like in them. I would have let things slide and just roll off my back. Life is short, and it's so, so good.

I would have counted my blessings, like that old church song. But it's not too late to do it now.

— Cassandra M. Brandt —

73

How Gratitude Saved My Life

The unthankful heart discovers no mercies,
but the thankful heart will find, in every hour,
some heavenly blessings.
~Henry Ward Beecher

For many years, I ran away when life became unbearable. I did whatever I could to escape emotional pain. It was worse when I became a pain-pill addict. When I finally got clean, I told another recovering addict about how I would get high when times were rough. She told me to do a gratitude list when it happened again.

"What good will that do? Will it make my problems go away?" I asked.

She simply replied, "Just try it."

A couple of months later, my world as I knew it was over, or so I thought. As autumn turned to winter, I struggled financially. It was hard to pay the bills and put food on the table, but I managed to do it. I often had anxiety attacks just thinking about my expenses and the need to buy Christmas presents.

One Sunday night in November, I walked in the door from a long day. The kitchen was dark, which was strange because I always left one light on. I brushed it off as forgetfulness. As I started up the stairs, I flipped the light switch. Nothing. *Hmm. The bulb must be out,* I thought to myself. I felt my way upstairs to the bathroom and then the bedroom. When neither of those lights turned on, I was concerned.

What were the odds that all those lights had blown bulbs?

I went downstairs and tried turning on other lights. Some lights worked but not others. I went through the checklist of problems my dad had taught me. The bill was paid, my neighbors had lights, and nothing was blown in the breaker box. When turning each breaker off and then back on didn't fix anything, I knew I had a bigger problem. I called a friend to see what he thought. After I told him I'd checked all the usual problems, he said the words I didn't want to hear, "You're going to have to call an electrician."

Now, anyone who's owned a house or had to call a repair person knows it's not cheap, especially for an emergency on nights and weekends. This was both.

When I bought the house a couple of years earlier, I needed an electrician to fix a few problems that the inspector had found. My dad suggested a company he knew and trusted, so I called them. While fixing the problem, they discovered and fixed a separate issue that could have burned down my house. I was so grateful that I told everyone I knew about them. So, I gave them a call again.

While the electrician was in the basement, I sat in the darkened kitchen surrounded by candles. I was on the verge of having a panic attack. I worried about how I'd pay for the repair because I knew the check would bounce.

I felt so powerless and not in control, which I hate. And then I thought about walking to the drug dealer's house next door and buying something. I stood up, took a step toward my shoes, but then stopped and said, "No, I can't." Just then, I heard a quiet voice telling me to do a gratitude list. I dismissed it, thinking it wouldn't fix anything. The voice in my head grew louder and more demanding. "Sit your ass down and do a gratitude list now, damn it!" the voice commanded. Out of sheer fear from what I'd just heard, I sat down and did what the voice said.

I thought really hard about something, anything, for which I was remotely grateful. I started with being grateful I had woken up that day. Next, I remembered the furnace and hot-water tank were still working. That led to being grateful that I wouldn't have to stay at someone's house that night and leave my two dogs and two cats behind. I was grateful when I heard the refrigerator turn on because I wasn't going to lose all the food I had just bought. Then I realized that the stove worked. I could cook dinner even though it would be by candlelight. Just as I finished the last thought, the kitchen lit up. The problem was fixed.

Now, how am I going to pay for it? I thought.

When the electrician came up from the basement, he said the problem was a bad connection that needed cleaning. Phew, it was nothing major. Then, like ripping off a Band-Aid really quickly to avoid the pain, I asked, "So, what's the damage?"

"Nothing," he said.

"What? What do you mean 'nothing'?" He went on to say that after his company worked on the house a couple of years earlier, I recommended them to so many people that they got a lot of business. This was their way of paying me back.

As much as I hate crying in front of other people, I couldn't hold back the tears. A couple of them snuck out of my eye and rolled down my cheek. As he was leaving, I thanked him profusely. When I closed the door, I stood in the kitchen thinking, *What if I hadn't called this company? What if I'd put on my shoes and gone next door, bought some dope and gotten high? What if…?* I thought of all the bad things I could've done but didn't. My heart filled with so much gratitude when I thought about the choice I had made to listen to that voice of reason.

Since that night, whenever times got tough, doing a gratitude list has saved me from doing something I'll regret later. It hasn't made everything rainbows and unicorns, but it's helped me find the blessings in the mess.

— Stephanie Stafford —

74

A Second Chance

If you are still breathing, you have a second chance.
~Oprah Winfrey

My mother and I had a relationship that could be described as "difficult" at best. We couldn't seem to get along or agree about anything. When we spoke on our weekly phone calls, she would push my buttons, and I would find myself annoyed and impatient. To compound the estrangement, my mother was beginning to show evidence of memory loss and would repeat her most offensive comments.

Then, a call came one Sunday morning with the heart-wrenching news that my father had suffered a fatal heart attack. I spoke to the police officer and my bewildered mother, who asked when I was coming over. I reassured her that I would be there as soon as I could, and arranged for someone to stay with her until I could make the four-hour drive from my home to hers.

The next week was a harrowing experience for both of us as I made funeral arrangements and endless phone calls, and prepared to bring my mother to live with us. She and I would have to find a way back to each other but in reversed roles. I would be the caretaker, showering and dressing her; I would be the cook, preparing all her meals; and I would be her chauffeur, driving her to the many doctors she had to see. I would also be her accountant and have her power of attorney, paying all the bills on her house, hiring painters and working with a Realtor now that the house would have to be sold.

When she first came to live with me, she fought like the lioness of old, snarling and striking out with razor-sharp claws. I would respond in kind — that is, until she would ask me in a timid and uncertain voice where my father was and if he was all right. Her vulnerability and disorientation dissolved my anger, and I would explain that he had passed. I realized she was hearing these words as if for the first time, and her sobs would break out again, as would mine.

I learned not to do that and, instead, when she asked, I would say that he was fine, he was golfing or bowling or at a meeting. These answers seemed to satisfy her, especially when I told her he would be home by dinner.

Lying went against everything I had been taught and every principle that structured my life. But these lies were less damaging than the harsh truth. So, I told them with less of a twinge of conscience with each telling because they provided her with something familiar, recognizable and comforting.

Gradually, she became accustomed to living with me and underwent a transformation. Even the smallest gesture was received gratefully and acknowledged with a thank-you or a compliment. I would look at her, bewildered. Who was this woman, and what had she done with my mother?

I had had to retire from my job to care for her, which meant long hours in her company. She would talk about her parents and her childhood, coming more alive as I asked questions about her past that she could answer.

Another way I came to enjoy her company was through music. Having grown up in a family where music was valued and singing along with the radio was encouraged, I knew the lyrics of nearly every song she did. I had a fairly good singing voice, but my mother sang like an angel. So, after dinner, we would sit by the living room fireplace and sing. It gave her such pleasure because music, for some reason, is untouched by Alzheimer's disease. She could relive some of the former joy she had taken in performing with the senior choral group. She had frequently sung solos. It was a special bonding time as we sang our duets.

Eventually, it was no longer possible to keep her with me. She would awaken at all hours, calling for me to dress her, insisting that people were waiting outside. Or I would awake to her calling for help and find her in the walk-in closet in a bedroom down the hall instead of in the bathroom across from her room. Making the decision to move her to the structured and safer environment of the care facility, while necessary, was difficult. I visited her at the times she would be most alert, and we would talk and sing together, drawing a small audience of fellow clients and aides who would join in our mini concerts.

While the music remained strong, her memories became more clouded. She no longer asked about my dad, thought she was a twenty-year-old, and forgot she had ever married or had children. Because I saw her every other day, I remained present in her mind longer than the rest. But one day, she no longer knew me as her daughter, and I was very sad indeed. Trying not to cry, I asked her, "Who am I if I am not your daughter?" Without hesitation, she said, "You're my friend."

I realized what a great compliment she had paid me with those three words, as powerful as if she had said "I love you." I was more than family to her. We can't choose our family. We love them despite our conflicts. But we choose our friends, and we choose to love and value them. I reached out and squeezed her hand and said, "You're my friend, too."

It's strange to be thankful for a disease as devastating as Alzheimer's, but I found the silver lining in it. It may have robbed my mother and me of some things, but it paved the way for us to find something deeper. It allowed us to find each other. It gave us a second chance.

— Kathleen Chamberlin —

75

Chased by the Garbage Collector

*Thankfulness is the beginning of gratitude. Gratitude
is the completion of thankfulness. Thankfulness may
consist merely of words. Gratitude is shown in acts.*
~Henri Frederic Amiel

Shortly after I moved to Nebraska from a metropolis, I was leaving my house to drive my young sons to school. A garbage collector waved at me as I backed out of my driveway. Knowing that men often found me attractive, I waved back coolly. Accustomed to big-city life, I kept my distance from strangers. I stayed alert, safety-minded, and prepared.

The garbage collector took off after me in his truck. And he wasn't alone. There were two men in the cab.

I sped up. The driver sped up.

I turned right at the next corner. He turned right.

I turned left at the next corner. He turned left.

He and his cohort passed by all the neighbors' trash cans in pursuit of me. Should I let them follow me all the way to my son's school? I had no idea where the nearest police station was.

I peered closer at the driver through my rearview mirror. He and the other man in the truck were now both yelling and waving at me. The driver honked his horn and gestured to the side of the road.

As if I were going to pull over!

I sped up. He sped up.

And then my seven-year-old son said something interesting: "Mom, they have your purse."

I looked down at the floor of the passenger seat where I kept my purse while driving. The spot was bare.

I glanced back at the garbage truck. The driver held a strangely familiar, oversized, black purse out the window.

Sheepishly, I pulled over as passersby stared at me and the honking, waving garbage collectors.

The driver of the truck ran to my window with the purse. "I saw you had this on top of your car," he said. "When you backed out, it fell on the street, so I picked it up before someone else could."

He had chased me nearly a mile to return my purse to me. What an introduction to small-town life! I sent a thank-you note and a gift certificate for doughnuts to the sanitation services after that, letting the owner know about his workers' good deeds.

— Ronica Stromberg —

Blessed Decision

A daughter is the happy memories of the past,
the joyful moments of the present, and the hope
and promise of the future.
~Author Unknown

I couldn't believe it when my doctor announced, "Alice, did you know you are three months pregnant?"

"Impossible! I'm forty-four years old. I'm just here for my yearly checkup." I shook my head, sure this was a dream. "How can I be pregnant at my age?"

My doctor slipped his gloves off his hands, smiled and patted my shoulder. "Well, you know, it happens the same way it does when you are twenty."

I choked back the tears that welled in the corners of my eyes. "Real funny. I mean, what will I do? I can't have a baby now."

My doctor, whom I'd known most of my life, took my hands in his. He said, "You know, Alice, lots of women today are having babies later in life. I'll send you to a neonatal doctor for tests. Everything will work out just fine."

My legs wobbled when I left the building. I scooted into the driver's seat of my car and let my head fall forward on the steering wheel. The floodgates opened. I scrounged around for tissues.

This can't be. Ray and I have so many plans to travel. We are building a new house. Where will we put a baby? Our friends will think we've lost our minds. My parents might have a heart attack when I tell them they'll

Saying Thanks |

be grandparents again. My co-workers are going to roll on the floor with laughter!

I don't know how I managed to arrive home without having a wreck. I put the car into Park but sat with the ignition on. *How will I tell Ray?* I continued to sit there as I thought *Maybe I shouldn't have this baby! Oh, gosh, did I just think that? Alice, what's wrong with you? Get it together!*

I slowly opened the front door and peeked inside to see Ray in front of the television. I turned toward our bedroom door. "Hi, honey, just putting my things away." By the time I entered our bedroom, I felt bile rise up in my throat. I quickly made a trip to the bathroom and emptied my stomach. I stood up, flushed my face with cold water from the faucet, and looked at my image in the mirror. Tears trickled down my cheeks. I managed to freshen my face and dry my tears before I headed to the family room.

"Hi, babe, how was your day?" Ray smiled and got up from the couch. He wrapped his arms around me. Newly married, Ray and I had grown children who pursued their own lives. We had been looking forward to a carefree life. I melted into his chest and buried my sobs into his neck. He pushed me back slightly. "Alice, what's wrong? Are you okay?" He held my arms firmly. "What's wrong, honey?"

I blubbered. "Oh, Ray, I don't know how to tell you."

He drew me back into his arms. "Silly, you know you can tell me anything."

"I know, I know." I sniffed. I blurted out, "I'm pregnant!"

I waited for Ray's response. His strong arms squeezed me closer. A low chortle escaped his lips, and I felt his tears mingle with mine against our cheeks.

"Oh, Alice, Alice. This is so wonderful. Are you sure?"

I squeezed against him. "Yes, yes, but do you think I should have it?"

He gently brushed my tears away and said, "I believe this is a gift from God that we should honor." He held me tighter.

We talked for long hours that night about what our lives might be like going forward. We talked about the new home we were building and how the sunroom we planned could be a nursery instead. We questioned whether I should quit work and become a full-time mom again. We fell asleep in each other's arms.

We went about our normal routines the next morning and left for work. My pregnancy blurred every thought in my head while I tried to work. A baby grew inside me.

At the end of my workday, I walked to my car. It was cloudy and a slight drizzle started to fall. Just before I put the car in gear, I looked up to see an enormous shaft of light break through the clouds. It shone directly on the hood of my car. I breathed in and out slowly. I whispered. "Okay, God, decision made." Immediately, the shaft of light disappeared.

Three months later, at twenty-seven weeks' gestation, I delivered our daughter. She weighed one pound, nine ounces. When a nurse wheeled me into the Neonatal Intensive Care Unit, I looked into the incubator that held our precious gift.

Before my eyes lay a tiny human who resembled a fragile bird. Her eleven-inch frame didn't look real. Blue veins ran through her transparent skin like the lines on a road map. Wires and needles pierced her chest, legs and arms. Tubes peeked out from her mouth and nose. A piece of gauze covered her eyes because of the bilirubin lights she needed for jaundice phototherapy.

Each decision we needed to make for our baby's care turned out to be the right one. Brain bleeds, blood transfusions, and the hurdles we jumped each day brought Ray and me closer together.

I learned how to be patient. A baby's growth can't be hurried. After all, she had come out of a safe haven in my womb to an artificial substitute. A sign above her incubator read, "Be patient. God isn't finished with me yet."

I watched nurses and doctors take care of our baby each day for three months. They remained considerate, compassionate, and humane no matter what circumstance arose. Their hearts never wavered from being gentle and loving.

I looked at priorities differently. My hair didn't need a touch-up, nor did I need to keep a nail appointment. I didn't need that new pair of shoes or the snazzy outfit hanging in the shop window. I knew that every penny needed to be saved for the mounting hospital bills.

During every moment in the hospital, I witnessed true compassion. I started to reach out to charity organizations. I realized how important family and friends, all relationships, really are... or should be. I quit hesitating when friends and family offered to lend a hand. I accepted graciously. I learned how to cry openly, laugh out loud and praise the milestones in our baby's care.

I am immensely grateful for the decision I made thirty-two years ago to bring our beautiful daughter into this world.

—Alice Klies—

77

Giving Life to a Stranger

*To know even one life has breathed easier because you
have lived. This is to have succeeded.*
~Ralph Waldo Emerson

T hrough my body surges the blood of people I've never met. An amalgamation of souls, hopes and dreams runs through me. The viscous red liquid creeping into my veins as these strangers share their life force with me when I can't sustain my own.

The first time, it scared me. I'd been having litres of luminescent yellow liquid pumped into me: chemotherapy—cytotoxic drugs—meaning "toxic to living cells." It kills off all your cells without discrimination, which is a terrifying thought. But it was specifically crafted by experts for that purpose: to kill the cancer growing within me, hopefully quicker than it kills the rest of me.

But blood is a force of nature, not something medical geniuses have synthesised. It's something older than humanity. It is personal, intimate. It is part of us, made for us, to keep us alive. To think that we can pull it out of one person and put it in another is mindboggling.

The first time that doctors hung a unit of dark red liquid above me, I watched it as they fiddled around, checking the blood type was right, checking my name and birthdate. When they hooked me up, my heart started to race as I watched the thick syrup creep toward my arm. The inches closed until it was centimetres, and then it was in. They had to take my temperature to make sure my body wasn't rejecting it. But my desperate, exhausted body welcomed it, as if it was always meant to be there. And in that moment, it became part of me.

I've now had more blood transfusions than I can count. Time and time again, strangers have saved my life. In the absence of being able to thank them directly, I send that gratitude out into the universe and down into my body. With each transfusion, I wonder what kind of person is flowing into me. Are they mathematical? Or a writer? A marathon runner? Do they have siblings? Are they musical? Are they a mother? Or are they a man? Could I have a man's blood in me? I wonder what music they listen to, what books they read. I weave stories around them as we become one. I marvel to think that the fabric of my cells is now made up of the kindness and generosity of others, and I feel those connections moving through me. Those people, who willingly donated their blood and its components, will be with me forever.

My soul is also made up of other people, even beyond a cellular level. I really feel that. I'm a combination of everyone I've ever met and loved. Everyone who has imparted wisdom, opinions, some hope, a smile — they're all part of me. It culminates in the person I wake up as every day, and I marvel at the behaviours and views I have picked up from others along the way.

I think of all the webs that link humanity, the connections we make and the effects we have, and I am eternally grateful for every ripple, every wave caused by another person that I have felt in my own life.

But, more than anything, I am grateful for the blood that courses through my veins that has been given freely by people who will never meet me. Without it, I would no longer be here. I cannot think of a greater gift to give someone: sharing a piece of yourself so that they might live.

— Jen Eve Taylor —

78

Flowers for Mother's Day

If you look the right way, you can see
that the whole world is a garden.
~Frances Hodgson Burnett

"Can we go now?" my son asked me once again.

I replied, "Okay, yes, but you don't have to do this, Dalton."

He stopped pacing, looked at me, and said, "I know I don't *have* to do this. I *want* to do this. Can we go now, please?"

I sighed. "Yes, let's go."

Mother's Day weekend was drawing near. I had recently been divorced from his dad, so we wouldn't have our usual Mother's Day this year. I knew he worried whether I would be okay. I tried explaining to him in the car, "Sweetie, I am fine. Please don't spend a lot of money on me! I know how hard you worked for that money shoveling snow!"

He just smiled and replied mischievously, "We will see. We will see."

As he left the store, he texted and asked me to open the truck with the key fob and close my eyes so he could hide my gift. A scene that would be repeated when he returned home.

When he got back in the car, he was smiling and happy. I asked him, "You didn't spend too much, did you?" He just looked at me and smiled from ear-to-ear.

That week, I noticed he was awake before me in the mornings. He'd rush to his room as soon as I got home from work.

Mother's Day finally arrived, and I was looking forward to what he had planned. As the morning turned to evening, Dalton said nothing. He just stayed in his room for the most part. I finally broke down and asked, "Dalton, did you forget that today was Mother's Day?"

He looked at me sadly and sighed. "Okay, but it isn't what I wanted to give you, and I don't want you to be disappointed."

I said, "Dalton, I would never be disappointed in anything you gave me. As long as it came from the heart, I would not be disappointed."

He disappeared into his room, only to return a couple of minutes later with a large bouquet of flowers still in their wrap. Most of them were dead.

As tears filled his eyes and his voice quivered, he explained, "I kept them hidden in the closet, but I knew that flowers needed sun and water to survive. So, every day I would bring them out of the closet, put them in water, and set them in the sun. As soon as you got home, I would take them out of the water and hide them back in the closet so you couldn't see them. As Mother's Day got closer, I saw that they were dying, so I started staying up nights after you went to bed to get them more water and then hide them back in the closet before you would wake up. After you went to work, I pulled them back out from the closet to get more water and sun for a few hours, and that is when I could sleep for a few hours."

I looked at my sixteen-year-old son, and my eyes filled with tears at the extraordinary effort he had put into this gift. You see, my son is on the autism spectrum and suffers from severe anxiety. I could not imagine what he must had been feeling for the past few days. I was the one in tears now as I said, "Dalton, how much sleep were you getting past few days?"

He said, "Aw, Mom, I got a few hours here and there. You know I don't need that much sleep. I really tried, Mom, I did!" He looked at me and said, "Why are you crying?"

I choked out the words. "Because this is the most wonderful Mother's Day gift I have ever received!"

Any visitor entering my home now will look into my china cabinet with a look of confusion. Sitting among the fine china is a bouquet of dead flowers.

— Vicky Webster —

79

A Friendship, Warmly Remembered

You can't forgive without loving. And I don't mean
sentimentality. I don't mean mush. I mean having
enough courage to stand up and say, "I forgive.
I'm finished with it."
~Maya Angelou

My best friend, the stranger at the bar, never noticed me sitting a few stools down. I wonder if he would have recognized me that night anyway. We hadn't seen each other in at least fifteen years, and we had stopped hanging out routinely several years before that. For a couple of thirty-somethings, our salad days were half a lifetime ago, before either of us had facial hair and forehead wrinkles.

I recognized Joe, though, as he looked down at his dinner. Like me, he was at the bar alone, perhaps refueling after a long, hard day of being an adult. No more bowl cut, no more comically large glasses framing his eyes. And yet, noticing his face was like hearing the opening notes of an old song. I knew him instantly and was glad to see him, which is why I should have gotten up, slapped him on the back, and bought him a beer.

Instead, I did what I have too often been guilty of doing when given an opportunity to act and live in the moment: I got stuck in my head, caught up in memories, reminiscing silently with the Joe I used to know.

I pictured the friendly boy who made room for the painfully shy, anxious me on the bus the first day of elementary school. From then on, we were an on-the-road team, regularly turning the bus into a race car or train or space shuttle to pass the time, with an array of imaginary buttons, levers and pedals spread on the seatback in front of us. The adventures were harrowing, but somehow we always safely made it to our destinations.

I pictured cross-town bicycle rides down winding, wooded roads by day and comfy sleepovers by night, during which we'd eat too much pizza, play too much Mario Kart, and make a too-long game of identifying anatomy in the scrambled adult TV channels.

I pictured the kid who motivated me to join town-league basketball, the only sport I ever played, and cheered me on even when he discovered how horrible I was at it, even when I decided midway through my first season that it was time to gracefully retire.

I pictured the funny guy who came up with silly nicknames for our peers and teachers, ribbed me constantly, fired off a killer Woody Woodpecker impression, and the night my father brought us to a cheesy haunted house for Halloween, peed his pants and didn't seem the least bit embarrassed.

The memories flooded me with gratitude — and laughter.

Joe always made me laugh, an ability I admired as a nervous, worst-case-scenario thinker. Every joke, every cartoonish giggle was balm for my high-strung soul.

The joy is what I remember most about our friendship. Joe was thoroughly good-natured. He and I never fought. We had no bitter rift. The end came slowly and quietly, simply and naturally. He went to one high school, and I went to another. Fifteen years later, I saw him at a bar.

I'm old enough now to know that some people enter our orbit only to gradually, almost imperceptibly, drift away until we awaken one day to discover they're not in our gravity anymore, and our universe has changed. Some friends are with us just as long as they need to be, and their presence is no less a gift when it disappears. That's because the memories remain, never failing to enrich and uplift us when we call on them. What would we be without the beloved people who become ghosts in our minds, frozen in age and appearance and a million little moments of shared experience? We wouldn't be us.

From the bar, I smiled at the memory of the Joe I knew and glanced at the stranger a few stools down, imagining who he had become and what his life was like.

We paid our bills. I walked out the door into the night a few steps behind my old friend. I watched his taillights fade from view as he left the parking lot. I sat in my car for a minute or two, wondering if he had noticed me when I wasn't looking and had talked himself out of saying hello. I wondered if I was in his head on his ride home, part of a grainy nostalgia loop of bike rides and video games and belly laughs, memories tucked safely in a place where we are eternally young and eternally friends.

And if that's true, I thought, maybe he's smiling and shaking his head all at once. Maybe he feels the gratitude I feel for the friendship we gave each other. And maybe he has come to the same bittersweet realization: We grew together until we had to grow apart.

— Phil Devitt —

80

Learning to Dribble

A friend may be waiting behind a stranger's face.
~Maya Angelou, Letter to My Daughter

I was the new kid in town. New home. New city. New state. And new school. My dad got a new job, and we had packed up our lives and moved from our old home, school, friends and everything. We moved over summer vacation, so I didn't have to deal with school right away.

But, wow, there were so many changes. We'd come from up north, and now we were almost as far south as possible. We'd landed in southern Florida, and we were total strangers.

The only neighbor we met right away came to find out whether I babysat, and I did. But, other than babysitting, I didn't know anything or anybody.

Summer whizzed by while we unpacked, arranged furniture, found stores we liked, and adjusted to the Sunshine State with its palm trees and canals everywhere — and the possibility of alligators on the front lawn. Oh, and with bugs the size of Vermont!

So many changes. School loomed over me, and I dreaded it. I was not an adventurous person. Shy and quiet, I read a lot and did not make friends easily.

My head teemed with fears and worries. Would I make friends? Would I fit in? Would I survive at all in this strange new world?

But there I was, bracing for a new school full of strangers I didn't know, but who all knew one another already.

And if that wasn't bad enough, I loved school.

I loved learning. I loved reading. I even — dare I confess? — loved homework. I was good at doing homework. I was good at school. Loving books and reading helped me to get good grades. Teachers loved that about me. Even a brand-new batch of teachers.

Other kids, though, did not. Other kids didn't like me getting top grades, answering questions in class, being delighted with school. I did not win popularity contests. But I couldn't stop being me — loving to read and learn.

I felt like a total failure. Nobody would like me. I tried not to be discouraged.

Then one day, a tall, muscular boy in English class strode right over to me. He introduced himself as being on the school basketball team. I knew that — he was the star player!

"Hey," he said. "You do really well in English class. Do you think you could help me?"

Yes, oh, yes, definitely yes. I could, and I would. We sealed the deal with an exchange of smiles.

From that moment on, life at school changed for me. I loved it! Basketball players asked me to help them out. I sat on the bleachers during practice and did lessons. Basketball players clustered around me, walked me to classes, and called greetings to me in hallways. All the girls were jealous, but they weren't mean about it.

Nobody gave me trouble about being smart anymore. I was the team tutor, a sort of mascot for them, and I fit in. I was thankful to be smart enough to help the team. I was forever grateful for the basketball star who helped me to change my life at school.

I taught the guys about commas and subject-verb agreement. They taught me how to dribble a basketball. And they taught me that being smart could be a real blessing — which I could use to help others.

And though I was only five feet tall, I walked the halls feeling as tall as those towering basketball players who helped me to fit in — in a new state, new city, new school. They gave me courage and confidence to be myself — and to be a short girl who really knew how to dribble a basketball!

— Karen M. Leet —

81

Keeping in Touch

Technology is best when it brings people together.
~Matt Mullenweg, Social Media Entrepreneur

With a serious tone in her voice, our seven-year-old grand-daughter told my husband and me that she had something important to discuss. "We haven't been together since last Christmas because of COVID," Leia said, "and that's a very long time." Her sister Andie nodded her head as Leia commented how important it was that we visit before they returned to school in a couple of weeks.

Allan and I were having a FaceTime visit with our granddaughters. Leia seemed to have quite a plan worked out, no doubt with assistance from her parents. She told us both families should have a COVID-19 test before we started our trip. If everyone's tests were negative, Leia suggested we consider driving across the mountains to avoid contact with other people rather than flying. Four-year-old Andie commented we should check with the government to make sure it was okay to travel to another province. "You can check with them online," she said.

We spent the next half-hour discussing all the activities we could do together if we did visit. Leia suggested we work on her Harry Potter puzzle or play Frozenopoly together. The girls talked about all the books we could read and all the Christmas crafts we could make during our visit.

A week later, Allan and I were on our way to Calgary. The girls called us on FaceTime a few times to check on our progress as we drove through various towns in the Rocky Mountains.

Their calls made me reflect on how much the world has changed, especially for our grandchildren's generation. They use various methods of video technology for communicating with ease. This technology has redefined distance and geography and made it easier for us to stay in touch with our entire family anywhere in the world. It has allowed my husband and me to watch our granddaughters grow up, and see our daughter's home in Calgary and our son's new apartment in Thailand from the comfort of our own home. Communications technology has definitely made life more bearable during the COVID-19 pandemic.

I sent our daughter a text when we were about ten minutes away from her home. Our granddaughters' faces were pressed to their living room windowpane waiting for our arrival as we drove up to their house. Allan and I stood next to our car watching the flurry of activity through their window. Within seconds, the front door flew open, and our two beauties were running down the sidewalk into our arms.

The days whizzed by as quickly as a speeding train. In no time, we were preparing for our return trip to the west coast. After numerous farewell hugs and comments about driving safely, my eyes filled with tears as we drove away from our daughter's home. Our two granddaughters waved to us through their living room window until we were out of sight.

During our eleven-hour drive home, we enjoyed the spectacular scenery while I took pictures of the mountains, valleys and emerald-colored lakes, texting them to our family. The highway weaved between majestic, forested mountains untouched by civilization, yet we could still communicate by video or text with our family members hundreds of miles away. I thought about how even road trips had been revolution-ized by technology.

We could hear the FaceTime ringtone on my cell phone within minutes of arriving home. Sure enough, our granddaughters were calling to check on the progress of our long drive. After a short chat, we blew kisses to each other before our granddaughters called out, "Goodbye, Nanny and Papa." Keeping in touch has never been easier, thanks to technology.

— Kathy Dickie —

Chapter
9

The Joy of Giving

82

Today You Are an Angel

Selfless giving is the art of living.
~Frederic Lenz

I was driving along US-80 about two hours from home after being gone for two days. I couldn't wait to see my wife, kids and bed. I was daydreaming as I listened to the truck drivers on the CB talking back and forth. My ears perked up when I heard one of the truckers say that a little old man and woman were standing behind their car with the hood up. They were saying that someone needed to get them help, or they were going to get hurt or killed.

Just then, I came over the hill and saw them. They reminded me of my parents. I remember thinking, *Okay, God, this is a test, right?* I grabbed the mic on the CB that a friend had loaned me for the trip and said, "I got them!"

I parked my pickup behind their car and put on my four-way flashers. I could hear the truck drivers thanking me for taking the time to help. It gave me a warm feeling inside.

I asked the couple if I could help and told them I was a mechanic. They were so happy and told me that they had been there for over two hours. They said that one truck driver had told them that he would call for help, and it shouldn't take very long. But that was over an hour ago, and they were getting very cold. However, they were afraid to sit in the car for fear that no one would see them. They told me they started taking turns standing outside after it started to rain.

I looked at their car and told them one of the fan belts had come apart. It needed a pulley. I knew I didn't have any parts to fix their car, so I told them I would get them help.

We walked back to my truck, and I cleared the maps and stuff off my front seat, giving them a place to sit. I turned my heater on high, and it felt so good knowing I could at least give them warmth.

The couple told me they were on their way to Michigan for the funeral of an old friend. I told them that was where I was headed. I offered to give them a ride to Michigan, but they declined, saying that I had done enough already.

As we drove down the road a few miles and got off the turnpike, they asked me to stop before the tollbooth so I wouldn't have to pay twice. I told them that they had already been through enough, and I wasn't letting them go until I knew they were taken care of.

I paid the toll and parked, and we all went into the toll station together. After the wrecker was called, I walked with them out to my truck. I got in and opened the window to say one more goodbye. The old man walked up to the door and reached through my window. Putting his hand on mine, he asked, "Son, are you a religious man?" I told him that I believed in God but admitted I didn't go to church as much as I should. He told me how he and his wife had finished praying just before I had come over the hill in my truck. He said they had asked God to send an angel to help them. He then looked deep into my eyes as he squeezed my hand and said, "Son, today you are an angel."

I will never forget the love I felt that day.

—William J. Garvey—

83

A Blessing in Disguise

The meaning of life is to find your gift.
The purpose of life is to give it away.
~Pablo Picasso

To the outside world, my husband Doug was the calmest person they knew. But that outward calm hid his inner stress. The job that he finally landed after two years of unemployment weighed on him. He didn't want to quit, but I could see that stress was eating away at him, so I insisted that he see a doctor.

On the day of the appointment, he called to say that he was not feeling well, so I brought him home to rest before his appointment. Doug was not doing well at all. I tried to help him to the bed, but he collapsed on top of me while still in the bathroom.

I did all the things that you see on TV. "Come on, Doug, stay with me! I'm right here." When I finally got out from under him, I called 911 and was the typical hysterical caller. The operator calmed me down, and I returned to Doug, holding him in my arms until the EMTs arrived — which, thankfully, happened very quickly.

The head EMT got Doug up on his feet. Doug asked me to "get my medicine so they'll know what I'm taking." That was a good sign. Then the EMTs put him in a mobile chair rather than flat out on the stretcher. Another good sign. Then, as they prepared to take Doug to the ambulance, they asked me to get his shoes and coat to bring to the hospital. Well, that was definitely a good sign.

I tried to follow the ambulance as closely as possible, but they got to go through red lights, and I did not. By the time I made it to the hospital, they took me directly to the "Family Room." That was not a good sign.

I asked to see him but was told to wait for the doctor. A few minutes later, the doctor came in. Anxiously, I asked, "I need to see him. Is he okay?" She stared at me for a moment and then said, "He's dead."

"What?" I yelled. "You made a mistake! Go back in and check! An hour ago, we were in a taxi. How could this happen?" The doctor was trying to console me, but all I wanted to do was see Doug. I sat with Doug's body for maybe an hour, holding him and talking to him. Finally, I realized I would have to make "the calls."

Hypertensive heart failure was the cause. All that stress had caught up to him. This man that I'd spent over half my life with was now gone. He was fifty-five.

I dragged myself through the days. One thing that kept me busy was all the paperwork when someone dies. I continue to preach, "Tell the people you love that you love them. And write down your passwords!" I spent months untangling everything.

Then a blessing appeared out of the blue, in the form of a letter. The letter told me that Doug's corneas had saved two people from blindness. I couldn't believe it. His beautiful blue eyes were still looking out at the world. Someone reminded me that the cornea does not account for the color of the eyes. All I know is that Doug was still helping people.

Then I was invited to a lunch to honor donor families such as mine. I met a few donor recipients who told of the guilt they felt receiving the gift of sight. They knew that someone had to die in order to save them from blindness. But the donor recipients were incredibly grateful for the miracle of sight.

The blessings didn't stop there. Not only had Doug's eyes saved people from blindness, but he helped others as well. There were forty-three bone grafts to fill bone defects caused by trauma or disease, such as cancer; fourteen skin grafts to save the lives of burn victims; and three tendon grafts to repair the anterior cruciate ligament (ACL) in the knee. These types of injuries are often sustained by professional athletes. Now Doug's ACL might be helping them. Could he possibly now be playing professional sports?

Even though I lost the love of my life, the blessings that he passed along after his death are being felt by many, many people.

Doug is now in many places. That is the true blessing.

—Francesca Peppiatt—

84

A Hostess's Blessings

God has blessed me with an amazing family, friends
and work colleagues that have been my joy,
my support, and my sanity. I don't know
what I'd do without them.
~Josie Loren

I am seventy-two years young. I live on my monthly Social Security check and a small monthly veteran's benefit. I'm grateful for these monthly blessings and the occasional check from books I have written. But things are financially tight for me.

Recently, I realized I was depleting the small savings account I have rather than adding to it. I also realized that it was time to earn some extra income. So, I prayed for guidance and then did an online search for a local job.

I have zero experience in the food industry, but there it was staring me in the face: "Hostess for restaurant. Full or part-time available." I definitely wanted part-time.

So, I texted HOSTESS to the number in the ad and waited all of fifteen seconds to hear back. I filled out their online form. Within minutes, I received a call to schedule an in-person interview the next day. I have since learned that restaurants and many other industries are desperate for people willing to work.

It had been forty-three years since I had been on a job interview. I dressed professionally and headed for my appointment. Paul seemed to be a courteous young man. Oops! I keep forgetting that almost everyone is young in my eyes! He was probably thirty-something, although he looked fourteen to me. I did alright with the interview. He asked me if I could come that week for training.

"Sure," I said. "I'm ready to start right now."

I have to admit it took me a little longer to get the hang of the job than it did the twenty-something prospective hostesses — at least the technology part. But with some help from one of those kind-hearted, almost-grown-ups, I figured it out. I kept reminding myself that I'm an intelligent, well-educated person. No seating software is going to get the better of me.

I work four-hour shifts. That's about all my body can take. At the end of the day, my back hurts. My knees hurt. My ankles hurt, too. And my feet feel like a thousand hot needles are poking them. But my heart feels full. The money I'm earning has been a huge blessing. I'm not dipping into my savings anymore. And there are other blessings, too.

I am blessed that God sent me an answer to prayers about my finances.

I am proud that I have become confident in the job I do. I now know for sure that I'm not too old to learn something new. And my boss says I work circles around those young whippersnappers. It's nice to be appreciated.

I think I'm even helping some of those almost-adults gain a different perspective on life. Or at least offering them a listening ear.

I enjoy smiling and chatting with customers. Almost all are nice in return. I try to notice those who seem low, exhausted or upset and give them a smile. And I try to express sincere gratitude for their patronage. There are plenty of other restaurants they could frequent.

We have several customers who, like me, are more than seventy years old. They live alone, so they come into the restaurant every day for a hot meal and a little human interaction. We know they are going to take their time, maybe read a magazine or book while enjoying their meals. They are genuinely happy to see me and the wait staff. I hope I'm enriching their lives a bit by chatting with them, showing them a little extra attention and letting them know that I am happy to see them. We all need frequent interaction with other people.

I try to find the closest seat for those who use walkers or wheel-chairs. Their gratitude for such a simple act of kindness is amazing. When I occasionally feel down myself, they make me laugh. We lift each other up. That's what friends do. And, though I may not know (or remember) their names, I consider these regular customers to be my friends.

Most of the other employees are considerably younger than me. I'm learning a great deal about the mindset and social characteristics of their generation, which happens to include my oldest grandchildren. That makes me smarter as I pray for them and more patient as I speak with them.

The restaurant is a beautiful mix of senior adults, young adults, middle-aged businesspeople, married couples, retired couples and even some families with four or five young kids. We are brown, black and white. And a lovely oasis of opportunities to show kindness. I never thought of any restaurant in that way before working here.

I do my job in such a way as to bless each person I interact with during the day. They, in return, make my day brighter. They give me a great reason for going to work other than my financial needs.

Yes, God was right. This little part-time job has been a good thing for me in more ways than one.

—Jean Matthew Hall—

85

Sergeant Santa's Warrior Spirit

Never doubt that a small group of thoughtful,
committed citizens can change the world; indeed,
it's the only thing that ever has.
~Margaret Mead

A young boy came sliding around the corner of his hospital room, the floor too slippery for his socks to get any traction. He came to a stop, stood up straight, and brushed his hands down his shirt. His hair was wet and messy. He still had a little bit of shampoo in it. He had a big smile on his face but tried to hide it with a more serious and professional demeanor. He was rushing to catch us on our way back because he was showering when we went by his room the first time. He was eager to meet the uniformed soldiers with Santa hats who were handing out presents.

"How are you, sir?" he asked me.

"I'm well. How are you?"

"I'm okay. I'm hanging in there."

This was an opportunity to spread more than cheer. This was my chance to be a mentor to the warrior spirit.

"You know, there's a difference between soldiers and warriors. Training and a uniform make someone a soldier. Attitude makes you a warrior. Never give up on yourself. If you keep fighting through whatever you're battling, no matter how difficult it seems, you're a warrior," I told him. We talked for a few minutes, and then he picked out a gift from Sergeant Santa's rucksack. As we walked toward the next room,

I heard him tell his father, "That was even cooler than Gronk's visit!"

The Sergeant Santa Project came from my idea to visit a children's hospital during the holidays. I thought I would make a quick phone call, do a one-time visit, and leave there feeling good about myself. It turned out it wasn't that easy. I was met with fierce opposition. Most of the hospitals told me they didn't have a program like that. One actually told me that too many soldiers have post-traumatic stress disorder. I was entrusted with safeguarding the country, but there was no confidence in me to visit a hospital and spread some holiday cheer. That stung a little.

A friend suggested that I refocus and put my efforts into helping the military community. I shrugged it off, but I thought about it for a few minutes. The world can be a dark and lonely place after experiencing war. Purpose and passion are often hard to find within a community that doesn't understand you. Isolation is a pervasive response, and suicide is the result far too often. There is a certain divide between the military and the rest of society because there isn't enough understanding.

I had a hard time reintegrating when I came home. I struggled to find a spark of purpose for years and basically hid myself away. As I thought about all of this, my newfound purpose suddenly ignited. Visiting a children's hospital was how I was going to help the military community. Society needed to see the positive characteristics that children have always seen in us. Children are inspired by soldiers because they recognize our values. They see our strength, bravery, and selflessness.

I needed to close the divide and restore the sense of belonging that can help our military feel comfortable at home. Volunteerism was the perfect way to accomplish my mission, so I built a program to enable it.

The next several years saw hundreds of soldiers giving thousands of hours to dozens of causes and interests. Sergeant Santa became a piece of a larger program that encompassed anything that any volunteer wanted to support. Other people started putting together their own initiatives with their unique spins. A volunteer saw a group across the state doing something similar to Sergeant Santa and said, "Hey! They're copying us!" I thought that was awesome. In fact, I fully encouraged it.

Kindness is inspiring and contagious. More people doing more things means society comes together even faster. It reflects acceptance and means we made a difference.

I often wondered how much of an impact we were making. On my last day of wearing a uniform, one of my soldiers told me somebody had bought him a coffee because of me.

Apparently, I had visited her son in the hospital a couple of years prior, and now she tries to show her gratitude through small gestures when she sees a military member. I smiled and said, "That's great. Now get to work!" I excused myself from my peers and went to the restroom because my eyes had some strange, watery substance building up. Somebody whom I had met one time had just bought a coffee for a soldier she had never met because I did something years ago that changed the way she saw the entire military community. I never thought I'd actually get to see this program come full circle, but this was the moment when I felt like I had succeeded.

I learned that helping others is perhaps the greatest way to help ourselves. It builds pride and purpose. It makes you feel good. It brings people together and reinforces your social support structures. Most importantly, it multiplies life satisfaction. Sergeant Santa saved at least two soldiers from suicidal thoughts. I know this because one of them told me. As for the other one… Well, the other one is me. Volunteerism helped me find my place in this world again. I just needed something to trigger that warrior spirit.

—Elton Dean—

86

Follow Your Dreams

Believe in your heart that you're meant to live a life full
of passion, purpose, magic and miracles.
~Roy T. Bennett, The Light in the Heart

What do you want to be when you grow up? Employment and Insurance Officer was definitely not on my list. I did not even know what an Employment and Insurance Officer did until I was hired by Service Canada in 1968.

An Employment and Insurance Officer helps people find jobs, apply for employment and insurance, and return to school for training. It is working every day on the front lines helping people. What could be more rewarding than to help someone find a job or change their career?

I have always said that people are at their worst when they are unemployed or sick. I must admit that some days were challenging. But I have one intriguing story that I would like to share.

One day, a lady came to the office with a dream to become a registered nurse. According to my client, her family did not approve. She was a mother with young children, and her husband had returned to school for training. It was not economically feasible for her to return to school.

It was clear that this lady had a passion for the nursing profession, so I encouraged her to realize her dream. I equipped her with the information necessary to apply for nursing school, and she left the office. At the time, the RN program was three years at the P.E.I. Hospital. She went on her way, and I never knew whether she followed her dream or not.

Many years later, I was diagnosed with breast cancer. I was admitted to the Queen Elizabeth Hospital in Charlottetown, Prince Edward Island, for a mastectomy. I must admit I was scared. My mother had died of breast cancer at age forty.

I had a husband and two beautiful children. I was only forty-eight years old.

The surgery was successful. It was, however, very painful. I prided myself on not being a bell ringer, but one night the pain was so bad that I had to call for a nurse. I rang the bell and waited for assistance. A nurse came through the door and offered to help. I apologetically thanked the nurse for coming to my rescue. I said, "I am not usually like this."

To my amazement, she said, "Oh, I know that, Mrs. Bryenton."

She went on to tell me that she had been interviewed by me many years before, and I had encouraged her to follow her dream to become a nurse. She subsequently returned to school for upgrading and later applied for nursing. And to think here she was at my bedside giving me pain medication in the middle of the night.

Goosebumps came to my arms as she relayed the story to me. I did remember this young lady. It was definitely a difficult decision for her to return to school, but she was determined to achieve her goal. And here she was fulfilling her dream as a registered nurse. You never know what impact your encouraging words will have on someone.

I always took pride in helping clients every day. It is amazing how many clients would return to say thank you. To this day, I am still approached by strangers and reminded that I was instrumental in changing their lives.

A job is definitely not a job if you love what you are doing. I count my blessings every day that I was able to fulfill my own dream of helping others.

Winston Churchill stated, "We make a living by what you get, but we make a life by what we give." I truly believe that God placed me on Earth for a reason and a season.

— Marlene Bryenton —

87

Random Acts

A single act of kindness throws out roots in all directions,
and the roots spring up and make new trees.
~Amelia Earhart

I was at high risk when it came to the pandemic. A childhood of respiratory illnesses had left me with scarred lungs, and I did what I could to avoid going out. I set a goal of getting supplies every two weeks, knowing that having lost my job meant budgeting my dwindling funds carefully. That particular day, I had twenty dollars to spend and had decided to make a large pot of turkey spaghetti. I could eat it for several nights. I added a jar of peanut butter, a loaf of bread and some jelly to my cart. With what I had at home, I could stretch things out and feel pretty good about my choices.

I had been in radio in my community for many years and was used to talking to lots of people when I went out, hugging my friends and loved ones, connecting to my community. Disconnecting from others was harder for me than I had anticipated.

In the checkout line I was behind a frail, elderly woman who was bundled against the cold in a mismatched jumble of scarves, gloves and sweaters. She greeted me warmly, and we chatted about the recent cold snap and how our families were faring being cooped up together.

She noticed my ingredients and mentioned she hadn't had a good plate of pasta in some time. We talked about the unexpected pleasure of sitting down at the family table for meals together and recipes we were discovering anew. Several other people around us began to chime in with their own recipes or ideas.

I couldn't help but notice what the woman was buying. She was counting out change to pay for some ramen noodles and canned tuna. I could see her furrowed brow and I realized she didn't have enough money to cover her meager purchase.

I looked at my items, things that now seemed luxurious and bountiful, and felt my eyes well up with tears. I had so much, and this beautiful woman, this grandmother, had so little. It wasn't a lot, but I could give her what I had.

I pointed to the elderly woman's items and asked the cashier if he would ring everything up together. As the lady was chatting with someone, she didn't notice. I had about seven dollars and change coming back, so I put it in the grocery bag that contained her items and mine. Over my shoulder came a gloved hand with a five-dollar bill. Across the aisle, a man handed me several dollars. A little boy darted over with a crumpled ten-dollar bill and put it in the grocery bag. I stood there, unable to see clearly for a moment. The young man who rang me up took a few dollars from his pocket and handed them to me, his eyes bright with tears.

By this point, Grandmother realized something was amiss. I turned, placed the bag in her little cart, and told her I thought perhaps she might enjoy a plate of pasta that evening. There was a little something for dessert if she so desired. I managed to get all the way outside before I peeked back at her.

She was at the end of the checkout counter with the bag in her hand. Her eyes went from the bag to the cashier as he explained that she was all taken care of. And, yes, I had meant for her to have the bag and its contents. I heard her ask if he was sure, and he replied again, "Yes, ma'am, it's for you to take." I somehow managed to make it to my car. The trip home was a blur. For the remainder of the afternoon, I alternated between tears and joyful laughter at the gifts I had received.

That day, in that ordinary place, I was taught a lesson in love. People I didn't know joined me in paying forward the kindness that had been shown to me — and likely to them — in earlier days. We stood against the fear of the pandemic and gave of ourselves in the only way possible in that moment. We were also reminded to see what we already had with a new respect and renewed gratitude.

It is said that random acts of kindness will change the world. That day, it changed for all of us.

— Cj Cole —

Every Day's a Gift

The quality of your life will be determined by the
quality of your contribution. When you work
to improve the lives of others,
your life improves automatically.
~Kurek Ashley

My wife and I were returning from a week's vacation in New York where we had a terrific time. We were flying back on Delta to Tampa, Florida, en route to our final destination: Clearwater.

Once we were seated on the plane, the flight attendant gave the usual safety speech. Finally, she demonstrated what to do in the case of an emergency when the overhead oxygen masks dropped down.

"First, place the mask securely on yourself and then, if necessary, assist a nearby child or passenger. First, help yourself. Then others."

When my wife and I arrived in Tampa, we headed for the baggage-claim area to retrieve our luggage. There, I spotted the flight attendant who had given the talk on our flight.

"Hi there. Did you have a nice trip?" she asked.

"Fine," I replied. Then, I added, "But, miss, I think you made a grave mistake when you gave your pre-flight presentation."

"Please. Tell me what the mistake was," she answered.

"You said to put the oxygen mask on yourself first. Correct?"

"Yes, I did," she replied, smiling gently.

"I think you meant to say that if a child or other passenger near you needs help to assist them first. Right?"

"No, sir," she answered firmly. "You must save yourself first."

I just shrugged my shoulders, grabbed my luggage and headed home, puzzling over that statement.

A few days later, while watching *Good Morning America*, the news commentator, Robin Roberts, closed the morning show with this. "All you gentlemen, fifty years and older, should make it a point to get a PSA test. It is a simple blood test and could save your life."

I called my doctor's office that very morning and asked about the PSA test. The nurse reaffirmed what Robin had said. So, I made an appointment to have it done.

Ten days later, I had an appointment with the doctor to get the results. Once there, he said, "Ray, you're a very healthy seventy-two-year-old. However, we got the results of your PSA test. It was high, and you probably have prostate cancer. I want to do a couple of biopsies to confirm it."

When the biopsies came back, I was called into the office once again. "You definitely have prostate cancer," the doctor said. He explained to me the various treatment options that were available. After hearing the various treatments and their after-effects, I decided to have the prostate removed and get rid of the cancer entirely, as it had not spread outside the prostate yet.

The next morning, my wife and I went to morning mass and prayed that we had made the correct decision. After going through several pre-surgery tests and donating a pint of my blood to keep on hand, the operation was scheduled at the nearby hospital.

I was scheduled to be the first person to undergo the new da Vinci method of removing the prostate. This is an operation where the patient and the machine are in one room, and the doctor is in the adjoining room operating the remote surgical controls.

Because this was the first operation of its kind in the local hospital, a medical provost had been assigned to monitor the situation. Unfortunately, he did not arrive on schedule, and I was kept sedated and with my head lower than the rest of my body for several extra hours. My wife said when she first saw me after the operation, my head looked like a pumpkin.

Doctor Gregg talked to my wife after the surgery and said all had gone well. My surgery was successful. All the cancer had been removed.

The next day, I was released from the hospital with post-operative instructions and directions on how to do the Kegel exercises to strengthen my abdominal muscles. I soon learned that all the body functions were working well.

What was even better was that my PSA level was zero. One morning shortly thereafter, my wife and I left morning mass and spotted a sign by the road requesting volunteers for Suncoast Hospice of Florida. We decided it was time to give back for our good fortune. After six informative classes, we became volunteers for Suncoast Hospice. After saving myself, it was now time to help others by regularly visiting nursing-home patients.

Now, years later, I am still cancer-free, and we are still hospice volunteers.

Our days volunteering for Suncoast Hospice have been very rewarding for us. Our first few visits with a nursing-home resident are to give him/her an opportunity to get to know us. Sometimes, our visits with the resident are very short, but sometimes they are quite long. There are days when the resident feels like talking, and there are other days when he or she just wants private time.

With the permission of the patient's nurse, we might bring cookies, books or flowers to the resident. One lovely lady, upon hearing my footsteps in the hall, would call out, "Look, here's the cookie man."

Whenever we visit a nursing home for Suncoast Hospice, we want to fit in, not stick out.

Recently, a ninety-year-old lady has come up with a new name for my wife and me. She said, "You two have so much energy, and I love your smiles. I'm gonna call you 'The Hospice Kids.'"

The license plate on the front of my car is from Suncoast Hospice. It reads: "Every Day's a Gift."

— Raymond Weaver —

Becoming a Book Lady

I hope these simple things are what I forever love about life,
for then I will be happy no matter where I find myself.
~R. YS Perez

"You know, if you need to work off some of your feelings, you could help us out here." I looked up from the shelf of used books that I had been examining. Amy, the woman who ran my favorite thrift store, and I had struck up a friendship since the store had reopened once the worst of the pandemic had passed. I'd had conversations with her about my very recent divorce, and I admit that part of the reason that I was at the thrift store every week was trying to deal with the end of my marriage.

Still, this was unexpected.

"Me, volunteer here?" I glanced at her. While I was the world's biggest bookworm, I'd never thought about actually doing anything with my obsession.

"It might help you deal with what you're going through." She smiled. "You could try it out... and you'd be helping out others at the same time."

I hesitated. I didn't have anywhere else I needed to be that day until the evening.

I managed a small smile. "Okay. I suppose I could give it a try."

That's when it started. I became a "book lady," one of several women who tended to the book room in the thrift store, processing donations that came in and getting them onto the shelves to be sold. It was dusty and at times difficult work because stacks of books in the donation room were always toppling over, boxes and crates were heavy, and trying to get shopping carts through could turn into a tug of war.

But I loved it. I was surrounded by my third favorite passion, behind my faith and my family: books. And now that passion could be passed onto others, and I could provide help to a desperately needed community organization. It was so rewarding to watch someone buy a book that I had just put on the shelf, to see empty shelves filled with books, or to give a book recommendation to a bewildered parent.

My time as a book lady has been filled with moments of grace — when I helped the new foster mother select books for the foster daughter she was about to bring home; when I searched the shelves for an older lady to find yet another of her favorite Amish romances; or when I located a large print copy of a cherished novel for a man with worsening eyesight.

When I volunteer, I always know that there are people waiting to welcome me who are grateful and appreciative for what I can do. The people there have become my friends. Regardless of how my life has been going or what I'm dealing with in that moment, I can walk in there and know that they will always be glad to see me.

Amy didn't know what she was starting that day when she invited me to help out, but I will always be grateful that I said yes.

So, yes, I am the "book lady." It's my way of giving back, but it has given so much more back to me.

— Anna Cleveland —

It's Not About Me

*Every child deserves a champion — an adult who will
never give up on them, who understands the power
of connection and insists that they become
the best they can possibly be.*
~Rita F. Pierson

"Is this our last stop?" six-year-old Dante said in a half-pleading and half-whining voice.

"I have to go by the bank, and that will be the last one… I promise," I answered. I usually tried to run all my errands while the children were in school, but this week they were out for spring break, so I had no choice.

"Grandma, look! McDonald's," five-year-old Sadie exclaimed. "That's where my momma took us!"

"Uh-huh," agreed Dante. "Momma bought me a Happy Meal."

"That's wonderful. Did she let you play a while in the outdoor play area?" I asked.

"Uh-huh," said Dante. "And she took us to the store, and we picked out a toy."

"And we went to the park and had ice cream, too," Sadie said.

"Wow, it sounds like you had a wonderful time with your momma. Did she watch the movie with you that you took to share?" I asked.

"No, 'cause we played video games, and we didn't have to go to bed 'til we wanted to," Dante replied.

"And Momma let us sleep in her bed all night with her," Sadie added.

"Well, you had a fun time, but now you're home, and things go back to normal, right?" I replied.

"She gets to spoil you, and I get to undo the damage," I mumbled under my breath.

For reasons I'd have to figure out later, I felt myself becoming perturbed with the whole conversation. Didn't my husband James and I take them to the exact same places? Yet, neither of them had ever exclaimed, "Look, that's where you take us!" And why did it matter anyway? Why was I feeling so envious of the children's birth mother? Isn't foster care all about healing and reuniting families? It's my job to keep the children safe and cared for until that can happen. It's not about me.

Knowing this, why was I reacting to the children's narrative so defensively? The visit with their mother had been a good visit, which is what we always hoped for.

"We're home, and we're finished with errands," I announced as we pulled into our driveway. "Who wants a nice, cold Popsicle?"

"Me, me!" they both chanted.

"Okay, Popsicles… then baths," I promised.

"Can I have a bubble bath?" asked Sadie.

"Sure, why not?" I answered.

"Me, too!" Dante exclaimed.

Of course, there it was, the infamous "Me, too." I didn't really have time to analyze my earlier thoughts or emotions until later in the evening. Baths taken, books read, and prayers said, both children now slept soundly in their beds. I checked in on them and watched them sleep. These two were siblings and had come to us at the ages of three and six. Both had made great progress in the two years since their arrival. I felt good about their time spent with us. To them, we were now Grandma and Papa.

Having grown up in foster homes myself, I asked God for a way to "give back." I am extremely grateful for the people who took me into their homes and families. Even those I detested taught me valuable life lessons. Also, as an adult I had worked in Child Protective Services as clerical support for three health nurses. Working there reminded me of the enormous need for foster homes in every state. I promised myself I would be a foster parent if I were ever able to do so. That chance came when my husband and I moved to Oklahoma.

Well-meaning people have told us, "Don't give these children your heart. It will only be broken. They are only on loan. Remember that." I had to disagree with that completely. I felt anyone who could not love these children (even for a brief time) should not be foster parents. The mandatory classes and special training required by the state of Oklahoma to become foster parents prepared us for many things. One thing our classes could not teach us was how to come to terms with loving them and then giving them up. Finding a balance between attachment and being able to detach is something everyone must do on their own.

My way of dealing with separation from Dante and Sadie was to put myself on the defensive, asking myself, "Why do I do all this? Who really notices or cares? Do I really make a difference? Am I doing this because God wants me to or for the wrong reasons? When these two children leave, can I take two more? If so, is it worth it all?"

These are the questions I ask myself each time we must say good-bye. But I know it's worth it! Even if I never get to see them again or know what will become of them, it's worth it. There have been children I've had for hours, others for years. With each child, I had a fragile, little human entrusted to my care. I had made a difference if only in keeping them safe and loved for a moment in time. I do my best with the ones I have, and I know there are so many more waiting, needing to be safe and loved. After all, it's not about me.

— Christine M. Smith —

A Stroke of Sweetness

The simple things can be really powerful.
~Jon Taffer

Halloween decorations adorned the walls, and some of the staff
were dressed in costumes. As we ventured down the hall to
physical therapy, my daughter Kari reluctantly held a leaf-
shaped bowl filled with candy.

We were doing a reverse trick-or-treat — handing out treats instead
of receiving. Truthfully, I hatched the idea; Kari scowled when I handed
her the bowl. "No, that's stupid." With her vocabulary limited by the
stroke, she had responded without a filter.

I understood her hesitancy. Never one to draw attention to herself,
my daughter liked to exist in the shadows. Therefore, this activity was
way outside her comfort zone. But I knew that after two months in the
hospital, Kari needed to experience the power of giving.

We turned the corner and offered some sweet treats to the patients
we passed. Some, we knew from our extended stay; others, strangers,
instantly joined our hospital family. All smiled, took the candy and
expressed thanks either with words or a gesture.

In the outpatient physical therapy waiting room, an elderly couple
sat on two chairs. I assumed they were husband and wife and deduced
the man was waiting for his appointment since he held a cane and
an expression that said he desired to be somewhere, anywhere, else.

Kari offered them candy by saying, "Want some carrots?"

Since stroke patients inhabited the halls, no explanation was necessary because everyone knew her meaning and why the words came out wrong. The wife simply picked through the selection, withdrew a piece of candy (not carrots) and said, "Thank you."

The gentleman's melancholy eyes looked up from the floor, and he said, "No." But then his eyes met Kari's and his face softened. Leaning toward the bowl, he cleared his throat. "Well, maybe I will." His hand released the cane and searched until it found a Reese's Peanut Butter Cup. We heard a polite, gruff voice say, "Happy Halloween."

Every person Kari encountered became supporters in her fight, and she in theirs. In this environment where individuals struggled with their own disabilities, the simple, edible gifts created a support system that reinforced them for battle.

In the physical-therapy room, more soldiers joined our army. A young woman with purple hair walked up a short flight of stairs supported by therapists on either side who clutched the wide cloth belt around her waist. At the bottom of the steps, one hand wrapped around a Snickers without releasing the handrail with the other. Each therapist tucked a bar of chocolate in their shirt pockets.

A stylish, elderly lady rode a stationary bike at a slow, steady pace. Pausing, she accepted a piece and continued her journey toward recovery. On the exercise table lay a middle-aged man with one leg in the air. His second leg was missing. He and his therapist each took a bar, and the therapist returned for a second before we exited the room.

Each person returned to their task a little less stressed and more determined.

At first, I feared that pushing Kari in this crazy scheme might backfire. But when we returned to our room after reverse trick-or-treating, my tired daughter was smiling and there was joy in her eyes. With grace in her heart, she lay down on her bed to sleep, ready to continue the healing process.

— Brenda Mahler —

A Change in Perspective

92

Living Life through Grateful Eyes

Happiness resides not in possessions, and not in gold.
Happiness dwells in the soul.
~Democritus

I scanned the vast Mongolian plains that stretched out in front of me for as far as the eye could see, wondering where I could seek privacy to go to the bathroom. There was no outhouse, tree or hill that could serve as a shield for many miles.

I glanced back at the yurt, the traditional, round white tent that I would be sharing with my Mongolian host family for the next couple of weeks. I wondered how they survived in this isolated location, hundreds of miles from anyone else, and without power or running water.

I entered the family tent, careful to observe the sacred nomadic traditions, which included stepping over an ancient wood piece at the entryway and staying on the left side of the tent (with the right side designated for the female head of the household).

I recited the formal greetings of respect that I had been taught to say to a shy gentleman and his spouse, both fashioned in traditional brown deels — the one-piece, loose cloak tied around the waist with a rope — and boots that were turned upward at the toe. Their faces were etched with deep character lines, which I suspected revealed the story of life's hardships versus age.

They stood gazing at me with bright smiles and presented their infant daughter, whom I would be caring for during the next two weeks while they sheared their sheep and tended to the horses. When I asked about the challenges of rearing countless animals and living in such a remote location — without any modern conveniences — they chuckled softly, expressing how grateful they were for all they had.

I handed over fresh fruit, infant cereal mixture, and sweets that I was told would be welcome gifts. While fruit was a rare treat — something the family might enjoy only once a year — the couple immediately started peeling it to share with me. They insisted I eat as much as they did.

As soon as the fruit was gone, they moved on to the sweets. Again, they insisted that I eat as much as they did.

As I scanned the inside of the yurt, I admired the tent's artistic wood frame, painted in deep reds and complemented with vibrant blues, yellows and greens. But, in equal measure, I couldn't help but be surprised by the sparseness of the space.

Western-type beds formed a circle around the outer walls of the tent, accompanied by a modest dresser and a small wood-burning stove that billowed smoke through an opening in the roof.

However, the only other items that could be found in the yurt were a couple of miniature wood stools set beside a worn trunk (which performed double duty as the dining table), a few items of clothing, and a couple of sacks of flour. Grass served as the home's natural carpet, and there was no refrigerator, lamp, television, or anything electronic.

My hosts caught me scanning the room and explained that their few possessions served them well. They went on in earnest tones to explain how pleased they were to be able to transport everything with ease when the animals needed a new grazing area.

Asked how they managed without water, they explained they had all they needed from the milk of their animals to drink, bathe, and boil food. They occasionally collected water from winter snowfalls.

Our conversation was interrupted by the sound of hooves galloping toward the tent. A husky male voice called out to us in Mongolian (which I would later learn means, "Hold onto your dog" — the typical nomad greeting before entering someone's tent).

As the visitor stepped inside, he exchanged greetings with my host family. Tseren, the woman of the household, poured warm milk into large bowls for us to drink. She refilled the bowls every few minutes, making sure we all had full stomachs of the warm liquid.

She then got to work making a thick noodle-and-mutton soup to feed the visitor and myself. Not much was said between the new arrival and the couple, and I suspected the three were strangers. As soon as the visitor had his fill of milk and soup, he began to take his leave.

The family motioned to the beds, offering him a place to spend the night, but he politely declined and was on his way. During my stay, this scenario would repeat itself time and again. On each occasion, the unknown guest was greeted with the warmest of hospitality, which always included food, milk, and an offer to stay as long as the visitor wished.

That night, as I curled up under my warm covers, staring up at the brilliant nighttime sky through the opening around the chimney, I realized that my host family had everything they needed. In fact, they had more than I could have ever imagined. They were rich in happiness and generosity, and truly grateful for all they had.

— Melissa Valks —

93

The Dog Days of Winter

Gratitude is one of the strongest and most
transformative states of being. It shifts your
perspective from lack to abundance and
allows you to focus on the good in your life.
~Jen Sincero

A wail pierced the air, overpowering the sound of ice crunching beneath my snow boots. This chilling sound could only have come from an animal in pain. I stopped to scan the frozen lake I was hiking around, and spotted a furry head frantically bobbing up and down through a hole in the ice about thirty feet from the shoreline. It was a large brown dog. His shoulders churned frantically in the bitter water as his paws splashed his face with icy water.

I yanked off my mittens and tapped out 9-1-1.

"911, state your emergency," a calm voice said.

"A dog has fallen through the ice on a lake. Please, can you send somebody to save him?"

"Do not go on the ice," the dispatcher said. "What is your location?"

"My location?" I hesitated. "I'm on a footpath walking around a lake." I had no idea what address to give her.

A second wail filled the air. That's when I saw a small boy ahead of me on the path.

"Please, Daddy, Buddy!" he bawled as he jerked on a man's sleeve beside him. His father left his side and gingerly stepped onto the edge of the lake, testing the ice beneath his Timberlands as he inched across the frozen surface toward the struggling dog.

"I see a man trying to rescue the dog," I reported to the dispatcher.

"No, do not go on the ice," she repeated. "If you see someone on the ice, tell them to get off the ice!" she firmly ordered.

I hurried over to the child. "Buddy, Daddy, Buddy!" his high-pitched voice continued to plead to his father's back.

"I have 911 on the phone," I yelled out to the man, but I stopped short of telling him to get off the ice. I wanted him to keep going. I wanted him to save Buddy.

I squatted beside the little boy, trying to comfort him and make sure he didn't attempt to follow his father. My shoulders tightened when the ice loudly crackled and white veins shot out from beneath the father's feet. I knew he had to turn around and come back.

But he didn't.

He carefully lowered himself to his knees and began crawling toward the whimpering dog. I pressed my phone tighter to my ear and prepared to tell the 911 operator there was now a man who had fallen through the ice. My other hand gripped tightly onto the boy's shoulder as he anxiously tugged away from me toward his father.

Reaching the watery hole, the father stretched his arm out to grab the dog. A chunk of the ice broke away, plunging his elbow into the numbing water. The dog moaned softly. It was obvious he was exhausted. Only his head quietly bobbled above the waterline now. With one last swipe, the man snatched the dog's red collar and jerked his shaking body out of the water, loudly snapping more ice beneath them.

Everything fell silent except for the anxious sobs and sniffling nose of the little boy squirming under my hand. Wriggling backward, the father dragged the chocolate Labrador by the collar as water seeped through cracks in the ice, soaking his jeans and flannel shirt until he reached the shoreline.

The boy flung himself over the shivering dog and buried his face into his wet fur. His father gave me a grateful nod and then collapsed over his son, wrapping his arms around him and his dog. I backed away to give them privacy as an unexplained surge of love flowed through me for these strangers as I watched them have a moment alone.

Buddy struggled to stand up on stiff, trembling legs, and the three of them limped down the path for home. I said goodbye to the 911 operator, turned back the way I had come, and headed for home myself.

Hiking back along the lake's edge, I noticed the sun glinting off a fallen tree limb on the water's edge. Half of it was submerged through a wet hole in the ice, while the other half jutted straight up, lodged tightly above the surface and held prisoner in a block of solid ice. How did the ice break under the weight of the dog, but the man didn't fall through it? It seemed against all odds, but they both made it off the thawing lake.

Stepping back into my warm house, I hugged my two boys and our cats. Feeling the same powerful connection to them that I had just felt for complete strangers, my heart danced with fresh joy for my simple life and healthy family. I marveled at my earlier timing, randomly deciding to go for a walk and then stumbling into another family's crisis at just the right moment to help them by safeguarding the little boy so the father could make his brave rescue.

I had left my house eager to take a break from my rambunctious sons. I returned with immense gratitude that I have what is truly important.

— Laura Savino —

94

Wrinkles

With mirth and laughter let old wrinkles come.
~William Shakespeare

We were in South Carolina for Easter this year. As is always the case when we spend time with our littlest grandsons, Drew and Wes, it was a delightful and exhausting time. Both boys got up much too early every day and crawled into bed with my husband and me.

That first morning, I woke at barely six o'clock to the sound of their feet pounding down the hallway. I had the fleeting thought that another couple of hours of shuteye would have been so lovely. The two jumped onto the bed, one after the other, and whispered loud enough to be heard in the next room, "Neena, are you awake?" This was followed by giggles as two squirmy, little bodies wriggled under the covers and nestled against me, warm from their own sleep, hair silky and fragrant against my face, one on either side. Drew reached up to stroke my cheek.

"Hmmmm," I said, eyes closed, enjoying the affection.

"Seven," he said.

"What?" I was still groggy and hoping to go back to sleep.

"The number of wrinkles on your face. See? One, two, three…" He traced each line with a small finger.

"Drew!"

"Each wrinkle is a memory," Wes said, his sweet, soft voice soothing on the other side of me. He must have gotten that from a cartoon or a book about grandparents or something. What seven-year-old would come up with that on his own? Whatever the source, I thought it was profound.

"Yeah, you probably got this one when Wes was three and burned his hand on your cookie sheet. This one might be from when we went to the beach together, and we wanted you to carry us back to the car because we were tired, remember?" Drew said.

Not to be outdone, Wes said, "The ones over on this side could be from last Christmas…"

I groaned.

"Your kind of wrinkles are the good kind." Drew was anxious to put my mind at ease. Pretty soon, all three of us were giggling and sharing stories of pirates and treasure chests full of chocolate and gummy worms.

I hugged them both and thought it was well worth it to lose a few hours of sleep and end up with wrinkles because I had my own treasure chest. It was full of memories of time spent with loving little boys.

"One… two…" I said.

It was their turn to ask, "What?"

"While you two count my wrinkles, I'm going to count my blessings. And you little monkeys are two of the best."

— Holly Green —

95

Giving Thanks

Cultivate the habit of being grateful for every
good thing that comes to you, and to
give thanks continuously.
~Ralph Waldo Emerson

I can be depressed I gained another pound,
Or be grateful I have plenty to eat.

I can complain because it's raining,
Or be thankful I have an umbrella.

I can be annoyed when my alarm clock sounds,
Or praise God I have a job.

I can be concerned about the price of gas,
Or remember when I had no car.

I can feel lonely when I miss my old friends,
Or look forward to finding new ones.

I can fuss about doing housework,
Or be glad I have a home.

I can be frustrated when I lose my glasses — again,
Or think about those who cannot see.

I can despair when a loved one dies,
Or rejoice that he's in Heaven.

I can complain about the cold,
Or provide help for those without shelter.

I can grouse about my neighbors,
Or work to get to know them better.

I can be sad when I don't get roses for Valentine's,
Or go outside and enjoy God's creation.

Praises turn gloom into gladness,
Make joy out of sadness.

— Maribeth Hynnes Stevens —

96

Drake the Duck

*Be like a duck. Calm on the surface, but always
paddling like the dickens underneath.*
~Michael Caine

O n the lake behind our house, it wasn't unusual to see a wide variety of waterfowl. Canada geese, mallards, and even an occasional heron stopped in for a drink or a swim. Yet, one morning, a new bird appeared.

I had been looking out my kitchen window, enjoying the show. The waterfowl blended into the scenery as they always had, in shades of gray, cream, black, brown, and green, perfectly camouflaged for their own safety. But, all at once, on the border of where the other birds flocked, I caught a glimpse of neon white. A duck was swimming near the wildlife.

I grabbed my binoculars for a close-up view and then searched online to identify the new visitor. His white feathers and orange bill marked him as a domestic duck, a Pekin. The feathers on his tail curled up, which apparently meant he was a male. Someone must have dumped him into the wild. All I knew was that he stood out like a beacon from the rest.

I spent a lot of time worrying about the little guy living in his strange new world. He walked in an awkward waddle, and he couldn't fly at all. How would he manage with no natural camouflage and no safe place to stay during the night when predators roamed? He at least deserved a name, so I christened him Drake the Duck.

Drake was smart enough to plunge into the water and swim away whenever a person or animal came too close. He hung out with the geese but preferred the mallards as friends, and I enjoyed watching him paddle happily around the lake every day.

Not long after Drake appeared, COVID hit. The entire world came to an abrupt halt. I, like so many others, isolated at home and felt shell-shocked thinking about the future. Predictions were dire, and tough restrictions were put into place. No one knew how long the restrictions, let alone the virus, would last. Uncertainty laced each day with huge dollops of fear, and I wondered if life would ever return to normal.

As weeks turned into months, I found myself watching the lake more than I ever had before. The waterfowl calmly swam as they always had, and the sight brought me a welcome serenity. Even though the wild birds calmed and comforted me, I still felt anxious for Drake. Every morning, I hurried to the window to look for him and felt a huge sense of relief when I saw him glide across the water.

During the extreme heat of summer, he appeared unfazed. When the frigid, frozen days of winter arrived, Drake braved whatever Mother Nature threw his way without as much as a ruffled feather. He seemed as nonchalant when he waddled across a patch of ice as he did while enjoying a beautiful spring day.

My morning ritual quickly became more than a pleasant diversion. Drake turned into a symbol for me. A survivor. A spark of hope. Whenever I saw him, my shoulders lifted, and a sense of gratitude washed over me. He had adapted without any fuss and kept his place among the wild birds, doing what he must to survive.

As I watched him interact with the others, it was as if he hadn't a care in the world, which brought a question to mind. If an abandoned Pekin duck could manage living a life he had never been cut out for, why shouldn't I handle the COVID virus with a deeper sense of serenity and grace?

I had nothing to lose. Then and there, I decided to discard my sense of powerlessness. I would learn to live each day in my own strange new world with the same purpose and courage I'd witnessed in one little duck.

The thought brought a much-needed smile. Drake would be okay. And so would I.

— Pat Wahler —

97

These Boots Are Made for Walking

Appreciation can make a day, even change a life.
Your willingness to put it all into words
is all that is necessary.
~Margaret Cousins

Sometimes, it takes a wake-up call to remind us of our blessings, and a few years ago I had such an awakening.

My husband and I had obtained teaching jobs at two different schools in Mexico City. We hailed taxis to take us to and from work each day. One afternoon, as I made my way toward the street to hail a taxi, I passed a blind beggar woman.

"Señorita, por favor," she said weakly, holding out a cup in my general direction.

I knew the only change I had was for my taxi ride home, but she was blind and had called me "señorita," which is a title given to younger or unmarried women, so I allowed my empathy and vanity to get the better of me. I dropped most of my taxi money into her cup, keeping just enough for a bus ride home.

"Gracias," I heard her say as I headed toward the bus stop.

Soon, I found myself standing on what had to be the world's most-overcrowded public bus and wondering what had possessed me to wear high-heeled boots to work that day. Each time the bus came to a stop, more passengers pushed their way inside until it was impossible to tell where one passenger ended and another began.

At one point, a stocky man entered the bus holding a large, live duck. *Are you kidding me?* I thought. *Isn't there some sort of regulation against live animals on passenger buses?* Almost as quickly as I had asked myself that question, I knew the answer. Of course, there wasn't. Otherwise, it would have been against the law to pile so many passengers onto a bus designed for half the number.

The atmosphere inside the bus was stifling, and my feet were killing me. Eventually, the man carrying the duck made his way toward the back of the bus and secured a position directly behind me. Each time that duck flapped its wings, I cringed and tried to squeeze closer to the person in front of me. I tried to get my mind off my discomfort by staring out the window of the bus.

There was always a bustle of activity on the streets of Mexico City, and normally the window in the back seat of my taxi provided me with a close-up view. I would see children running into the streets to clean windshields or musicians performing on street corners. One time, I even saw a mime decked out in full white make-up, reaching into imaginary pockets, finding no money to his obvious disappointment, and shrugging at passersby. So, I had become pretty familiar with the various money-making tactics used by the homeless or impoverished there. That is why I was caught off-guard by what I saw from the window of the bus that day.

During one of the bus stops, I saw two men sitting in the median sharing a sandwich. Because they seemed lost in the moment and oblivious to the world around them, it did not register with me that they were beggars. They did not have that fixed expression of hopelessness and dread I had noticed on the faces of so many others. In fact, they were laughing between generous bites of their shared sandwich and seemed engaged in lighthearted conversation. Occasionally, they would toss their heads back with amusement, so caught up in the moment that they were completely unaware of any prying eyes. I wondered what they were taking about; their laughter seemed infectious.

Somehow, the bus driver managed to close the door after yet another passenger squeezed inside, and we were off again. As we pulled away from the curb, I took one last glance at the two men on the median and found myself shocked to realize that neither of the men had legs! How had I not noticed that? I had been so enthralled by their joyous expressions, their obvious appreciation for each other's company, a soft place to sit, and a sandwich to share, that I had not even allowed my eyes to travel past their faces.

What a wake-up call! There I was complaining to myself about having to stand in high heels on a bus packed with people and their livestock, while two legless men sat oblivious to the world around them, enjoying each other's company.

"I hear you loud and clear, God," I whispered as I exited the bus several blocks before my stop. I wasn't alone, though. With each step I took, my boots were there to remind me of the excruciating pain that high heels inflict upon the vain and unwise. Yet, I was determined to use the legs I was so blessed to have, so on I walked... counting my blessings every step of the way.

— Cynthia Zayn —

98

The Wedding Photo

The highest compliment I could receive is that I've
turned into my mother. I can only hope!
~Author Unknown

"Two heads are better than one," I said as I handed my husband the photo taken of the family at our daughter Tina's wedding.

"I don't get it," he said, staring closely at it.

"It's a double exposure. My mother has two heads."

"You'd better look again." He handed me back the picture.

It took me a while to see it, perhaps because I didn't want to, but the second head, a dead ringer for my mother's, belonged to me. I had rolled Mother, in her wheelchair, into her place in the family lineup for the picture taking. I stood behind her chair while Tina's friend took a few pictures. Mother's height in her chair put the top of her head just beneath my chin. It truly looked as if someone had stacked two identical, gray, bushy-haired heads — totem-pole style.

So, how could this be? I was sixty years old and believed I had never, ever looked like my mother. I had always been Daddy's girl — and that included my looks. Mother was eighty-five, and if pictures didn't lie, not only was I the spitting image of my mother, but most people also saw me as an octogenarian. It wasn't that my mother was unattractive. When younger, she looked a lot like Judy Garland.

Seeing myself in the wedding photo was a real eye-opener for me. Had I been fooling myself all my life thinking I was like my father, the fun parent? In what other ways, besides my appearance, did I take after my mother, and how had her influence made me who I am today?

I decided to give it some thought. Surely, my sense of honesty and integrity came from Mother. I have often said that "I am honest to a fault" as I have worked to temper my honesty and directness with compassion — something Mother needed to work on, too. Mother loved the old hymns. She knew all the words to every verse. In my career as a mail carrier, I spent hours alone in my mail truck singing aloud all the words to the hymns and praise songs I learned in church. Perhaps, I was a little like Mother after all.

But, as I sat pondering this wedding photo — remembering the incredibly special summer day, the lovely outdoor setting, and seeing my gorgeous daughter and my fine-looking son standing with the family — I realized what a wonderful gift my mother had given me.

When I was a very small girl, my mother kept foster children. She loved every one of these babies. It did not matter what their nationality or disability was. They came into our home and were treated like family. They did not have to share our DNA to be accepted or considered equal.

She made those children beautiful clothes and rode the city bus to take them to the pediatrician. She scattered Cheerios on the trays of their highchairs for them to eat with pudgy fingers. She wanted to adopt each of them. This was not long after World War II. Having a Japanese baby was not popular in our Navy town. But Mother proudly carried Japanese Sandra everywhere she went and returned the hostile stares with her own strong, brown eyes. Gary was born without sucking muscles. Mother patiently massaged his cheeks, allowing the formula to slowly drip down his throat so he wouldn't choke until his glass Evenflo bottles were empty. Without giving birth to any but my sister and me, she was a mother to many.

As I searched the photo looking for ways that Mother had influenced me, I saw my daughter in her wedding gown, grown-up and lovely. My son, Kurtis, a handsome young man in his tux, beamed with pride. I had adopted these kids. My children came with their own special needs, but Mother loved them despite their challenges, just as she taught me to do by the example she set so many years ago.

I didn't adopt Tina and Kurtis because I couldn't have children of my own. I did so because Mother had shown me that reproduction wasn't a parental requirement. She had set an example of love that reached way beyond the boundaries of DNA and had a depth far deeper than our family's gene pool.

I eventually became comfortable with the wedding photo. Actually, I kind of like it. I am okay with having Mother's head — since I also have her heart.

— Mason K. Brown —

99

Pictures in the Sky

*There are only 940 Saturdays between a child's birth
and her leaving for college.*
~Harley Rotbart

I t was a perfect summer afternoon: warm and mild, breezy and bright. My daughter and I were at a park where we'd spent countless hours together. We had picnicked by its pond and peered in, spying flashes of fish. We had watched the geese who made their nests each spring on a tiny island in the middle of the murky green, keeping a respectful distance when they ventured out onto the banks.

Sarah had had her first ride in a swing at that park on a cool April morning when she was not quite a year old. She had worked her way up three slides of increasing size. Braving a larger slide was a big deal back then, and I always waited for her at the bottom, cheering. We'd celebrated her fourth birthday with a handful of friends over in the pavilion with pizza, cupcakes and a piñata. We had brought Sarah's first bike to this park on an unusually warm Christmas afternoon for her first wobbly attempt in the empty parking lot. We had visited with school friends. We had flown kites on windy evenings.

Sarah and I crested the hill and followed the path that wound through athletic fields and stretched behind the middle school and high school. We sat down on the grass.

This was the path we'd followed to the park so many times when I pushed Sarah in the stroller. I remembered telling her that these would be her schools — someday, when she was a big kid. In those days of naps and board books, school seemed light years away. Now she already had one year of middle school behind her.

I started to feel the old nostalgia, recalling all those walks. I missed the days when we had all the time in the world to spend at the park or to visit the library for story time. My heart ached as I smiled, trying to stay focused on what Sarah had to say.

She had a lot to say. She talked about the nature walk her science class had taken along this very path in the spring. She mentioned the things they had studied that year: owl pellets, life cycles, producers, consumers and decomposers. When we passed the school courtyard, she told stories about rowdy recesses and games of kickball in P.E. class. She pointed out the window of her language-arts classroom.

As I listened, I marveled that the same kid who'd once needed my hand to scale the playground's wooden maze was now learning how to play the flute and solve math problems for x.

Sarah glanced up at the sky, where clouds curled and uncurled against the sunny blue, and pointed out what she saw.

We lay back against the warm grass. We pointed out pigs and pelicans to one another. Several dragons roared across the sky that day, breathing out wispy white smoke. There was an elegant lady with hair blown wild, glancing back over her shoulder. There was a headless horseman.

Some shapes were harder to spot than others. *There! No, up a little. Over there, to the right.* Sometimes, by the time I found what Sarah was trying to show me, the wind had already begun to pull it apart. I felt a twinge of sadness, wanting to see what she had seen. Wanting the sky to hold still.

Each time one of those images stretched and faded, though, new images revealed themselves: mermaids, dachshunds, dancing elves. They, too, were a delight to see — if I kept my eyes open to them.

I could miss what was no longer in front of me, or I could notice the new things that had taken shape.

I could grieve the old days, or I could give thanks for this day —

right now, with the warm green beneath us and the breeze brushing our faces, laughing with Sarah at those ever-shifting pictures in the sky.

— Kelly Close —

100

A Habit of Gratitude

Happiness is a habit — cultivate it.
~Elbert Hubbard

"Can we look at the school supplies while we're here?" my nineteen-year-old daughter, Julia, asked during a recent trip to the store.

She already knew the answer. Although I'd left my job as a kindergarten teacher more than a decade ago, my love of school supplies had stayed with me. Julia and I loved to shop for gel pens in every color of the rainbow, notepads with inspiring quotes on the covers, and Post-it Notes shaped like hearts and stars. But my favorite school-supply item to shop for is the daily planner.

Because I struggle with organization, I'm always on the lookout for the perfect planner. I dream that the perfect planner will somehow cure me of my procrastination and transform my life into a utopian paradise of order and productivity.

Julia and I headed to the school supply section and got lost in all the wonderful options. She picked out some gel pens in colors she didn't already have, and I chose a package of binder clips with smiley faces on them. Neither of us actually needed the item we'd chosen, but they made us smile, so we threw them in the cart.

Julia turned to leave the aisle, but I pointed at the planners. "I'm just going to look for a minute," I said.

"Didn't you already buy a planner for this year?"

I'd actually bought two, but I didn't say that. Instead, I said, "Yes, but I'm going to see if they have a different kind that might help me more than the ones I have at home."

Julia smirked, and I realized I'd given myself away. I shrugged and said, "Planner shopping is one of my hobbies, okay?"

Jules laughed. She picked up a planner, flipped through it, and then showed it to me. "Look, Mom, this one has a habit tracker. Do your other ones have that?"

I thought for a minute. "No, I don't think they do, but that could be really helpful." I thought of all the good habits I wanted to cultivate in my life. Exercising regularly. Drinking more water. Decluttering a junk drawer or closet each week. Reading more books and watching less TV. Procrastinating less on work deadlines. Spending more one-on-one time with each of my kids and reaching out to out-of-town family and friends more often. Making special meals, playing more games, and doing other things to make my loved ones feel loved and special on a more regular basis. Developing a more consistent prayer habit. The list of changes I wanted to make was long.

I motioned for Julia to put the planner in the cart. "Can I get one, too?" she asked.

"Don't you already have a planner for this year?" I teased while grabbing a second one for her.

The next day, I filled in the habit-tracker section of my new planner, determined to make some positive changes. As I sipped a glass of water — instead of my usual Diet Coke — I felt excited that maybe I'd finally found the perfect planner to help me get my act together.

Over the next few days, I was able to check off several items on my habit tracker. I exercised more often and cleaned out a linen closet that had been bothering me for months. I was pleased with the progress I'd made on my task-related habits, but I hadn't done much with the habits I wanted to develop to improve my relationships. I tried to put more focus on those habits, but on busy days I simply ran out of time to do everything.

One Saturday morning, I opened my planner and realized that I'd grabbed Julia's by mistake. The first task on her habit tracker was "Write in my gratitude journal." The second one was "Do something nice for someone else."

Both items were checked off every day that week. Julia was a busy college student who worked two jobs. How did she find time to journal and do random acts of kindness?

When I asked her about it, she smiled and said, "Those two habits go together. Writing in my gratitude journal makes me want to do nice things for other people."

I motioned for her to tell me more.

"Every morning, I write down three things I'm thankful for. It's a great way to start the day, and it reminds me that I'm blessed to have a great family and wonderful friends. It makes me so happy, and it usually prompts me to do something nice for another person."

"Like who?"

"Well, sometimes I want to do something for the person I'm thankful for. But, more often, it makes me want to find someone who doesn't have as much to be grateful for and do something kind for them." She smiled. "Last week, I wrote in my journal that I was thankful for you and Dad and the support you always give me. It reminded me of my friends on campus whose families are far away, who can't go home on the weekends like I can. I realized that they might be homesick. So, when I was home last weekend, I made chocolate-chip cookies and took them back to campus with me. One of my friends said they tasted just like the ones her mom makes."

"What a wonderful thing to do, honey," I said. "I'm so proud of you, and I love that your gratitude fuels your acts of kindness."

I realized that I'd spent years searching for the perfect planner when what I really needed was a gratitude journal. I grabbed a plain, spiral-bound notebook and wrote, "I'm thankful for… my husband who brings me coffee every morning, supportive friends who want to 'do life' with me, and my daughter who inspires me to be a kinder, more grateful person."

Just as Julia said, as soon as I'd written the words, I felt compelled to do something kind for someone else. I prepared my husband's favorite dinner, sent an encouraging text to a friend, and baked another batch of cookies for Julia to share with her friends.

Following my daughter's example, writing in my gratitude journal became an item on my habit tracker. And, like Julia, being grateful for the blessings in my life made me want to bless someone else. It was a double win.

I've discovered that gratitude can fuel kindness, and that is definitely a habit worth tracking.

— Diane Stark —

Lessons of the Season

Blessed is the season which engages the
whole world in a conspiracy of love.
~Hamilton Wright Mabie

"I s this all I got?" asked my daughter, Allison. "I asked for a new cell phone and a laptop!"

"Where are the rest of the presents?" asked my son, Blake. "I wanted a set of golf clubs and a skateboard!"

Money had been tight, and as a single parent, I was doing the best I could. My children received almost everything on their wish lists when their father was alive, but things were different now.

Blake was now thirteen years old and Allison twelve. I knew we had somewhat spoiled them, but I had no idea it was this bad. I was in shock. I looked at my children and their confused faces. My feelings were hurt, but I didn't want to show it. I was also very disappointed in their reactions to their presents.

"What kind of Christmas is this?" asked Allison.

"I know! Right! Are we being punished for something?" asked Blake.

I was starting to get angry now. How selfish and unappreciative could my children be? What had we done? I was on my own now, and I couldn't maintain our old lifestyle.

"Okay! I want you to remember how you are acting this Christmas and the hurtful thing you have said because I will certainly remember this next year. We will be celebrating Christmas in a whole new way!" I told them.

The months went by quickly. I was planning our next Christmas celebration in my head a little every day. I knew my kids thought I would forget all about their actions the previous Christmas, but I was determined to teach them a lesson. I contacted agencies to find a family that desperately needed help. That's how I found a family that lived on a farm about an hour away. There were four children in the house ranging in age from three to eight. The father had lost his job when his company went bankrupt. He had not found steady work since. They were a low-income family, and my children needed to know they existed and what they had to endure.

That next Christmas we did all the usual traditions, such as putting up a tree, baking cookies, making candy, and singing Christmas carols. But as Christmas Eve drew closer, there were still no presents under the tree. I knew Blake and Allison had to be wondering what was going on. Finally, they asked where the gifts were. I explained that we would be giving gifts to a family that truly needed them. They needed to see what it was like to need essentials such as clothing and food. I went on to explain my disappointment in their actions and words the prior Christmas.

We went shopping that weekend and bought gifts for all the children. We purchased gloves, hats, socks, shoes, and coats for them. Then, we picked out age-appropriate toys. We bought three toys for each child. Next, we needed coats, hats, gloves, socks, and shoes for the adults. Then, it was off to the grocery store. We purchased everything they would need for a nice Christmas dinner and then picked out some things to help them get through the winter.

Blake and Allison didn't seem happy with the situation, but I was sure I had them thinking about their attitudes last Christmas. I had a couple of gifts hidden in my closet, but they would only get them if they were polite and respectful to this family and to me.

It was the day before Christmas Eve, and the day we would deliver the food and gifts. I woke the kids and told them to get ready for breakfast because we would be leaving soon. They groaned in protest but did what I said.

The drive there was beautiful. It was mostly down back roads with amazing views of the countryside.

"What do people do here?" asked Allison. "There are no stores or fast food or anything."

"They are probably bored out of their minds," replied Blake.

"I'm sure they get out and go shopping or out to eat occasionally, just not every day as some people do," I said.

We arrived at the small home of this family in need, and we were welcomed inside with smiles and appreciation. They offered beverages and homemade cinnamon bread they had just baked. We accepted the treat. I knew it made them feel better about taking the things we had brought for them. The bread was delicious. I asked for the recipe, which seemed to delight the mother.

The parents let the children put the packages under the small Christmas tree in the living room. They were picking them up, shaking them, and guessing what was inside. They were so excited. Allison and Blake joined the children. Before long, they were laughing and playing with the little ones.

The smallest one wanted Allison to hold her, and she did. Blake was rolling a ball back and forth with the others. I think their hearts were full of joy to be able to give happiness to this family. We all enjoyed the day with them. They explained how they came to be in this situation, and I felt so sorry for them. I also knew that this could happen to anyone.

It was time to go home, and we said our goodbyes. The children handed out hugs and kisses, and I could tell our visit had touched Blake and Allison. Their eyes were full of tears that they didn't let fall.

The drive home was quiet.

When we arrived home and went inside, Allison looked at me and said, "Thanks, Mom," and gave me a big hug. Then, Blake said, "Thanks, Mom. Lesson learned."

I sat on the couch and sighed. "Mission accomplished," I said to myself.

The gifts that were waiting in my closet could now go under the tree. I knew my children had learned a lesson that would stay with them for a long time.

— T.K. Curry —

Meet Our Contributors

Kristi Adams loves sharing all aspects of military life, including hard-won lessons in gratitude. Kristi now calls Alaska home with her husband of sixteen years and is a regular contributor to *Military Spouse* magazine, *Stars and Stripes*, and the *Chicken Soup for the Soul* series. Learn more at www.kristiadamsmedia.com.

Sarah Budka Ammerman lives in upstate New York with her beloved daughter Mina, and her equally beloved cat, Kita. She is a cancer survivor who is passionate about sharing her experiences with others. Sarah enjoys watching the sun set from her balcony, writing, learning new things, and spending time with her daughter.

Dave Bachmann is a retired teacher who worked with special needs children in Arizona for thirty-nine years. He now resides in California with his wife Jay and their fifteen-year-old Lab, Scout, writing poems and stories for children and grown-ups.

Joanna Baghsarian is a graduate of Saint Basil's Teachers College (now Hellenic College in Brookline, MA). She also studied at Arsakion Teachers College in Athens, Greece. She worked in public relations at the Greek Archdiocese in New York City and as Director of Christian Education at the Armenian Prelacy in New York City.

Lori Kempf Bosko lives in Edmonton, Canada. She graduated from Grant MacEwan's journalism program in 1990 and has written many feature articles for newspapers and magazines. She enjoys spending time with family and friends, and playing with her rescue pup, Lucky.

Norma Bourland is a retired non-profit director who blogs for women in their grand finale stage of life at www.vibrantoldwoman. com. She loves being Granny to her six grandchildren, enjoys collage and fabric art, volunteering in her community, having coffee with her husband, and walking her Bichon.

Cassandra M. Brandt was born and raised in rural Arizona. A single parent, she became a traveling tradeswoman and studied human services and sociology by night. At age thirty-three she sustained an injury leaving her paralyzed from the neck down. Now Cassandra writes full time and is in grad school to teach literature.

Linda B. Breeden lives in the foothills of the Georgia Blue Ridge Mountains. She is an avid volunteer, reader, and writer. She has two children and one grandson. Her stories are published in *Redbook*, *Guideposts*, *Southern Writers*, *Birmingham Arts Journal* and *Chicken Soup for the Soul: Count Your Blessings*.

D.E. Brigham lives and writes in Tellico Village in eastern Tennessee. He enjoys pickleball, kayaking, bridge, hiking, bicycling, gardening, cooking, and traveling. E-mail David at davidebrigham@gmail.com.

Mason K. Brown has homes in Forest Grove and Seaside, OR. She is the author of over 150 publications, mostly in the inspirational and humor genres. Mason travels extensively collecting water from around the world. E-mail her at masonkbrown@frontier.com.

Dr. Marlene Bryenton's first story appeared in *Chicken Soup for the Soul: Angels All Around* in 2019. She received the Order of Prince Edward Island in 1998. Marlene is a children's storybook author, and has written *Anna's Pink and Purple Glasses*, *Jaya's Magic Wheelchair* and *The Magic Toothbrush*. E-mail her at ghizpark@eastlink.ca.

Patricia Bunin writes the weekly "Senior Moments" column for the Southern California News Group. She is the author of two books, *Password: SeniorMoment* and *Do You Think We Could Have Made It?* Learn more at patriciabunin.com or e-mail her at patriciabunin@sbcglobal.net.

Jill Burns lives in the mountains of West Virginia with her wonderful family. She's a retired piano teacher and performer. She enjoys writing, music, gardening, nature, and spending time with her grandchildren.

A long-time contributor to the *Chicken Soup for the Soul* series, **Jack Byron** is proud to share the remarkable life of Sgt. Navarro. José's own account of his life from his service days until the present, *Unbreakable, Unstoppable. An American Soldier's Story of Coming Home* is available on Amazon.com.

Eva Carter is a freelance writer with a background in finance and telecommunications. She and her husband live in Dallas, TX with their two cats.

Kathleen Chamberlin is a retired educator living in Albany, NY. She enjoys reading, gardening, genealogy, and grandchildren. Her short stories and poetry have appeared in several anthologies and online publications.

Leah Angela Cioco is a ludicrously passionate individual who wears many hats. She's studying applied math while running a production and media startup. In her other life, she's a computing enthusiast, public speaker, and writer. Most passionate about innovation and social impact, finding creative solutions to problems is her "why."

Christina Ryan Claypool is an award-winning journalist who has been featured on *Joyce Meyer Ministries* and CBN's *700 Club*. She is a graduate of both Bluffton University and Mt. Vernon Nazarene University. Christina adores being with her husband and son, a good movie, and hot coffee. Learn more at www.christinaryanclaypool.com.

Anna Cleveland has a degree in English. She resides in North Carolina with her parents where she teaches in a local school system. She enjoys reading, writing, and listening to music and hopes to publish her own book someday.

Kelly Close grew up in McMurray, PA. She began writing at age eight. After many years and many detours, she found her way back to writing. Kelly works in library services and enjoys reading and spending time outdoors. She lives with her family in North Royalton, OH.

Cj Cole is a retired radio diva and newspaper advice columnist living on the eastern shore of Virginia. A fan of dogs, horses and sushi, Cj now works from home under the watchful eye of her little Jackchi Tink.

T.K. Curry is currently working to complete a course on writing for children and teens. She has completed other writing courses and has had a short story published in an online publication. She likes to travel (especially by cruise ship), crochet, walk, read, and, of course, write.

Melissa Cutrera, M.Div. is a pastor's wife and homeschool mom.

She is the author of *God's Great Plan*, a picture book that shares the gospel with children. She enjoys reading, hiking, visiting museums and parks, and teaching for her local homeschool co-op. Melissa writes devotions for women at www.melissacutrera.com.

Geri D'Alessio lives on Long Island, NY with her husband and five-year-old blessing. She is Mom to Rebecca and Grandma to Ashley. She loves trees, birds, books, early morning walks along the shore and escaping to Starbucks with Ashley.

A frequent contributor to the *Chicken Soup for the Soul* series, **Barbara Davey** is a graduate of Seton Hall University where she received her bachelor's and master's degrees. She is an adjunct professor at Caldwell University where she encourages her students to put down their phones and pick up a pen. She and her husband live in Verona, NJ.

Tammy Davis is a teacher and a writer, finding lessons in everyday life. Her first book, *Chin Up, Buttercup*, is a collection of essays about the power of perseverance and a positive attitude. Davis lives in Columbia, SC with her dog, Rosebud. E-mail her at tammydavisstories@gmail.com or visit www.tammydavisstories.com.

Elton Dean is a college instructor and U.S. Army combat veteran with a passion for helping others. He has served on the board of directors for multiple non-profit organizations. Elton received his Master of Business Administration with distinction from Post University and has been inducted into three honors societies.

Phil Devitt is an award-winning writer and editor in Massachusetts. For his work in community journalism, he was named one of *Editor & Publisher* magazine's 25 Under 35 and twice, GateHouse Media's Feature Writer of the Year. He enjoys hiking, rowing, traveling, pondering life, and making memories with family and friends.

Kathy Dickie is the proud grandmother of two amazing granddaughters who fill her life with constant joy. She enjoys traveling, family visits, quilting, ancestry research and writing. Kathy and her husband live in Calgary, Alberta. She has contributed to previous titles in the *Chicken Soup for the Soul* series.

Mark Dickinson is an international teacher and freelance writer who has taught on three continents, currently in Whitfield County, GA.

When not in the classroom, he wanders the globe, having visited more than seventy countries. Mark's travel memoir, *Sleeping in the Homes of Strangers: A Month-Long Journey of Trust,* is available on Amazon.com.

Pat Dickinson is a retired teacher and legal secretary who lives in North Carolina with her husband Dan, daughter Meredith, and dog Tennyson.

Donna Arthur Downs is a professor at Taylor University. She seeks to touch hearts and inspire people to tell their stories so future generations will understand the value of relationships and seek to create memories worth sharing. A graduate of I.U. and Ball State, Downs has two sons and three remarkable grandchildren.

Dana Drosdick is an account manager living in Boston, MA with a passion for all things stewardship, faith, wellness, and personal enrichment. Her work has been featured in various *Chicken Soup for the Soul* anthologies, *Peaceful Dumpling*, and The Banner Magazine. Follow her work on Instagram @danadrosdick.

Alexis Farber is seventeen years old and attends Beacon High School in New York City. She enjoys writing, working out, traveling, and hanging out with her friends!

Tracy Farquhar is a professional psychic medium, teacher, and author. She has three published books: *Frank Talk*, *Channeled Messages from Deep Space* (co-authored with NY Times bestselling author Mike Dooley), and *Tarot for Today*. Learn more at TracyFarquhar.com.

Shaista Fazal is a graduate in home science and a postgraduate in law. She is a freelance content writer. She loves painting, embroidery, cooking and playing with little kids and telling them stories. She likes their sense of wonder and awe of little things.

Gail Gabrielle joined the Chicken Soup for the Soul family in 2018. She enjoys creating written memories about her own family as she continues to add to her repertoire of publications. Her children Danni, Zack and Alex always serve as inspiration. Leisure time is spent with her kids or at work on her book *Zack Attack*.

William J. Garvey was employed by Consumers Energy for thirty-five years, working in many departments. William now enjoys retirement with his wife Lorraine. They have three children: Will, Tim and Natalie. All three have moved on to other places and things, but they all stop by to help make memories or to give their opinions on the latest news.

Kathleen Gerard is an award-winning writer. She is the author of the novels *The Thing Is*, *In Transit* and *Cold Comfort*. Learn more at www.kathleengerard.blogspot.com.

Angela Williams Glenn teaches and lives in Maryland with her husband and three children. When she's not writing with her students for their school newspaper, she writes personal essays and articles for "Her View from Home" and other women and family sites. Her story "Already There" is dedicated in memory of Lorrie Glenn.

Holly Green is a wife, mother, doting grandma, novice gardener, retired nurse, and author. She wrote nonfiction for years, a book on domestic violence, and numerous articles for women's and family magazines. Under the name Anne Ashberg, she's written four novels: *What Julia Wrote*, *Linger*, *Exactly Enough*, and *Swan in Winter*.

Jean Matthew Hall lives in LaGrange, KY with her old-lady dog Sophie. Jean has been published in numerous magazines and anthologies. Learn more at jeanmatthewhall.com and on Facebook at Jean Matthew Hall Author.

Michelle Hanley is inspired by family, fairy tales, and odd blurbs on news sites that can't possibly be true. When she isn't writing, you can find her paddleboarding, fly fishing, gardening, or reading. Look for her other work in *Dread Naught but Time*, *MOJO*, *Gingerbread House*, *Pure in Heart Stories* and *Tall TV*.

Heather Hartmann resides in O'Fallon, MO with her husband, two sons, and four crazy animals. She is working on self-control in the area of multiple manuscript writing. This will be her first national publication, fulfilling a lifelong dream. Heather is determined to achieve the next goal, a published novel.

Darlene Carpenter Herring, a native Texan, received her Master's in English from the University of Texas. She enjoys spending time with her two daughters and three grandchildren. After teaching high school for many years, she now enjoys her travels with her grandchildren, from river rafting to roller coasters to mountain hiking.

Kate Hodnett has been published numerous times in the *Chicken Soup for the Soul* series. For more of her inspirational content, you can check out Kate Hodnett on TikTok, or shop at www.etsy.com/shop/TheAsterArtistStore.

Kayleen Kitty Holder is a journalist and children's book writer. She published a fun kid's book, *Hello from the Great Blue Sea,* with another A-T warrior who illustrated it. All profits will go to the A-T Children's Project. Purchase one to help find the cure for a disease called A-T, which her four-year-old niece is battling.

Amita Jagannath is an IT professional, a restless wanderer, a vegetarian chicken soup member, a student of life and a voracious reader. Her uncanny knack of reading finds powerful utility in reading her husband's mind and her teenager's cryptic texts. She lives in Chicago, IL with her husband and daughter.

Margaret Johnston is a writer who resides in Washington, D.C. For the past twenty years, she's been married to a man who's married to Uncle Sam. It's a torrid love triangle, but it makes for great writing. She enjoys reading, cooking, and collecting passport stamps.

Jill Keller is a novelist living in a small town in Southern Indiana with her husband and two children. When not writing, she enjoys making desserts for her bakery, running a business helping those suffering from baby loss, perusing library aisles, and reading to her children. Learn more at kellerjf.wixsite.com/authorjillkeller.

Lynn Kinnaman has been writing and publishing nonfiction and fiction since college. She teaches courses on writing, resilience, and creativity, as well as other writing services. She's also an instructor at Montana State University. Her latest memoir is about growing up with a narcissistic mother. E-mail her at Lynn@lynnkinnaman.com.

Alice Klies is president of Northern Arizona Word Weavers. She is a twelve-time contributor to the *Chicken Soup for the Soul* series and has been published in eighteen other anthologies including two *Guideposts* compilations. She lives in Arizona with her hubby and hopes her stories cause a reader to smile or giggle. Learn more at aliceklies.com.

Carol Anne Lake and her husband Jim spend most of their days running a small business. In their free time, they love exploring. Carol is a freelance writer and has written many magazine articles reflecting her current interests. She self-published a book: *Mr. Rude is not a Cool Dude*, a children's tutorial on basic manners.

Rosemarie Zannino Law researches, writes, and performs living-history portrayals as the American spy Virginia Hall and American poet Emily Dickinson. She guides children and adults to express their lives through poetry and memoir writing. She shares a Music and Memories singalong program for seniors with her ukulele.

Karen M. Leet loves to write and has been at it since age ten. Her writing has appeared in numerous publications. She has two books from The History Press: *Sarah's Courage* and a Civil War nonfiction.

Crescent LoMonaco used her knowledge from years working behind the chair and owning a hair salon to write the "Ask a Stylist" column for the *Santa Barbara Independent*. She is a frequent contributor to the *Chicken Soup for the Soul* series. She lives on the California coast with her husband and son.

Brenda Mahler retired from public education. Working as a teacher and administrator, she followed her passion to support America's youth. She is a mother of two and grandmother of four. Brenda enjoys traveling, playing with her dogs, and writing stories to inspire others. Follow her blog, "I AM My Best!" at iammybest.org.

Jane McBride dreamed of writing from the time she was a small child and often made up stories to entertain her friends. These fanciful tales sometimes enchanted, sometimes delighted, and sometimes horrified her audience. Being published in the *Chicken Soup for the Soul* series is a dream come true for Jane.

Gloria Shell Mitchell, author of *The Garbage Man's Daughter* series, grew up in South Carolina with a passion for education. An ordained minister and retired educator, Gloria enjoys writing, travel, counseling, and spending time with her two daughters and granddog, Typo.

Gwen Mulkey is a human resource professional originally from Evanston, IL, currently living in League City, TX. She is married to a wonderful husband and has two beautiful stepdaughters. Gwen is an avid reader who also loves to garden and knit. She plans to continue writing as she considers it her passion!

Rachel Dunstan Muller is a professional storyteller, author, and children's podcaster. She is married to her best friend of thirty-plus years, and they have five children and four grandchildren. Home is on Vancouver Island, on the west coast of Canada. Listen to her podcast at www.sticksandstonesandstories.com.

Jeannette Nott is an actor, playwright, and stand-up comedian. She is a 2010 Colorado Voices competition winner and guest columnist for *The Denver Post*. Her story, "A Mother Never Forgets" appears in *Adoption Reunion in the Social Media Age: An Anthology* edited by Laura Dennis, 2014. Jeanne is the reigning Ms. Colorado Senior America.

Carole Olsen is an author and freelance writer. Carole enjoys hiking, kayaking, and volunteering at a local animal rescue. She resides outside of Richmond, VA with her husband Eric and her two rescued pups, Zoey and Dobby.

Francesca Peppiatt is a writer and speaker who works in theatre, film and TV. She has an Emmy nomination for writing and won the title of Funniest Person in Chicago on WGN-TV. Her program How to Re-write Your Life guides members to the exciting next chapter in their lives by skillfully using their writing and humor.

Linda Kaullen Perkins taught second grade at Washington Elementary in Sedalia, MO. Her writing has appeared in the *Chicken Soup for the Soul* series, *Woman's World* magazine, and various other publications. She enjoys life on the farm with her husband and pets.

Evan Purcell writes the award-winning *Karma Tandin: Monster Hunter* book series for children. He also travels the world, teaching English and creative writing to students everywhere from Bhutan to Zanzibar. *Remember*, his first screenplay, is currently being filmed.

Dorian Leigh Quillen is a licensed professional counselor and award-winning journalist. She is a magna cum laude, Phi Beta Kappa graduate of the University of Oklahoma where she earned a B.A. in Journalism and an M.Ed. in community counseling. She recently authored the book, *Captured by Grace: The Jamie Jungers story*.

Taylor Reau is an Ohio native. She's a busy homeschooling mom of two, and in addition to working multiple jobs, still finds time to follow her passion of writing. She also edits books part time. Taylor loves collecting indoor house plants, listening to music, and mostly, the outdoors.

Rachel Remick lives in Tampa, FL where she writes, swims, and cares for dogs. Both her fiction and nonfiction short stories have been published in literary and women's magazines. An avid reader and road-tripper, this is her third story published in the *Chicken Soup for the Soul* series.

Melissa Richeson is an author, content writer, freelance editor, and assistant literary agent. As a resident of coastal Florida, she enjoys swimming, running, and paddle boarding, and can often be found visiting the beach or Walt Disney World with her husband and four sons. Connect with her on Twitter @MelissaRicheson.

Mariann Roberts is a Canadian writer who received her Bachelor of communication studies with a major in journalism in 2020. She has been writing stories since she was old enough to print her name and plans to complete her first novel shortly. Mariann enjoys reading, hiking, camping, music, and going on new adventures.

Laura Savino is an author, motivational speaker and STEM education advocate. Using her experience as an international widebody pilot for United Airlines, her book *Jet Boss: A Female Pilot on Taking Risks and Flying High* brings the reader inside the cockpit and empowers women everywhere! Learn more at https://laurasavino747.com.

Rebecca Schier-Akamelu works as a copywriter in Kansas. She also writes short stories, personal essays, and has a novel in the works. When she is not writing, she enjoys spending time with her husband, three children, and her dog. Learn more at rebeccaschierakamelu.com.

Rachel Schmoyer is passionate about helping Christians find simple truth in hard parts of Scripture. She is the author of *Take It to Heart: 30 Days through Revelation, A Devotional Workbook for Women*. She blogs at ReadtheHardParts.com. She lives in the Lehigh Valley of Pennsylvania with her husband and four teenage children.

Laurel L. Shannon is the pseudonym of a NW Ohio based author who lives on her hobby farm along with three cats and an Australian Terrier who would rule the world if she had a thumb.

Christine M. Smith is an aging mother of three, grandmother of fourteen, great-grandmother of thirteen, and foster mother of many. She is retired and lives with her husband of fifty-three years in Lane, OK. Christine enjoys reading, writing, sewing, and spending time with family. E-mail her at iluvmyfamilyxxx000@yahoo.com.

Jane R. Snyder is a Syracuse University (MFA) and Parsons School of Design (BFA) graduate. Her work has appeared on jewishfiction.net, everydayfiction.com, *Nashville Arts*, *The New York Quarterly*, *Response* and more. She is an ASCAP member, and her songs can be heard on CDs, TV, and film. Learn more at janersnyder.com and thisjane.com.

Stephanie Stafford is a recovering addict with a few twenty-four hours clean. Since she's been in recovery, she has relapsed three times, one time of which she nearly died. Unable to return to her previous line of work, she found a new way of life. Stephanie enjoys gardening, hiking, beachcombing, writing, and photography.

Diane Stark is a wife, mother, and writer. She is a frequent contributor to the *Chicken Soup for the Soul* series. She loves to write about the important things in life: her family and her faith.

Maribeth Hynnes Stevens is a member of the NC Scribes. As a volunteer for Trans World Radio, she has contributed to the TWR Women of Hope prayer calendar. She is also featured in the book, *9/11 That Beautiful Broken Day*. She enjoys spending time in God's great outdoors with her husband Tom and is currently working on a devotional book.

Marv Stone is a software engineer sneaking dangerously close to sixty. He has always enjoyed reading, thanks to the many hours his mom spent with him during summer break in the local library. He now enjoys sitting on the other side of the typewriter, telling stories about his family and his childhood.

Ronica Stromberg writes fiction and nonfiction for books, magazines and the two National Science Foundation programs she manages. Her children's books include *The Time-for-bed Angel*, *The Glass Inheritance*, *A Shadow in the Dark* and *Living It Up to Live It Down*. Her stories appear in more than twenty anthologies.

Jen Eve Taylor is originally from Sydney, Australia, but now lives in London — the city she considers her life's one great love story. When not writing essays or working on her novel, she can be found tackling the ups and downs of life on her website www.thecancerchronicles.blog.

June E. Taylor, a recently retired French teacher, has a doctorate in French from the University of Illinois at Urbana Champaign. Living on the North Shore of Massachusetts, she enjoys walking at local beaches and parks. She is an avid reader of mysteries. Her hobbies include botanical drawing and crossword puzzles.

Becky S. Tompkins enjoys working with words, both professionally — as a former teacher of English, proofreader/copy editor, and freelance writer — and in her spare time. She also enjoys cooking, gardening, and spending time with her family.

Eve Turek, M.Photog., is an internationally awarded nature photographer as well as a lifelong writer. She owns SeaDragon & Yellowhouse Gallery in Duck, NC, and leads workshops on photography and creative/spiritual practice. She loves to travel and return home to her dogs and cats. E-mail her at evetureknaturephotography@gmail.com.

Melissa Valks is a four-time contributor to the *Chicken Soup for the Soul* series, with her pieces focused on being welcomed into the homes and hearts of people from Syria to Central Africa. She remains grateful to her boss who allows her time off to wander the globe and share her tales.

Pat Wahler is a Missouri native and proud contributor to nineteen books in the *Chicken Soup for the Soul* series. Pat is the author of four novels and is currently at work on her next book under the supervision of one bossy cat and a lively Pekingese-mix. Learn more at www.PatWahler.com.

K.M. Waldvogel is a retired teacher who has enjoyed writing since she was a child. She belongs to writing groups in Arizona and Wisconsin and has several published children's books. Waldvogel loves traveling and spending time with family. She and her husband split their time between Wisconsin and sunny Arizona.

Suzettra L. Walker is the mother of two beautiful and intelligent people, Brionna and Sienna. Suzettra is also the author of the children's book, *Don't You Dare Touch Me There* which teaches children to create touch boundaries and focuses on body autonomy. Suzettra loves butterflies, travel, and beautiful minds.

At age seventy-five, **Diana L. Walters** continues to work part-time enriching the lives of seniors in a retirement community. She and her husband also develop material through their nonprofit (Center for Bold Action) to help people with dementia remember their faith. E-mail her at dianalwalters@comcast.net.

Samantha Ducloux Waltz is delighted to be part of the Chicken Soup for the Soul family. Her writings include anthologized and award-winning essays, several books on parenting, and the Seal Press anthology *Blended: Writers on the Stepfamily Experience*. She lives in Portland, OR where the smile of a stranger changed her life.

David Warren resides near Springboro, OH with his wife Angela. They have a daughter, Marissa, who just had her own wedding. David is Vice President of Sales for Lutz Blades and a freelance writer. He has had two children's books and various magazine articles published and has had stories appear ten times in *Chicken Soup for the Soul* books.

Writing coach **Roz Warren** works with writers to improve and publish their prose and writes for everyone from the *Funny Times* to *The New York Times*. She has appeared on both the *Today Show* and *Morning Edition* and has been included in sixteen *Chicken Soup for the Soul* books. E-mail her at roSwarren@gmail.com.

Ray Weaver has been writing for over sixteen years. He's about to have his twelfth novel published. He and his wife Ellie have been Suncoast Hospice Volunteers for over sixteen years. They were selected as the Suncoast Volunteers of the Year in 2021.

Vicky Webster lives in Missouri and is the proud mother of two children: Cheyanne and Dalton. In her spare time she enjoys trying new restaurants, writing, and traveling with the love of her life, Larry. This marks the third time Vicky has been published in the *Chicken Soup for the Soul* series.

Marsha Shepherd Whitt was born and raised in SW Ohio, the youngest of seven children. She has always had an entrepreneurial spirit that has brought her success as an adult. (Her first foray into business was at age eight, selling garden seeds to neighbors.) Her love of writing began in high school, where she was elected president of the creative writing club.

Lisa Workman lives on a farm in the Blue Ridge Mountains with her husband, three sons, and many pets. In her spare time, she enjoys riding her horses, running, and geocaching with her family. You can find other stories by her in *Chicken Soup for the Soul: The Magic of Dogs*, *Guideposts*, *All Creatures*, and *Backwoods Home*.

Vic Zarley lives with his wife Eva in southern Indiana. He and his wife have written many Christian songs. He shares a song, an original poem and a teaching from his books in his podcast, published twice a week. His podcast can be Googled and is entitled, "Leaving the Grandstand World." Learn more at https://www.buzzsprout.com/1765402.

Cynthia Zayn is the mother of three children and three grand-children. She lives outside of Atlanta, GA and is a frequent contributor to the *Chicken Soup for the Soul* series. Before retiring to pursue a full-time writing career, she taught literature and composition inside and outside the United States.

Meet Amy Newmark

Amy Newmark is the bestselling author, editor-in-chief, and publisher of the *Chicken Soup for the Soul* book series. Since 2008, she has published 183 new books, most of them national bestsellers in the U.S. and Canada, more than doubling the number of Chicken Soup for the Soul titles in print today. She is also the author of *Simply Happy*, a crash course in Chicken Soup for the Soul advice and wisdom that is filled with easy-to-implement, practical tips for enjoying a better life.

Amy is credited with revitalizing the Chicken Soup for the Soul brand, which has been a publishing industry phenomenon since the first book came out in 1993. By compiling inspirational and aspirational true stories curated from ordinary people who have had extraordinary experiences, Amy has kept the twenty-nine-year-old Chicken Soup for the Soul brand fresh and relevant.

Amy graduated *magna cum laude* from Harvard University where she majored in Portuguese and minored in French. She then embarked on a three-decade career as a Wall Street analyst, a hedge fund manager, and a corporate executive in the technology field. She is a Chartered Financial Analyst.

Her return to literary pursuits was inevitable, as her honors thesis in college involved traveling throughout Brazil's impoverished northeast region, collecting stories from regular people. She is delighted to have

Meet Amy Newmark |

come full circle in her writing career — from collecting stories "from the people" in Brazil as a twenty-year-old to, three decades later, collecting stories "from the people" for Chicken Soup for the Soul.

When Amy and her husband Bill, the CEO of Chicken Soup for the Soul, are not working, they are visiting their four grown children and their spouses, and their five grandchildren.

Follow Amy on Twitter @amynewmark. Listen to her free podcast — Chicken Soup for the Soul with Amy Newmark — on Apple, Google, or by using your favorite podcast app on your phone.

Thank You

We owe huge thanks to all our contributors and fans. We received thousands of submissions for this popular topic, and we spent months reading all of them. Laura Dean, Crescent LoMonaco, Jamie Cahill and Kristiana Pastir read all of them and narrowed down the selection for Associate Publisher D'ette Corona and Publisher and Editor-in-Chief Amy Newmark.

Susan Heim did the first round of editing, D'ette chose the perfect quotations to put at the beginning of each story, and Amy edited the stories and shaped the final manuscript.

As we finished our work, D'ette Corona continued to be Amy's right-hand woman in working with all our wonderful writers. Barbara LoMonaco, Kristiana Pastir and Elaine Kimbler jumped in to proof, proof, proof. And yes, there will always be typos anyway, so please feel free to let us know about them at webmaster@chickensoupforthesoul. com, and we will correct them in future printings.

The whole publishing team deserves a hand, including our Vice President of Marketing Maureen Peltier, our Vice President of Production Victor Cataldo, Executive Assistant Mary Fisher, and our graphic designer Daniel Zaccari, who turned our manuscript into this beautiful, inspirational book.

Sharing Happiness, Inspiration, and Hope

Real people sharing real stories, every day, all over the world. In 2007, *USA Today* named *Chicken Soup for the Soul* one of the five most memorable books in the last quarter-century. With over 110 million books sold to date in the U.S. and Canada alone, more than 300 titles in print, and translations into nearly fifty languages, "chicken soup for the soul®" is one of the world's best-known phrases.

Today, twenty-nine years after we first began sharing happiness, inspiration and hope through our books, we continue to delight our readers with new titles, but have also evolved beyond the bookshelves with super premium pet food, television shows, a podcast, video journalism from aplus.com, licensed products, and free movies and TV shows on our Popcornflix and Crackle apps. We are busy "changing your world one story at a time®." Thanks for reading!

Share with Us

We all have had Chicken Soup for the Soul moments in our lives. If you would like to share your story or poem with millions of people around the world, go to chickensoup.com and click on Submit Your Story. You may be able to help another reader and become a published author at the same time. Some of our past contributors have launched writing and speaking careers from the publication of their stories in our books!

We only accept story submissions via our website. They are no longer accepted via mail or fax. Visit our website, www.chickensoup.com, and click on Submit Your Story for our writing guidelines and a list of topics we are working on.

To contact us regarding other matters, please send us an e-mail through webmaster@chickensoupforthesoul.com, or fax or write us at:

Chicken Soup for the Soul
P.O. Box 700
Cos Cob, CT 06807-0700
Fax: 203-861-7194

One more note from your friends at Chicken Soup for the Soul: Occasionally, we receive an unsolicited book manuscript from one of our readers, and we would like to respectfully inform you that we do not accept unsolicited manuscripts, and we must discard the ones that appear.

Changing lives one story at a time®
www.chickensoup.com